DELUGE

UNIVERSITY PRESS OF NEW ENGLAND ✺ HANOVER AND LONDON

PEGGY SHINN

DELUGE

Tropical Storm Irene, Vermont's Flash Floods,
and How One Small State Saved Itself

University Press of New England

www.upne.com

© 2013 Peggy Shinn

Manufactured in the United States of America

Designed by Eric M. Brooks

Typeset in Fresco Plus Pro by Passumpsic Publishing

University Press of New England is a member of the
Green Press Initiative. The paper used in this book meets
their minimum requirement for recycled paper.

Library of Congress Cataloging-in-Publication Data
Shinn, Peggy.
Deluge: tropical storm Irene, Vermont's flash floods,
and how one small state saved itself / Peggy Shinn.
    pages cm
Includes bibliographical references.
ISBN 978-1-61168-318-9 (cloth: alk. paper)—
ISBN 978-1-61168-404-9 (ebook)
1. Hurricane Irene, 2011. 2. Disaster relief—Vermont.
3. Hurricane damage—Vermont. 4. Floods—Vermont.
5. Vermont—History, Local. I. Title.
HV636 1999 .V5 S55   2013
363.34'92209743—dc23   2013002825

5 4 3 2 1

TO MY PARENTS,

Ferguson & Jane McKay

I love Vermont because of her hills and valleys, her
scenery and invigorating climate, but most of all because
of her indomitable people. They are a race of pioneers who
have almost beggared themselves to serve others. If the
spirit of liberty should vanish in other parts of the Union,
and support of our institutions should languish, it could
all be replenished from the generous store held by the
people of this brave little state of Vermont.

§ CALVIN COOLIDGE, September 21, 1928,
from a speech given in Bennington, Vermont,
after President Coolidge, a native Vermonter,
viewed the ravages of the 1927 flood

CONTENTS

Color photographs appear after page 82.

PREFACE

Every book has a story behind it. The idea for this book came as I rode my mountain bike home from Pittsfield, Vermont, at the end of August 2011. And it wasn't a pleasure ride.

On August 28, the remnants of Hurricane Irene had left Pittsfield, along with a dozen other Vermont towns, isolated from the outside world—at least by car. My sister, Betsy McKay, the Atlanta bureau chief for the *Wall Street Journal*, was working on Irene coverage (hurricanes usually hitting the Southern states the hardest). Given the hundreds of washed-out roads in Vermont, it was difficult to get a reporter into many of the towns where damage was the worst. A writer and an avid cyclist, I offered to ride my mountain bike on a trail through the woods to reach Killington—and, I hoped, Pittsfield—then report what was happening in those cut-off towns.

Loaded down with a ham sandwich, two energy bars, a half-gallon of water, cell phone, camera, notepad, pens, and digital recorder, I pedaled up the road and through the woods on what would soon be dubbed the Woodchip Parkway. Thanks to Killington resident Paul Buhler and his daughter Alison, who gave me a tour of the worst damage, I saw and heard far more than I'd expected. The devastation was astounding. Roads I had driven just days before were gone—not only flooded but completely washed away. Houses lay tipped every which way, with possessions strewn through the woods and washed far downstream. At least two houses were completely gone. This was not pastoral Vermont. It was a war zone.

Then I began talking to people. I myself had never lived through a natural disaster, and I was struck by the fact that no one was waiting for outside help, and no one was waving a white flag of surrender—not even those who had lost everything. Instead, people had rolled up their sleeves and were digging out themselves and their neighbors. The recovery brought out the best in people and illustrated what we can do when we are entirely focused on a goal, either removing hurdles or finding a way around them. The stories of their selflessness and stubborn can-do spirit warranted far more than a couple of newspaper articles. If Vermonters could respond like this against impossible odds, the future suddenly seemed brighter.

This book does not aim to tell every Vermonter's Irene story. There are simply too many. Instead, my goal has been to tell the story of the storm and the state's recovery through the experiences of the following characters: Lisa Sullivan in Wilmington, whose bookstore was flooded, as well as town clerk Susie Haughwout, who saved the town records; Tracy Payne in Jamaica, who lost her home, everything in it, and the land on which it had sat; Geo Honigford, an organic vegetable farmer in South Royalton, who put his own mess on hold to help out others; the village of Pittsfield, which became a model of town unity and survival; and the guys who put U.S. Route 4, a major east-west artery, back together.

My hope is that their stories encapsulate some of what we all coped with in the days, weeks, and months after the remnants of Hurricane Irene ravaged Vermont—and what many people will continue to cope with for years to come. These are stories that show how one small state saved itself, and what we all might want to ponder before the next Irene hits Vermont.

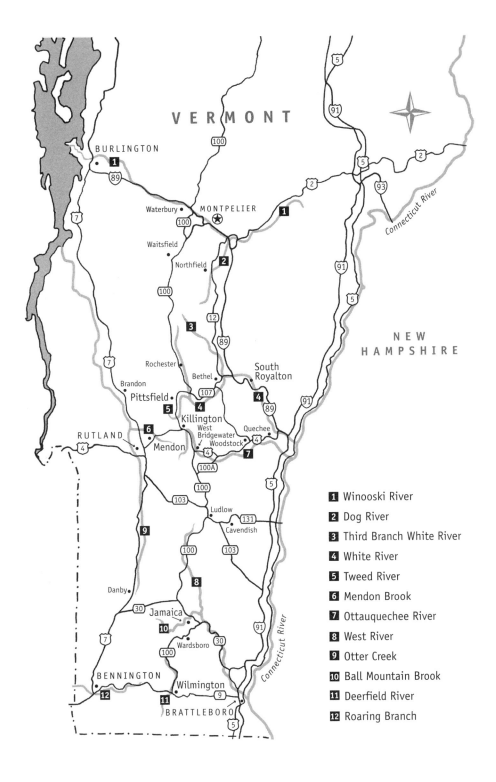

VERMONT

BURLINGTON **1**

89

7

Waterbury • MONTPELIER ★ **1**

Waitsfield

Northfield **2**

100

12

3

89

Rochester •
Bethel • South
Royalton

Brandon • **107**
Pittsfield • **4**
5 **4** **89**

RUTLAND **6** Killington
West **91**
4 Bridgewater Quechee
Mendon • Woodstock • **4** **7**

100A

100

103 **5**

Ludlow
9 **131**
Cavendish

100 **103**

Danby • **8**

30
Jamaica
10
Wardsboro **30**
100

7 **91**

BENNINGTON
12 Wilmington
11 **9**
BRATTLEBORO
5

100

MONTPELIER **1**

5

91

2

93

Connecticut River

5

91

5

NEW
HAMPSHIRE

Connecticut River

1 Winooski River

2 Dog River

3 Third Branch White River

4 White River

5 Tweed River

6 Mendon Brook

7 Ottauquechee River

8 West River

9 Otter Creek

10 Ball Mountain Brook

11 Deerfield River

12 Roaring Branch

PART I

THE STORM

FLASH FLOOD

Flash flooding is the leading cause of weather-related mortality in the United States (accounting for approximately 200 deaths per year).

    ⑤ U.S. Centers for Disease Control and Prevention

FROM THE MOMENT THEY SAW THE CUTE HOUSE in Pittsfield, Vermont, Heather Grev and Jeremy "Jack" Livesey knew they wanted to live there. It was a classic little square house with two stories, white clapboards, and a green tin roof—the kind of picture-perfect house a child might draw. When it became available to rent in 2007, they jumped at the chance. At the time, it never occurred to them that the Tweed River and its West Branch, which meet behind the house, would ever be anything but an asset. Sleeping in the summers with the upstairs bedroom windows open, they could hear the streams babbling softly in the night air.

Surrounded by high mountain ridges in the heart of Vermont's Green Mountains, Pittsfield is the kind of village where people live to hear the streams babble. Home to 546, the village sits on State Route 100 in a narrow valley about fifteen minutes north of Killington, a town known for its big ski resort, and about thirty minutes northeast of Rutland, once Vermont's second largest city (now fourth, behind Burlington and three of its suburbs). In the village, two general stores, an inn, the town hall and library, a church, and several homes with lovely porches surround an oblong green complete with—of course—a little gazebo. Heather and Jack chose to live in Pittsfield because Heather, a New Jersey native, had traveled across the country after she graduated from college, and of all the places she visited, none was as perfect as Pittsfield.

"They've got the store and the hotel and the breakfast place and everything," she said. "It's just a Vermont local town."

And it was home to this perfect little white house. It had once been Pittsfield's school—a classic one-room Vermont schoolhouse. At some point in the last hundred years, the building had been set on a foundation and renovated into a house. It sat near Route 100, in a low spot just before the road ascends a small bluff into the village proper.

After the couple that lived in the little white house moved out West, in 2007, Heather and Jack rented the place and moved in, along with Cody, a German shepherd mix that Heather had rescued from a shelter in Connecticut when she was still in college in the 1990s. Over the next four years, Heather, who is the head of youth services at the Killington Town Library, and Jack, who works at Pittsfield Standing Seam, a metal roofing company, made the rental house their home. In the spring of 2011 they added another puppy to their household, a mutt named Irie.

In the big backyard that sloped gently from the house to the two brooks, Heather built three gardens. By August, she had finished the third garden and was looking forward to the summer of 2012, when all she would have to do would be to plant the gardens and weed them. She had also recently purchased a riding lawn mower so they could more easily cut the grass in the big backyard, where they loved to hang out. They often swam in the brooks and invited their friends and family over for dinner or just to visit—a relaxing afternoon in a place that many might consider paradise. Every July Fourth, Heather's family came up to Pittsfield from New Jersey for a huge party.

In late August 2011, with Hurricane Irene bearing down on the East Coast, Heather was more concerned about her family in New Jersey than she was about herself. This is Vermont, after all, and locals around the state like to joke that nothing *ever* happens in Vermont. Still, with high winds forecast in the state for Sunday, August 28, Heather and Jack prepared just in case the power was knocked out. They stocked up on food, did their laundry, filled buckets and the bathtub with water, and made extra ice. They ensured that their flashlights worked, and they put candles in every room. And they made plans to attend a hurricane party on Sunday afternoon hosted by their friends Matt and Dana, who also live in Pittsfield.

"We were ready," said Heather. "We were ready [to be without] power for days."

What they were not ready to do was flee their house with no warning.

♬ ♬ ♬

AROUND LUNCHTIME on Sunday, August 28 — with rain falling hard in Pittsfield — Heather was upstairs in the cute little white house folding laundry and trying to find the dog bed, which she wanted to bring to the hurricane party for Cody. Over his fourteen years Cody had seen his share of accidents and injuries: he had torn the anterior cruciate ligament in one knee, been hit by a car, and once had jumped from a second-story window. Heather loved Cody as she would a child and wanted him to be comfortable at Matt and Dana's, even if they planned to stay at their friends' party for only a few hours.

As Heather was gathering what they would need for the party, the phone rang. Jack answered. It was his mom, Judy Livesey, who also lives on Route 100, just two houses north. Judy was screaming into the phone, but Heather couldn't make out what she was saying and assumed it was an issue between mother and son.

Suddenly Heather heard water running downstairs. She went to the top of the stairs and looked down. Water was pouring into the house under the front door. She ran downstairs, grabbed a towel from the spare bathroom, and set it on the floor in front of the door.

It was just after 1:00 p.m.

She then ran into the kitchen and looked out the side door. About a dozen neighbors were standing across Route 100 in the Piccarello's Pizza parking lot. Between the little white house and the parking lot, what was once lawn and road was now a wide swath of swiftly moving brown water. The water was already up to the axles on their Subarus, which were parked beside the house.

"Get out of the house!" the neighbors screamed. "You have to get out of the house!"

Heather's first thought was of Cody — get the old fellow out of this mess. She called to Jack, who grabbed a backpack, threw in a few odd items, picked up the dog, and walked out the side door, stepping into the fast-moving water. It came to his knees. It was now 1:18 p.m.

As Jack came around to the front of the house, the full force of the current hit him. The water was now up to his thighs, and he was fighting to maintain balance, let alone pick up his feet and walk toward higher ground.

Greg Martin, Don "Ziggy" Ziegler, and James Marcroft, Jr. — all Pittsfield locals — saw Jack struggling. Ziegler lives about a mile up a nearby side road off Route 100. After watching it rain all morning, he had decided to take a ride into town to see what was happening and asked his two boys, ages seven and nine, if they wanted to come. The three Zieglers had piled into the family's minivan; Ziggy's wife, Kelly, had stayed home baking cookies. When they reached Route 100, they could go no farther. Water was covering the road. It was then that Ziegler saw Jack trying to walk through the thigh-deep water with a large dog in his arms. Ziegler, a member of Pittsfield's volunteer fire department and a former ski patroller at the Killington Resort, threw open the car door and yelled to his kids to stay put.

Almost at the same moment, Marcroft said to Martin, "We've got to do something."

Instinctively, Marcroft waded into the current toward Jack. Martin and Ziegler followed. As the force of the current hit him, Ziegler remembered a hike in Alaska he had taken with Kelly in the summer of 1990. They had had to traverse wide rivers swollen with glacial melt. Although the water from Pittsfield's Tweed was warmer than those of the icy Alaskan rivers, the force of the current brought back memories of how to stay upright in rushing water — face the current and walk diagonally into it.

"Let's hold hands," Ziegler shouted to Martin and Marcroft. The three men formed a human chain and, bent forward against the strong current, waded out toward Jack. Martin, at the front of the chain, reached out and grabbed Jack's arm. Then the human chain slowly worked back toward dry land. Jack handed Cody to Ziegler and turned to head back into the raging waters. Everyone standing in the parking lot shouted at him to stop, but he needed to help Heather.

While Jack had been carrying Cody to safety, Heather ran upstairs to find Irie, who had run to hide after Jack picked up Cody. She found the puppy under a bed and pulled him out by his tail. She then ran back downstairs, swept whatever was on the kitchen counter into a canvas bag with her free hand, and wondered if she should put Irie into the bag as well. She decided to carry the puppy under her arm instead. Swinging the bag over her shoulder, she secured her grip on Irie. Two minutes after Jack had left the house with Cody, Heather walked out the kitchen door and stepped into the flood. The torrent immediately ripped the flip-flops off her feet, but she kept moving. As she struggled to walk around the side of their Subarus, she met Jack. The floodwater was now up to their hips, and the current so strong that they almost couldn't move against it.

Greg Martin knew that Heather would need help, but there was no way he was going to wade back into that angry brown torrent. The water level had risen two feet in twelve minutes. He ran to get his Ford F-350 truck — the "biggest, baddest truck in town," as Marcroft called the pickup. It had a far better chance of withstanding the current than a human chain. If Martin backed the truck toward the house, he could always rev the truck's diesel engine and drive out to dry land if he realized he was in trouble. And the water level was still below the engine's air intake. From the back of the truck, Marcroft might be able to reach Heather and Jack and pull them to safety.

Ziegler realized they might need a rope, so he jumped back into his minivan, did a U-turn, and floored it home, where he had a 150-foot-long heavy section. As he searched for the rope, he told Kelly to take the children. She had never seen her husband so panicked.

There was no time, however, to wait for Ziegler to return. Martin's father walked up with a piece of webbing used for towing and handed it to Marcroft. Martin backed his big pickup into the torrent as close to the little white house as he dared. The big truck weighs about eight thousand pounds, but both Marcroft, standing in the bed, and Martin could feel the current rocking it. Behind Heather and Jack, the current had started to move the Subaru. Martin's mother, Ellen, was standing nearby, her heart in her throat. From the back of the truck, Marcroft threw one end of the tow strap toward Heather.

Heather had no way of knowing, just then, that eighty-four years earlier, only a few hundred yards upstream from where she was struggling, a woman named Mrs. French had died under similar circumstances. On Thursday, November 3, 1927, as rain poured down onto already sodden soil, the Tweed River had suddenly jumped its banks. Around 4:00 p.m., floodwaters surrounded the Charles French farm with Mr. and Mrs. French still inside. Rescuers backed a truck up to the farmhouse as far as they dared and threw a line to Mr. French. He tied the rope around his waist, took his wife in his arms, and signaled the rescuers that they were ready. As the rope pulled Mr. French into the full force of the current, his wife was swept from his arms. The next day, they found her body at Daley Bend, where the Tweed makes a sharp turn to the north just below Heather and Jack's little white house. The Flood of 1927 is still today considered Vermont's worst natural disaster.

This time the rescuers threw webbing, but Jack didn't tie it around his waist. Instead, Heather grabbed it and handed Irie, who was paddling at the water with her paws, to Jack. But even with the truck pulling Heather, she found it difficult to move. The current was so strong that her legs were pinned in place. If she picked up a foot, she might lose her balance. And waterborne debris was pelting her legs.

"I can't do it!" she screamed.

IRENE'S TRIP TO VERMONT

The main effect of tropical storms on Vermont is the enhancement
of the normal rainfall. The intruders from the south usually bring
northward vast quantities of warm, humid, tropical air that results
in heavy precipitation when the cyclonic whirl reaches New England.
    ⅋ David M. Ludlum, *The Vermont Weather Book*

HURRICANE IRENE WAS BORN ON AUGUST 15, 2011, a tropical wave
in the warm Atlantic waters off the west coast of Africa. As the wave
tracked west at about twenty miles per hour along a line just north of the
equator, it was a well-defined weather disturbance on satellite images.
As it neared the Lesser Antilles, the chain of Caribbean islands dropping south in an arc from Puerto Rico toward Venezuela, shower activity
within the tropical depression showed signs of organizing into a tropical
storm. At 8:00 a.m. on the morning of Saturday, August 20, forecasters
at the National Hurricane Center in Miami gave this tropical depression
an 80 percent chance of developing into a tropical storm during the next
forty-eight hours.

Within ten hours, conditions had changed explosively. At 6:00 p.m.
on August 20, National Hurricane Center forecasters upgraded the disturbance to a tropical storm and gave it a name: Irene. The ninth-named
storm of the 2011 Atlantic hurricane season, stretching from June 1 to
November 30, Irene would be the first tropical storm in 2011 to develop
into a hurricane: tropical storms Arlene, Bret, Cindy, Don, Emily, Franklin, Gert, and Harvey all died out before their winds achieved hurricane
force (greater than seventy-four miles per hour).

With thunderstorms swirling around her cyclonic center, tropical storm Irene continued her march west through the Caribbean. By

Sunday, August 21, she had reached the Virgin Islands—the northernmost islands of the Lesser Antilles—and showed her potential for destruction. In the wee hours of August 22 she unleashed a lightning bolt over tiny Necker Island, part of the British Virgin Islands and privately owned by Virgin Airlines founder Sir Richard Branson. The bolt set Branson's island home afire. Inside were twenty people, including Branson's ninety-year-old mother and actress Kate Winslet. Everyone escaped, but the mansion was destroyed.

Later that day Irene was upgraded to a Category 1 hurricane. According to the Saffir-Simpson hurricane wind scale, that meant her winds were now sustained at more than seventy-four miles per hour. When the storm made landfall in Puerto Rico, high winds downed trees and power poles, leaving about 1 million people—half of Puerto Rico's population—without electricity. Flooding left some five hundred people homeless and killed one woman, who had tried to drive across a swollen river. After battering Puerto Rico, Hurricane Irene skirted north of the Dominican Republic, where she caused more heavy flooding and claimed at least three lives.

On the evening of Monday, August 22, as she steamed northwest toward the Turks and Caicos islands and the Bahamas, Irene strengthened to a Category 2 hurricane. According to the Saffir-Simpson scale, that meant her winds were now sustained between 96 and 110 miles per hour. Forecasters at the National Hurricane Center predicted she would make landfall in North Carolina by the end of the week.

After wreaking havoc on the Turks and Caicos, Hurricane Irene intensified yet again. Now a strong Category 3 hurricane, with sustained winds of 111 to 130 mph, she headed northwest toward the Bahamas. On August 24 and 25 she battered roofs, downed trees, and flooded streets and homes across the archipelago, and knocked out power in Nassau. Her eye passed directly over several of the Bahamian islands, and she reportedly swept away 90 percent of the homes in Lovely Bay on Acklins Island.

Done with the Bahamas, Hurricane Irene then shifted course and took a more northerly direction. Landfall on the Eastern Seaboard of the United States was now less than two days away, and coastal residents from South Carolina to New Jersey began worrying that Irene would intensify into a Category 4 or 5 hurricane—with winds greater than 155 mph—as she refueled over the warm Atlantic waters for two days.

So far, she was following the same path Hurricane Floyd had in 1999. Floyd was an enormous storm that hit the East Coast of the United States in mid-September 1999. A Category 4 hurricane as it crossed the Bahamas, Hurricane Floyd's damaging winds stretched across its entire 580-mile diameter: most hurricanes average 300 miles in diameter. Floyd made landfall at Cape Fear, North Carolina, around 1:30 a.m. on September 16, 1999, as a Category 2 storm and dumped up to twenty inches of rain on parts of North Carolina. Following closely on the heels of Hurricane Dennis, which had drenched the mid-Atlantic states, Floyd's torrential rains caused devastating flooding in the Tar Heel State.

From North Carolina, Hurricane Floyd had accelerated up the Atlantic Coast and, though his winds lost strength, the storm continued to unload enormous quantities of rain from North Carolina to New England. In all, fifty-seven deaths were directly attributed to Floyd—most from drowning in freshwater flooding. North Carolina suffered the worst, with thirty-five reported fatalities. It was the deadliest hurricane in the United States since Hurricane Agnes in 1972 and one of the most costly. Property damage was set at $1.325 billion. But thanks to a drought in New England that had extended back to the first of the year, flood damage in Vermont and surrounding states was isolated. To most Vermonters, Floyd was no more than a much-needed soaking rainstorm.

If Hurricane Irene behaved like Floyd—and so far, she was acting very similarly—the mid-Atlantic states were in for a walloping. And 2011 was not a drought year in the New England states. Far from it.

But Floyd wasn't the only hurricane haunting coastal residents in late August 2011. Although no hurricane had struck the mainland United States since 2008 (when Hurricane Ike hit Texas), memories of the death toll and property damage inflicted on the Gulf Coast by Hurricane Katrina on August 29, 2005, kept residents in Irene's strike zone busy preparing for flooding, storm surge, and flying debris. Or they were evacuating. Hurricane Katrina had killed up to eighteen hundred people and caused more than $80 billion in damage from central Florida to Texas. Would Irene cause similar damage to the mid-Atlantic states?

At 5:00 p.m. on Thursday, August 25, 2011, the National Hurricane Center issued hurricane watches and warnings from South Carolina to New Jersey. Forecasters predicted that Hurricane Irene would make landfall on the continental United States on Saturday morning. Forecast cones put New York City in the center of Irene's projected path.

From the beaches of South Carolina to the streets of New York City, authorities ordered people to evacuate. In New York alone, more than 370,000 people were ordered to leave low-lying areas. Airlines canceled more than twenty-four hundred flights at airports along the Eastern Seaboard, and Amtrak canceled all trains running in its busy Northeast corridor. New York City mayor Michael Bloomberg ordered New York's mass transit system shut down for the first time ever. Buses, commuter trains, and the subway would stop running at noon on Saturday. Even Broadway went dark.

However, as the media was hyping her potential for destruction, Irene lost some of her punch. Spinning toward the East Coast that Friday, she did not intensify to a Category 4 storm, as many had feared. Instead, she was downgraded to a Category 2. Still, her size was daunting. The National Hurricane Center reported hurricane-force winds greater than 74 mph extending outward from Irene's eye up to ninety miles, with tropical storm–force winds reaching out another two hundred miles in each direction. Like Hurricane Floyd, Irene was about twice the size of a typical hurricane. From edge to edge, she had a wind field of almost six hundred miles, as well as a huge swath of rain.

Those on the East Coast either evacuated or stocked up on water, food, and fuel, then battened down the hatches. While they had power, most Easterners watched satellite and radar images of the huge, swirling storm on the many TV news broadcasts and the Internet. And then they waited for the wind and rain to start.

§   §   §

HURRICANE IRENE hit North Carolina's Outer Banks by midmorning on Saturday, August 27. She came ashore just east of Morehead City as a Category 1 storm, with winds around 85 mph. Over the next few hours she crossed North Carolina from south to north, dumping some fifteen inches of rain. She then paralleled the mid-Atlantic coast as she churned northward that Saturday. Wind and rain knocked out power to almost 800,000 in North Carolina and Virginia, and nine people, from North Carolina to Maryland, were killed. Falling trees and limbs caused six of the nine reported fatalities.

In the wee hours of Sunday morning, August 28, Hurricane Irene made landfall again near Atlantic City, New Jersey, with sustained winds of around 75 mph. More than 1 million people had evacuated the Jersey Shore, a popular destination on summer weekends. But the coastal communities did not suffer the expected damage. Rainfall totaled just over 4.5 inches along the coast. "We dodged a bullet," Police Chief David Wolfson of Margate City told a Reuters reporter. Margate City sits on a barrier island five miles southwest of Atlantic City.

But Irene was far less kind to inland New Jersey, where property, roads, and power lines were damaged by downed trees and flooding. About 650,000 people lost power in the state. North of Trenton, rainfall totals topped ten inches, and flooding closed more than 250 roads. Irene was the first hurricane in more than a hundred years — and only the second in recorded history to date — to make landfall in New Jersey.

With New York City next in Hurricane Irene's sights, the nation seemed to hold its breath. What damage would the strong storm inflict on the skyscrapers and densely populated coastal areas? No major hurricane had struck New York City since Floyd brought 40-mph winds and several inches of rain to the metropolitan area in September 1999. But, for the most part, Floyd had spared the city significant destruction. Most of the damage from that hurricane — downgraded to a tropical storm long before hitting New York City — occurred upstate, where the storm dropped ten to fifteen inches of rain.

Throughout Sunday morning, many people were glued to the Weather Channel, perhaps waiting to witness the devastation in New York unfold behind the intrepid Jim Cantore, the Weather Channel meteorologist who frequently reports live from the middle of blizzards and hurricanes. But as Hurricane Irene's eye passed over Coney Island, just east of the city, around 9:00 a.m. on Sunday, little of the feared damage occurred. "Windows in skyscrapers did not shatter. Subway tunnels did not flood. Power was not shut off pre-emptively. The water grid did not burst. There were no reported fatalities in the five boroughs. And the rivers flanking Manhattan did not overrun their banks," reported the *New York Times* on August 28. Three hours later, Irene moved over Carmel, New York, sixty miles north and slightly east of New York City. She was now downgraded to a tropical storm, with winds around 65 mph.

That, it seemed, was the end of Irene. By Sunday afternoon, commentators on national television were almost celebrating. Except for some flooding in low-lying areas, New York City had escaped Irene relatively unscathed. Story over.

ʄ ʄ ʄ

BUT IRENE was far from finished. Although her winds were winding down, she still carried a huge load of rain, and she was bearing down on New England—which was already experiencing one of the wettest Augusts on record. The National Climatic Data Center reported that August 2011 was the second wettest in the Northeast in 117 years, surpassed only by August 1955; and four states—New Hampshire, New Jersey, New York, and Vermont—were having their wettest August since 1895. The region had already averaged 7.34 inches of rain in August alone, 189 percent of the normal total. And this rain came on the heels of the third snowiest winter on record and a very wet spring. All this precipitation had left the soil highly saturated, from New Jersey through Vermont, New Hampshire, and northern Maine. Any new rainfall on New England's sodden earth would therefore become runoff.

Throughout Sunday, flooding and storm surge destroyed at least twenty homes in Connecticut. The wind took down power poles, and the state's two main electric companies, Connecticut Light and Power and United Illuminating, reported that a record 754,000 customers—about half the state—had lost electricity. A week later, many were still without power. At least two people died, one in a capsized canoe, the other in a house that caught fire after live wires fell on it. In neighboring Rhode Island, another 256,000 were without power, and flooding and storm surge caused some damage. But a hurricane barrier that had been built after the infamous 1938 hurricane, which descended on New England with no warning, protected the city of Providence at the head of Narragansett Bay.

From Connecticut, Irene marched into Massachusetts, with the eye of the storm over the state's southwest corner by early afternoon. Most damage occurred in the Berkshire Mountains, where the Westfield and Deerfield rivers flow. The seventy-six-mile-long Deerfield, with headwaters in Vermont, flows southeast into Massachusetts and drains into the Connecticut River near Greenfield, Massachusetts. In a matter of hours on Sunday, August 28, the Deerfield rose twelve feet and was flowing nearly 38,000 cubic feet per second (cfs) when the gage* stopped working around 10:45 a.m. Normal flow rates in the Deerfield are closer to 1,000 cfs. The Massachusetts Department of Transportation closed Interstate 91 because they feared that the Deerfield would undermine the highway's bridges near Greenfield. The seventy-eight-mile-long Westfield River, which originates in the Berkshire Mountains and drains into the Connecticut River near Springfield in south-central Massachusetts, rose fifteen feet in twelve hours and topped out almost seven feet above flood stage. By the end of the storm on Sunday, more than a half-million residents and businesses in Massachusetts were without power.

Farther west, in the Catskill Mountains of New York, Irene caused floods that took out roads and bridges and left residents trapped. Similar damage occurred in New York's Adirondack Mountains, where flooding wiped out the fire station in Keene, a town on the road to Lake Placid. About 900,000 people lost power in upstate New York.

ꞩ ꞩ ꞩ

IN VERMONT, as elsewhere, people had prepared for wind. Lots of wind. Employees at Central Vermont Public Service (CVPS),** the state's largest electric utility, serving 160,000 customers in almost all of southern and central Vermont as well as a few towns in the north, were particularly uneasy. High winds would no doubt bring massive power outages.

"Our private weather forecaster scared the daylights out of us when the National Weather Service (NWS) forecasts were barely raising an eyebrow over the storm [in Vermont]," said CVPS spokesman Steve Costello. "By the morning of [August] 25th, we concluded that we had to move quickly or face a potentially life-changing storm without any outside resources."

By the end of the day on Thursday, August 25, CVPS had firm commitments from hundreds of contract utility and tree workers from as far away as Illinois, Missouri, Kansas, Texas, and Ontario. This outside help began traveling to Vermont on the Friday before the storm (utilities in other Eastern states were not willing to free up any linemen, given the

*Gage (rather than gauge) has been the accepted spelling for stream measurement activities and equipment in the water resources documents of the U.S. Geological Survey since before 1900.
**In June 2012, CVPS merged with Green Mountain Power.

threat that Irene posed to their own customers), and crews were pulling into motels and hotels around the state by Saturday evening. These crews, along with CVPS employees, expected to chainsaw downed trees and right power poles taken out by the high winds. Power might be out for several days in some locations, warned CVPS. The utility, along with local and state officials, urged Vermonters to stock up on food, water, batteries, and fuel for cars and generators; fill bathtubs with water (to flush toilets when power outages make private water-well pumps inoperable); have a hard-wired telephone on hand (one that does not require power from the grid); and clear yards of anything that could become a wind-blown projectile.

Still, few in Vermont seemed worried about Irene. Although weather forecasters predicted devastating flooding in the state, that did not seem to sink in with many residents, perhaps because Vermonters don't have much experience with hurricanes. To many people in Vermont—New England's only inland state—the word "hurricane" conjures up images of palm trees blowing sideways and huge, wind-driven waves—not water spilling over the tops of riverbanks, ripping out roads and flooding valley floors. The last hurricane (or rather, hurricane-downgraded-to-a-tropical-storm) to hit the state was Floyd, and most Vermonters do not remember that storm. Floyd had dumped three to six inches of rain on the state, but the dry ground meant that flooding was localized. In comparison, by the time Irene hit Vermont, the state had already had more precipitation than it typically sees in an entire year (about forty inches). Record snowfall plus heavy spring rains had already caused damaging flooding, especially along Lake Champlain. Although the month of July provided some relief from incessant rain in Vermont, heavy rains had returned in August. By the end of the month, the soil was almost completely saturated, especially in southern and central Vermont.

In fact, it had been almost seventy-three years since a hurricane had caused major damage in Vermont. The Hurricane of 1938 hit the state on September 21, 1938—fifteen years before the National Hurricane Center began naming hurricanes. And it arrived as an unexpected guest. The storm had formed over the Bahamas, and the National Weather Service predicted that it would veer out to sea south of New York, not roar straight north, make landfall over Long Island, and then barrel straight into New England. The storm traveled with such speed—sixty miles per hour, according to David Ludlum in *The Vermont Weather Book*—that it arrived before weather bureaus in New England could issue warnings. The storm killed more than five hundred people in New England, over half of them in Rhode Island. In Vermont, the storm claimed eight lives.

The eye of the Hurricane of '38 blew into Vermont near Brattleboro and then veered northwest, "crossing the Green Mountains on a diagonal along a Marlboro-Weston-Rutland-Brandon-Middlebury-Vergennes line," wrote Ludlum. Wind speeds had diminished from those experienced in the southern New England states; Burlington and Northfield recorded maximum sustained winds of 47 mph, with gusts probably half again as strong at higher elevations. Nevertheless, the winds are what many remember. Barn roofs blew off and chimneys toppled, and most of Vermont—especially the northern and eastern parts of the state—was littered with downed trees, particularly the state's beloved maples. At a farm in Cabot, the wind uprooted or broke off twenty-four hundred maples in a sugarbush of thirty-five hundred trees. In South Royalton, a thousand young pine trees were destroyed. In other parts of the state, apples were reportedly blown off trees.

The Hurricane of 1938 also brought devastating floods. Worst hit was southeastern Vermont, which was on the western side of the storm's eye as it tracked northwest from Brattleboro to Vergennes. While higher winds are almost always found on the eastern side of advancing hurricanes, the western sectors typically see the heaviest rainfall. This phenomenon occurs because hurricanes and tropical storms transition into extratropical storms as they move into New England. During that transition, they develop temperature differentials from one side to the other. Spinning counterclockwise around the storm, the air currents on the western side of the storm carry cooler air from Canada southward. Meanwhile, warm and moist tropical air on the eastern side of the storm continues to surge northward. Aided by interactions with a strengthening jet stream high in the atmosphere (as was the case with Irene), that moisture-laden tropical air is forced to rise over the cooler air, resulting in prodigious amounts of rain, primarily to the north and west of the storm's center. The region's mountains also cause the tropical air to lift and cool, wringing out the moisture.

Precipitation totals from the 1938 hurricane bore this out. Ludlum reported that Burlington, on the eastern side of the storm's eye, received

2.85 inches of rain, while Woodstock and Brattleboro, on the eye's western side, totaled 4.45 and 5.50 inches, respectively. But the rainfall from the hurricane was not the only cause of flooding. In the week before the 1938 hurricane hit Vermont, the state had received heavy rains from several smaller storms. Just days prior to the hurricane, a rainstorm had brought more than two inches of rain to Rutland and one inch to Woodstock, followed by showers that dropped another couple of inches onto southern Vermont.

With the soil already saturated, water poured from the hills in southeastern Vermont during the 1938 storm. Roads were washed out, such as U.S. Route 4 in Mendon Gorge, where Mendon Brook cut a deep gash in that important cross-state route, making it impassable. In Brandon, the Neshobe River, which flows through downtown, "swirled through the streets," reported the *Rutland Herald*, and the high-water mark, according to one observer, was three feet above the 1927 flood mark.

In Wilmington in far southern Vermont, the Main Street Bridge, then only four years old, collapsed on one side and smashed the town's water main; bridges and roads leading in all directions were washed out. Just north of Wilmington, in West Dover, flood levels were reported to be twice those of the 1927 flood.

The impact of Tropical Storm Irene on Vermont, then, would depend on exactly where her eye tracked. Forecasters predicted that if Irene's eye traveled west of Vermont, through New York, the Green Mountain State would get strong, damaging winds but less rain. If the eye moved up to the east of the state, Vermont would get hammered by rain, and most rivers in the state, if not all, would reach flood stage.

As Irene approached, models put her eye traveling up the Connecticut River Valley between Vermont and New Hampshire—the scenario that would bring torrential rains to Vermont. Still, many people seemed to fixate on the word "hurricane" and were anticipating only high winds; they stocked up on food, water, and provisions such as batteries in case the power was out for a day or two. Not even the weather forecasters were prepared for the devastation that would follow.

§ § §

ON SATURDAY, the eve of the storm in Vermont, the air was still, warm, and heavy—literally the calm before the storm. Rain began falling in southern Vermont sometime during the night — a light sprinkle that was barely audible to those sleeping.

But not everyone was sleeping well. In the village of Wilmington, in southern Vermont, Susie Haughwout was lying in bed listening to the Weather Channel's continual Irene updates. Haughwout, Wilmington's town clerk, was one of the few in Vermont who was more concerned about rain than wind. Nestled against the Deerfield River, Wilmington is prone to flooding.

Located almost exactly halfway between the southern Vermont cities of Bennington and Brattleboro, Wilmington hasn't always sat on the river. When the town was chartered in 1751, its eight houses, store, and Masonic Hall were on a nearby hill. In either 1832 or 1833 the town moved down to its current location on the Deerfield River. The river originates near Mount Snow, a popular ski resort about ten miles north of the village. After meandering through lush farm fields, the Deerfield funnels into a rocky gorge just north of town. This rocky gorge was the perfect place to build the saw and grist mills needed by the rural dwellers for their livelihood and survival. The village grew up around the mills, and the Old Red Mill, now a restaurant and inn, was once a sawmill, which closed down in the 1930s. The historic buildings that line state routes 9 and 100 — meeting in Wilmington between the police station and the concrete Main Street Bridge over the Deerfield — are now home to some forty-five shops and restaurants. The town itself is home to just under two thousand people.

Given its proximity to the Deerfield River and its topography, downtown Wilmington lies almost entirely within the floodplain. In 1938 the village paid dearly for that location when rains from the hurricane of that year caused the Deerfield to fill downtown with almost five feet of water. Over the intervening years high water has intermittently threatened Wilmington — notably on August 10, 1976, when the remnants of Hurricane Belle deluged the state with about four inches of rain: Lilias MacBean Hart, who had opened the Quaigh Design Centre in downtown Wilmington in the 1960s, remembers water from the Deerfield River pouring over the Main Street Bridge and flooding the town about a foot deep. In fact, flooding is such a concern in Wilmington that a water height scale is painted on one of the Main Street Bridge abutments. The scale starts at eleven feet — far above the river at normal summer flow rates—and tops out at eighteen feet. If the river rises above eighteen feet, it is almost at street level. A flood marker is painted on the side of the police station, which is adjacent to the town office. At about eye level, two wavy lines, with the words "1938 Flood" written between them, mark the height of the water during Wilmington's worst flood ever. Haughwout saw that flood reminder every day as she walked into the town office.

Haughwout had grown up in Wilmington but moved to Miami, Florida, in the late 1970s and worked for a boutique real estate agency. Then Hurricane Andrew hit Florida in 1992. The Category 5 hurricane devastated southern Florida, destroying 25,524 homes and damaging 101,241 others in Dade County, including 90 percent of all mobile homes. More than a quarter-million people were left homeless. After the storm, almost all Haughwout's friends left Miami. So she decided to return to Vermont and visit her family. She never thought she would stay in Wilmington. But the town clerk at the time asked her to work as her assistant. In 1995, Haughwout ascended to the role of town clerk.

Her experience with Andrew turned Haughwout into a "perennial hurricane worrier," a concern most people pooh-poohed.

"They go, 'Pshaw, you're just worried because you're a worrier,'" she said.

When forecasts for Hurricane Irene showed the storm moving into New England, Haughwout became concerned. On Friday, August 26, she talked to the Wilmington fire chief.

"What do you think about potential rainfall?" she asked him. "Should I get everything off the floor in the office about six inches in case we get a little water?"

"That's a good idea," he responded.

That afternoon, Haughwout and assistant town clerk Patricia Johnson moved town records that were on bottom shelves onto tabletops in the town office. But Haughwout couldn't stop worrying. What if the flooding were more significant than people were saying? She went to bed Saturday night with the TV on, the Weather Channel forecasters giving storm updates throughout the night. Every couple of hours she would wake up and watch the next update. Her gut told her, "We're in trouble."

҉ ҉ ҉

IN MENDON, Doug Casella was home with his wife, Maureen, which was unusual. As the founder of Casella Waste Systems and Casella Construction, one of Vermont's largest construction and earth-moving companies, he usually spends the busy summer construction season driving around the Northeast, from Massachusetts to New York, checking on his company's various jobs and sleeping in hotels. But during the summer of 2011, his company had a job close to home. Casella Construction was demolishing Peak Lodge, atop nearby Killington Mountain, so Casella spent a few more nights than usual sleeping in his own bed. And he was looking forward to an upcoming long weekend — a rare break in his busy schedule. Every year for the past six or seven years, Doug and Maureen have taken the train to New York City on the last Sunday in August and spent two days watching the world's best tennis players — such as Roger Federer, Rafael Nadal, and Serena Williams — compete at the U.S. Open.

But this year, Irene was threatening to be a third wheel on their date. With Amtrak canceling rail service on August 28 in the Northeast, they knew they wouldn't make it to the city on Sunday. The Casellas went to bed Saturday night thinking that they would spend a rainy Sunday hunkering down at home. Then they would probably be able to make it to the courts at Flushing Meadows on Monday.

3

NOT JUST A RAINSTORM

The surging waters carry an assemblage of debris, composed
of limbs of trees, fragments of buildings, spans of bridges, and
any other loose object that is buoyant.... Together these serve
as battering rams to smash and destroy any obstacle along the
way such as dams, bridges, and mills. Riverfront buildings are
undermined and sometimes collapse to join the floating debris,
adding to its destructive power. Railroads and highways are
severed, and the lines of communication and power cut.
Whole communities become isolated.

    💲 David M. Ludlum, *The Vermont Weather Book*

ON THE MORNING OF SUNDAY, AUGUST 28, Tropical Storm Irene
seemed to many in Vermont like an overblown rainstorm. Compared
with summer thunderstorms, which can dump several inches of rain in
a couple of hours (on July 8, 1914, for example, eight to twelve inches
of rain fell in Jericho, Vermont, within an hour and a half), Irene's rainfall in Vermont's valleys appeared steady, not torrential. And throughout
much of the state, her winds were no worse than what the state experiences during the many Nor'easters that bring deep snow in winter. In
Rutland, wind speeds stayed under twenty miles per hour for most of
the day, with gusts hitting thirty-seven miles per hour in the evening.
These gusts were the only indication that Irene, until very recently, had
been a hurricane.

But the steady rain was falling on already sodden ground that was unable to absorb any more water. As the morning wore on, the state's rivers
and streams began to swell rapidly.

௫   ௫   ௫

IN WILMINGTON, town clerk Susie Haughwout was out of bed at 5:30 a.m. and pacing. It was raining outside—not hard, but coming down. Sometime around 7:00 a.m. she drove her Mitsubishi SUV to the fire station, where her husband is a volunteer firefighter. She asked one of the firefighters if she should be preparing for worse flooding than that of the 1938 hurricane. He said, "I would."

Haughwout jumped back in her car and drove two blocks to the town clerk's office. She parked in front of the police station next door—directly in front of the 1938 high-water mark—got out of her car, and walked over to the Main Street Bridge. She looked down at the water level scale painted on the bridge abutment. The water was at the twelve-foot mark. Six more feet and it would reach the top of the scale . . . and the bottom of the bridge. It was 8:00 a.m.

Haughwout walked back to the police station and stood in front of the 1938 high-water mark. She followed the line with her finger from the mark back toward the town clerk's office. She stopped at the front door and looked at where her finger was. If the water rose to the 1938 flood level, it would be waist high in the town clerk's office.

She walked next into the vault where the town records are kept and surveyed what she would need to move to the building's second floor— huge books of land records; books containing birth, death, and marriage certificates; property deeds; plat maps; everything needed to run a town, as well as documents that home and business owners would need to get loans or insurance payments should they suffer storm damage.

During her sleepless night, Haughwout had been pondering how best to save the town records. She knew she had to get them to the building's second floor, and the most efficient way to accomplish that was by elevator. But if the power went out, the elevator wouldn't work. She figured that she had until at least noon or 2:00 p.m. before the storm got that bad. From the office phone, Haughwout called assistant town clerk Patricia Johnson and asked her and her boyfriend, Larry Nutting, to come in and help move the records. She also called select board member Jim Burke and his wife, Patti. Both Johnson and Burke said they would be in as soon as they could.

Tropical Storm Irene Rainfall - Vermont

August 27th & 28th, 2011

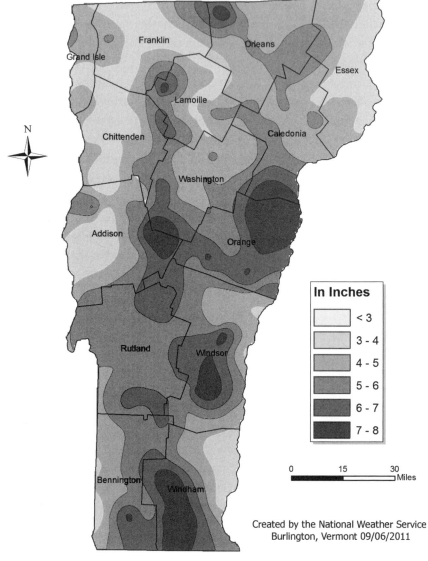

Franklin
Orleans
Grand Isle
Essex
Lamoille
Chittenden
Caledonia
Washington
Addison
Orange
Rutland
Windsor
Bennington
Windham

In Inches

	< 3
	3 - 4
	4 - 5
	5 - 6
	6 - 7
	7 - 8

0   15   30 Miles

Created by the National Weather Service
Burlington, Vermont 09/06/2011

186 reports were used from NWS Cooperative Observers, Automated Weather Stations, CoCoRaHS, Mesonets, Trained Spotters, Personal Weather Stations, Public Reports This map is an interpolation of actual reported values but should be considered an estimation only. Due to the influence of terrain, amounts may vary greatly over a short distance.

With a morning of heavy lifting in front of her, Haughwout headed to Dot's Restaurant, a town mainstay that sits adjacent to the Main Street Bridge. The building was originally constructed in 1832 and served as the town post office and general store until it became a restaurant in the 1930s. Despite the fact that the restaurant is literally cantilevered over the Deerfield River, the structure survived the 1938 flood (other buildings along the river were not as lucky). After the flood, the restaurant, then called the Green Shutter at Village Square Diner, underwent a complete renovation to repair water damage. Since then it has undergone ownership and name changes, from Dairy Bar to Dot's Dairy Bar. In the 1980s, John Reagan purchased the restaurant and renamed it Dot's. It soon became the place to go for blueberry pancakes in the morning and homemade meatloaf in the evenings. It was also the place that John met his future wife, Patty, who worked there as a waitress for a short time. And over the years, Dot's has become Wilmington's gathering place—what some call the town's "water cooler."

Crossing the Main Street Bridge, Haughwout looked at the water level scale again. In the ten minutes since she had arrived downtown, the river had risen one foot. It was now hitting the thirteen-foot mark.

Inside Dot's, Patty Reagan looked askance at Haughwout, who's not known as a morning person.

"What are you doing here at this hour?" asked Reagan.

"I'm moving all the town records out of the vault," replied the no-nonsense town clerk.

"You're not making me feel very good," replied Reagan.

"I'm sorry," said Haughwout, "but I don't think this is going to go very well."

Haughwout ordered a breakfast sandwich—a "McDot"—and started talking to the other locals. Phil Taylor, owner of Bartleby's Books along with his wife, Lisa Sullivan, was also ordering breakfast sandwiches and coffee at Dot's. Worried that downtown Wilmington might flood when Irene hit, Sullivan and Taylor had returned home from a family reunion in Rhode Island a day early. But now they were uncertain what steps they should take to protect their store. Bartleby's Books sits in a building about fifty yards west—and slightly downhill—from Dot's on Wilmington's West Main Street.

Taylor looked at the town clerk and said, "You're going to move stuff out of the vault? What do you think I should do? Fill sandbags?"

"No, you don't have time," replied Haughwout, who was basing her reply only on gut instinct. "Go home, be with your family, be safe."

Taylor took the egg, bacon, and cheese sandwiches and coffee and returned to Bartleby's, where Lisa was starting to move a few books and other valuables to upper store shelves. Less than five months earlier, Taylor and Sullivan had lost their other bookstore, the Book Cellar in Brattleboro, to fire. It was unthinkable that they might lose two businesses to biblical-scale disasters in less than half a year. Rather than that, they thought they might get a couple of inches of water in Bartleby's that afternoon — more a nuisance than a disaster.

Seated at Dot's, Haughwout began talking to Ann Manwaring, the Wilmington state representative, who offered to help the town clerk move the records to the second floor. The two women walked back across the bridge to the town office and started loading books from the vault onto the office chairs and rolling the chairs to the elevator. Haughwout knew that the office chairs could double as dollies because a couple of other times over the past sixteen years she had moved documents from the lower shelves to the second floor in the face of flood threats — threats that had not materialized. She had never moved this many, though. This time, "I knew we were screwed," she said.

Johnson, Nutting, and the Burkes arrived around 8:30 a.m., and they and Haughwout and Manwaring continued moving the town's vital records, computers, and copiers to the second floor — with Haughwout barking out orders about what documents could be left behind. They focused on land records and indexes, recorded land surveys, town meeting records, election records, vital records, grand lists, and town reports. On the fly, Haughwout told them to leave behind voted ballots from the 2010 general election (they were scheduled to be destroyed in August 2012 anyway), school registers, and grand lists that were well over a hundred years old (many of which had been damaged in the 1938 flood), twenty- to forty-year-old lien documents that had been noted in old lien volumes, and land records that had already been digitized.

At one point during the process, Manwaring borrowed Haughwout's car to get a camera. The town clerk wanted to take photos of the vault before they moved too much. Manwaring drove home, picked up her camera, then drove back downtown and parked the suv in front of the town office. She ran back into the office and began snapping photos. Focused on the impending disaster, she had no memory of where she put Haughwout's car keys.

ᔕ   ᔕ   ᔕ

AT 9:30 A.M., the National Weather Service received its first report of flash flooding. The stream along Centerville Road in the hills above East Wallingford in central Vermont was over its banks and washing out the road. Just over an hour later, someone reported to the NWS that a large culvert near the intersection of Vermont Route 155 and Maple Hill Road in Mount Holly — about seven miles from East Wallingford — had washed out. Bonnie MacPherson, an East Wallingford resident, had driven down to the village by Route 103 to see how the Mill River was doing. She was amazed to find the water level above the embankment but not flowing over it, as if some unseen force were pulling the water downstream so fast that it couldn't flow out of its channel. At least for now. Farther downstream, the Mill River burst through its bank as it rounded a corner and began turning the fields of Evening Song Farm into a new riverbed.

By 11:45 a.m., reports of damage were coming in fast — many of them from the Ottauquechee River valley in central Vermont. With headwaters in Killington, the forty-one-mile-long Ottauquechee flows due east to the Connecticut River through the towns of Bridgewater and Woodstock and the village of Quechee. For twenty-six miles, U.S. Route 4 parallels the river from Killington to Quechee.

Craig Mosher lives along U.S. 4 near the Killington/Bridgewater town line — and very near the Ottauquechee's headwaters. The owner of Mosher Excavating, Mosher was out at midmorning on Sunday helping his neighbor try to save his ski shop. A small stream pouring out of the mountain behind the First Stop Ski Shop and Board Barn was flowing across the parking lot and clogging the culverts under U.S. 4 that normally channel the stream's water into the Ottauquechee. Mosher was on his knees clearing the culverts with his hands. When the quantity of water and debris began to overwhelm him, he went home to get an excavator.

Later in the morning — he doesn't remember exactly when — Mosher looked across the road at his own property. The Ottauquechee flows right through Mosher's land and separates his home and business from a twenty-one-acre pasture, home to two shaggy Scottish Highlanders, two sheep, and an ornery donkey named Pedro. Since Mosher first acquired the animals in 2006, they had become a local attraction, with passersby often stopping for photos or to pet them. On that Sunday, as Mosher worked to clear the culverts near the ski shop, he noticed that water was beginning to flow across part of his pasture, and that the river had already flooded an area behind his equipment garage, where he stored magazines of dynamite.

Mosher jumped off the excavator and ran back to his house to try to save the dynamite. By the time he'd started up his loader and maneuvered it behind the garage, the magazines were almost underwater. As he was moving them to higher ground, he noticed that his four pigs—not in the pasture, but in a small yard behind the garage—were swimming. He waded into the water, grabbed them by the hind legs, loaded them into makeshift crates, and put the crates inside a hay trailer on higher ground.

Water from the river was now flowing down his driveway and toward his house. But Mosher had to check on his animals. The Scottish Highlanders, named Big and Rob by Mosher's son (after an MTV show), were already on higher ground in the pasture, as were the sheep, Byron and Jessie. But Mosher couldn't find Pedro, so he waded out to a shed where Pedro often sheltered and found the donkey hiding inside. He put a halter and lead rope on Pedro and pushed him out the door and through the water. The animal, normally quite vocal, didn't make a sound.

Shortly after Mosher had pulled Pedro to higher ground, the shed, along with a larger one in which Big and Rob often sought refuge, was carried off by the water and tangled in debris just downstream, by Blackie's, a deli and gas station on U.S. 4. At that point, one of the Scottish Highlanders (Mosher is not sure which, but a neighbor thinks it was Big) began to head for his now displaced shed. Highland bulls typically weigh between fifteen hundred and two thousand pounds, but Big nevertheless struggled in the force of the river current. His legs started to wobble.

"Quick, throw me a feed bucket!" shouted Mosher to the neighbor, who was standing near the pasture fence along U.S. 4.

Big saw the bucket and began walking toward Mosher. But before he was out of the current, a tree with its root ball and leaves still attached came floating with the current through the pasture.

"As the tree was floating by, he stopped to have a salad!" said Mosher of his opportunistic bull. Big finally gave up snacking and walked to safety.

૭   ૭   ૭

PEOPLE WHO LIVE in the mountain town of Pittsfield are accustomed to the inconveniences caused by bad weather. With the nearest large grocery store thirty minutes away, they keep their kitchens stocked in case a snowstorm makes traveling treacherous for days at a time, or a summer thunderstorm, often severe in the mountains, washes out their roads and driveways. After almost a week of warnings about Irene, Pittsfielders knew they should gas up their cars, buy food and other provisions, and fill their bathtubs with water. Still, some people were heading to Home Depot in Rutland on Sunday morning to buy last-minute items.

Heather Grev and Jack Livesey were already well stocked for the storm. With little else to do except watch it rain, they headed out for a late breakfast at the Swiss Farm Inn, a local establishment that advertises the "World's Best Breakfast." The inn is on Route 100 about a half-mile north of Pittsfield's downtown. They ate pancakes and eggs, chatted with locals about the storm, and watched the rain fall.

Just down the road at the Amee Farm, sixty or so people, mostly from the New York City area, were partaking in a "farewell brunch," the final event of Evan Leibowitz's and Janina Stegmeyer's wedding weekend. An artist and bar manager in Brooklyn, Leibowitz met Stegmeyer, who hails from Germany, while she was studying English in New York. Engaged to be married the previous Christmas during a flight over the Atlantic, they had planned a Vermont wedding for August 28 at Pittsfield's Riverside Farm, a wedding venue owned by Joe and Courtney De Sena.

The De Senas had purchased Riverside Farm in 2000, and Joe, a Wall Street trader, has become known for his Death Race, a twenty-four-hour suffer-fest around Pittsfield that can involve carrying thousands of pounds of rocks, cinderblocks, wood, stumps, even onions; building fires; crawling through mud; chopping cords of wood; and other such grueling challenges. Its website is titled youmaydie.com. Within

Pittsfield, De Sena is known as Millionaire Joe, since he owns Riverside on the south end of town, the Original General Store in the village itself, and the Amee Farm (another lodge and wedding venue) on the north end of town. The recently constructed Amee Farm lodge commands a hillside just north of town. But not all the wedding guests were at the lodge enjoying the brunch. Some were still sleeping at Riverside Farm. When they awoke, they noticed that the Tweed River was striking the bottom of the covered bridge that accesses the farm from Route 100. As covered bridges go in Vermont, this one was relatively new: it was built in 1976.

After enjoying their breakfast at the Swiss Farm Inn, Grev and Livesey returned to their little white house. The rain was really coming down now. The Tweed River and its West Branch were still within their banks, but they were no longer babbling mountain streams. They were more like raging torrents. Grev and Livesey decided to bring up a few items from the backyard and shed: Livesey's toolbox, their bicycles, and the new riding mower. Friends stopped by to help, and they put everything in the driveway beside the little white house and two Subaru wagons.

A few minutes later, the Tweed jumped its banks and the water quickly reached the basement windows at the back of the house, where the slope of land makes the basement more like a first floor. Livesey checked the basement and was surprised to find it dry. What he didn't know was that the Riverside Farm's covered bridge just upstream had given way, bursting apart in the raging river. Along with trees and other debris, pieces of the broken bridge had jammed against the Parmenter Place bridge that crosses the Tweed upstream from the little white house. The clog formed a dam. Almost simultaneously, a similar tree dam was forming at the Route 100 bridge over the West Branch. That bridge sits almost directly in front of the little white house.

Around lunchtime Grev called her family in New Jersey, where Irene was supposed to hit hard. The wind was bad, said her parents, but they were fine. Grev told them that all was well in Pittsfield and that she and Jack were headed for a hurricane party later that day. She said good-bye and hung up, unaware that the water was rising alarmingly just outside.

Pittsfield town clerk Patty Haskins saw the water starting to flood Route 100 near the West Branch bridge. Pittsfield has an emergency plan written in 2001 by Haskins in conjunction with the local regional planning commission. But in the ten years since she had written the plan, she had never had to implement it. Haskins and Peter Borden, Pittsfield's emergency management coordinator, would open the book every year, make a few minimal changes (mostly adding or deleting names of the people considered vulnerable in a disaster, such as the elderly), then close it—because nothing was ever going to happen in Pittsfield.

As the floodwaters rose on Sunday, Haskins realized that they should start checking on people who live in the high-risk locations and those living alone, as well as the disabled and elderly. She called Borden and then rang up town road commissioner George Deblon, who is also on the select board. He was on Hawk Mountain, a development on a steep hillside east of the village. In the steady rain, the roads and driveways on Hawk were starting to wash out, and Deblon was trying to divert water away from houses in the hillside development. He told Haskins that he couldn't leave. She then called Mark Begin, a selectman who lives on the other end of town. He said the river was already flooding there too.

"It was like a switch went off, and there was water everywhere," said Doug Mianulli, Pittsfield's second constable, who was out checking on people around town.

Haskins instituted the emergency plan.

§   §   §

IN SOUTH ROYALTON, Tom "Geo" Honigford had planned to take the day off. The forty-nine-year-old farmer had been working seven days a week since April—growing organic fruit and vegetables on his thirty-seven-acre farm on the banks of the White River—and he figured the weather was a good excuse to rest. He and his wife, Sharon O'Connor, had purchased the farm in 1995, though it took some convincing on Honigford's part. The farmhouse, built in 1780 after the original house was burned in the Royalton Raid—a British-led raid involving three hundred members of the Mohawk tribe against the towns of Royalton, Sharon, and Tunbridge in what was then the Vermont Republic—needed lots of work, and the fields had been "monocropped" for years. The previous owner had planted only corn in the fields and the soil was dead, said Honigford. He gradually rehabilitated the soil and began growing a large variety of organic produce, from melons and sweet potatoes to lettuce and other mesclun greens, tomatoes, you name it. From April through October, he carts his produce to farmers' markets in nearby Norwich,

Vermont, and Lebanon, New Hampshire. He also runs his own farm-stand. The farm is named Hurricane Flats.

With Hurricane Irene coming, Honigford and his farm manager, Mark Edsell, had buttoned down the two greenhouses that sit on his fields, as well as a smaller one up by the barn, in anticipation of high winds. "They were closed up tighter than a drum," Honigford said. Inside one of the greenhouses were five thousand pounds of onions ready to be sold. Inside the other were red, ripe tomatoes still on the vines.

About a half-mile farther downriver, David and Peggy Ainsworth were expecting people for a "corning party," in which friends sit around a table and help freeze corn. The Ainsworths own a fifth-generation dairy farm along the White River and grow corn and hay on about forty acres. After the wet summer, the corn stalks were twelve to fourteen feet high. It was going to be a banner year for silage. Ainsworth was figuring he would get eight hundred tons of silage, or twenty-five tons per acre, to feed his forty-six-cow milking herd and the calves.

Around 12:30 on Sunday afternoon, Honigford went online to check the U.S. Geological Survey's river gage twenty miles downstream of South Royalton. The White River was running at 3,870 cfs and was 6.51 feet deep at the gage—up from 1,030 cfs and 4.55 feet at 9:00 a.m. The water volume was rising quickly, he realized, but that was not unusual. Twice in August the river level had jumped significantly in a short period of time: on the evening of August 15, the river had gone from 941 cfs to 2,460 in three hours, then continued to climb another 3,000 cfs over the next five hours. The Sunday before Irene hit, the river flow had increased by 4,000 cfs overnight. In both cases, the water did not top the river-banks and had quickly receded.

At 3,870 cfs and 6.51 feet, the river was still well below its flood stage of eighteen feet. Honigford logged off his computer and lay down for his second nap of the day.

He woke up around 1:00 p.m. and, out of curiosity, checked the White River gage again. It now read 5,260 cfs, up 1,600 cfs since he had last checked, a half-hour earlier. One cubic foot of water per second is equal to approximately eight gallons. In just thirty minutes, the rate of flow had increased by 12,800 gallons per second. The river level was at 7.70 feet—still well below the 18-foot flood stage, or what's called bank-full.

Honigford looked out a back window of his house, which sits on a bluff above the river's floodplain and his farm fields. Water was starting to flow onto his field. The river, he realized, was not at 7.70 feet. It was bank-full.

"Oh shit, the gage isn't reading right," he mumbled.

He put on his boots and, with his wife and one of his teenage daughters, walked down the hill onto the field. They walked across the field toward the river until the water was up to their ankles. They weren't worried, just curious.

"We were just playing around, it was all fun and games still," he said.

Around the same time, a friend called the Ainsworths to say she wasn't going to make it to the corning party. The police had closed Route 14 northbound in South Royalton, and she was worried they might also close the road traveling south. Ainsworth looked out his window. Water was starting to flood his lower meadow. But he wasn't worried yet. The water had been that high in the Flood of 1973, a June flood that bent over his corn, which was three feet tall at the time. After that flood, the stalks had recovered.

Just upstream from the Ainsworth's farm, Honigford was standing in his field, watching the river and chatting with his wife and daughter. Suddenly they realized that tufts of grass and other vegetation they had been looking at just a few minutes before were no longer visible. They were underwater. Honigford reached down and held his finger where the water hit his ankle. In one minute's time, his finger was under an inch of water.

"It was at that point that I realized this is not good," he said.

As Honigford and his family hustled back toward his two greenhouses that sit near the back of his field, he looked down at the ground. Brown river water was flowing over his vegetables as if the tide were coming in.

§ § §

AROUND 1:00 P.M. a call came in to Rutland police dispatch that the bridge was washed out on Medway Drive, four miles east of the city. The bridge crosses Mendon Brook near Medway Drive's intersection with U.S. Route 4, where that major east-west thoroughfare begins its ascent across the spine of the Green Mountains. There, in the town of Mendon, U.S. 4 shares a narrow mountain valley referred to as Mendon Gorge with the normally placid brook. Mendon Brook helps drain the Green

Mountains' western flank near 4,235-foot Killington Mountain, Vermont's second highest peak. The caller had reported that people were trapped on the other side of the washed-out bridge. The Rutland City Fire Department, which is contracted by the town of Mendon to respond to emergencies, sent a truck to check on the situation.

As the fire truck rounded a sweeping corner on U.S. 4 and entered the narrow mountain valley, Rutland deputy fire chief Brad LaFaso looked out the truck's window at Mendon Brook and suddenly realized that Tropical Storm Irene meant business.

"There was a lot of water coming down the brook, *a lot* of water," he said. "A lot of brown water and trees just going right down the brook."

The water in the brook—now the size of a river—was acting like a giant, hungry serpent, eating the roadbed where it clung to the valley wall, as well as huge chunks of asphalt. U.S. 4 was rapidly disappearing. By the time LaFaso arrived, the raging water in Mendon Brook had eroded U.S. 4 to the yellow centerline. The steep embankments above the brook were collapsing in landslides into the maelstrom. LaFaso had never seen anything like it in his life—except on TV.

If this was what Irene's rain was doing to little Mendon Brook, the rest of the region was about to face serious flooding, LaFaso realized. He picked up his radio and alerted the Rutland City fire station to call a third alarm. This procedure would call in the two previous shifts to the fire station—or all the Rutland City firefighters. Then LaFaso jumped out of the truck and, with a megaphone, tried to convince a man across the brook to stop building a wall out of firewood, a flimsy dyke that was not going to hold back this much water and debris. Giant trees, complete with their root balls and branches, were being carried violently down the valley in the torrent. A wall of cordwood didn't stand a chance.

Around the same time, Mike Garofano left his home with his twenty-four-year-old son, also named Mike, to check on Rutland City's Davis Reservoir. A Rutland native, the fifty-five-year-old Garofano was well known in this central Vermont city of 16,495 people, and not just as the city's water treatment and resource manager. A third-generation Rutlander, he was also the father of three sons, Thomas, Robert, and Mike, all of whom had grown up in Rutland, then stayed in town as adults. Tom worked for Rutland's Public Works Department along with his dad. Robert had been an engineer at Casella Construction until he died tragically from a fall in April 2010. And Mike—who was said to be very close to his dad—worked for a local country club and was a self-employed landscaper.

The elder Garofano had worked for Rutland's Public Works Department for thirty years, and he took his job as water treatment and resource manager seriously. That was obvious. More than eighteen thousand people draw drinking water from the reservoir, and Garofano had always wanted to ensure that the water was of the best quality. The thirteen-acre Davis Reservoir, which sits on a hillside about four miles northeast of Rutland near the Mendon town line, was built in 1954 after a flood in June of 1947 caused by the bursting of the East Pittsford dam. The disaster had wiped out the city's water system. In that flood, days of heavy rain caused water to overflow the Chittenden Dam, which impounds the 702-acre Chittenden Reservoir. Downstream, the East Pittsford Dam could not hold back the deluge, and shortly after 8:00 p.m. on June 3, 1947, the dam, located six miles northeast of Rutland, burst, sending a fifteen-foot wall of water into Rutland. En route down East Creek, the floodwater severely eroded the earth near the old reservoir and washed out sections of pipe, leaving the city without water for days. It was the worst flood in the city's history, surpassing the 1927 flood.

The Davis Reservoir was built on land 120 feet higher than the old reservoir. Although the asphalt-lined reservoir was almost fifty-seven years old by the time the remnants of Hurricane Irene hit Vermont, the lawns around the reservoir, the slow sand filter, and the holding tanks were immaculate. Even the fences, railings, and entry gates were well maintained, as if the entire facility were an elegant country estate.

The reservoir is recharged with water from Mendon Brook, which flows through an intake valve more than a half-mile upstream from the reservoir. The water flows by gravity through thirty-four hundred feet of pipe into the ninety-million-gallon reservoir. Water from the brook enters the system through a trash rack and leaf screen in a building beside the brook. That building also houses a turbidity meter (which measures how "dirty" the water is), chlorinating equipment, and a manually operated valve.

An electronic valve was installed in the 1980s and is located in a manhole over the pipeline a few yards downstream from the intake building. The controls for that valve are wired so that the valve can be closed by either of two methods if a water quality problem develops in the water-shed (such as an accident on U.S. 4 that might cause gasoline or other chemicals to spill into Mendon Brook). In the case of such an emergency, the valve can be closed by dialing a telephone number that Garofano, police, and other emergency personnel had on file. In addition, the valve will close automatically if the turbidity meter and hydrocarbon sensor in the intake building detect that the water coming into the system is too turbid or "dirty," or if the water contains hydrocarbons above a safe, predetermined level. This prevents petroleum-laden or silt-filled water from contaminating the reservoir. But the automated valve can be opened only on site, in order that the water treatment plant operator can see first-hand what the conditions are at the intake structure. Prior to the installation of the electric valve in the 1980s, keeping the reservoir free of dirty or contaminated brook water depended entirely upon "the alertness, responsiveness, and weather forecasting abilities of the water treatment manager," wrote Rutland Department of Public Works commissioner Alan Shelvey in a history of the city's water supply.

Generally, though, the automatic valve was closed in anticipation of, or at the start of, every heavy storm and — as required — during spring runoff. As Irene bore down on Vermont on Saturday, Garofano had closed the valve.

No one knows exactly what Big Mike and Young Mike — as they were known when they were together — did once they arrived at the reservoir on Sunday, August 28. But with Irene dumping multiple inches of rain throughout the Mendon Brook watershed, Garofano no doubt had wanted to ensure that mud and debris in the brook wasn't going to compromise the city's drinking water supply. According to those who knew him, the water treatment plant operator always wanted to check personally that the intake valve at Mendon Brook was closed and everything was in good order.

As the Garofanos drove along the access road that connects the reservoir to the intake at Mendon Brook, their jaws must have dropped. Mendon Brook was so full of roiling, brown water that it had left its banks and was flowing where the access road had once been. Garofano parked the truck in a pullout along the road about two hundred yards downstream of the intake. If they wanted to reach the intake valve, their only choice was to climb a steep, tree-covered embankment that paralleled the brook and walk upstream along the embankment.

AT 1:45 P.M., the Otter Creek in Rutland reached flood stage of eight feet and topped its banks. Doug Casella was worried about the Casella Waste System's customer care center on Belden Road. That facility sits in the one-hundred-year floodplain near the confluence of East Creek and Otter Creek. Casella had started the waste system company in 1975, and though his brother John is now president, Doug sits on the board and says that whatever happens inside the building is his brother's responsibility, whatever happens outside the building is his.

With water rising in East and Otter creeks, Casella Waste System's customer care facility parking lot was starting to flood. East Creek flows down into Rutland from the Chittenden Reservoir about eleven miles up in the hills northeast of the city (and Mendon Brook flows into East Creek a few miles outside the city); Otter Creek flows north through Rutland from its headwaters in Danby and eventually drains into Lake Champlain. Worried that the building itself would flood, Casella and his twenty-three-year-old son Joe, who works for Casella Construction, brought pumps and set them up in the building. As they worked, Doug Casella watched propane and fuel tanks float through the parking lot, and "they were moving," he said. By midafternoon the parking lot looked like a muddy lake, and water was encroaching on the building. Casella had his pumps running hard.

4

ALL HELL BREAKS LOOSE

When descending the narrow defiles of the upper slopes, the
mass of water is given an irresistible force by gravity, causing
extensive erosion of soil and ground cover. Fields of crops are
covered and roadways washed away.

⌐ David M. Ludlum, *The Vermont Weather Book*

WHEN IT COMES TO NATURAL DISASTERS, Vermont is fairly lucky.
The state experiences very few tornadoes. Winds rarely top fifty miles
per hour in the valleys. Summertime temperatures infrequently hit 100
degrees. And earthquakes—if they are felt—do little more than rattle
the china cabinet. The most frequent statewide weather events worthy
of note are snowstorms—Nor'easters that blow up the East Coast in
winter and can dump feet of snow in the Green Mountains. With ten
major ski resorts and at least nine smaller ski areas in Vermont, from
tiny Cochran's in Richmond to giant Killington, the state drew more
than 4.3 million skiers to the snowy pistes in winter 2010–11. Tourism
dollars brought to the state by skiers account for $750 million a year in
direct spending. So the storms are mostly welcome—except when Vermonters have to shovel the snow, or drive in it.

The state does experience periodic flooding, but it tends to be localized. According to David M. Ludlum in *The Vermont Weather Book*, the
first recorded flood—or freshet (a deceivingly appealing word), as it was
called back then—in Vermont occurred in January 1770, when a rainstorm inundated all of New England. Details are few, but it was noted
in the *Annals of Brattleboro* that an island in the Connecticut River was
under water. Ludlum then describes twenty-three more floods that occurred in the state over the next two hundred years, ending with Hur-

ricane Belle's flooding in August of 1976. It works out to an average of one devastating flood somewhere in the state once every 8.3 years. In the second half of the twentieth century, flood damage tallied at almost $17 million in the state.

Often, damaging flooding in Vermont is caused by intense thunderstorms that travel across the state in the late spring or summer—as happened in towns from Cabot to Montpelier on the evening of May 26, 2011. On that warm, humid spring evening, a series of strong thunder cells paraded across Vermont. One of the largest stalled over Washington County and parts of Caledonia County in the north-central and northeastern parts of the state and dumped up to six inches of rain in six hours near the headwaters of the Winooski River. In Cabot, a stream overflowed a culvert that runs under the tiny downtown and washed out the town garage and the hardware store's parking area. Up the street, trees washed up against a bridge, creating a dam that caused the torrent to overflow the road and erode it deeply. Twenty miles south, the town of Barre was buried in up to three feet of silt when the floodwater receded. Although devastating, the flooding was localized.

The state also experiences less violent flooding, when ice jams in winter or runoff in spring may cause what is referred to as localized inundation flooding—especially after heavy snow years. In the spring of 2011, after the third snowiest winter on record (with 128.4 inches of snow recorded in Burlington) and record rainfall between March and May (24 inches), Lake Champlain rose to its highest recorded level. In Burlington, the lake hit 103.27 feet on May 6, more than three feet above flood stage. It did not drop below flood stage for well over a month (June 19). Flooding damaged lakeside houses, overflowed roads and the causeway leading to the Grand Isles, and closed marinas and beaches.

Every few decades, the state experiences flooding on a more statewide basis. The worst such flood occurred in 1927. It hit unexpectedly over the course of two days in early November that year and became Vermont's worst statewide disaster. It all started after a very wet October, in which total rainfall was 50 percent higher than normal. By early November, locals were finally enjoying warm air and fair skies. On Wednesday, November 2, 1927, the *Rutland Herald* weather forecast called for fair weather, showers overnight, and a return to fair but colder conditions on Thursday.

But two storms were about to meet over Vermont and make a mockery of the forecast. On that Wednesday evening, a storm blowing north, the remnants of a hurricane laden with tropical moisture, became trapped between a cool, low-pressure system moving into New England from the Great Lakes and a high-pressure system extending northeast from Maine over the Canadian Maritimes. This high-pressure system stalled, trapping the moisture-laden storm over New England. The predicted overnight showers never gave way to sun on Thursday. It began raining across the state early in the morning on Thursday, November 4, 1927, and didn't stop for close to forty-eight hours. Rainfall exceeded eight inches in many locations across the state. Rivers rose quickly, and some of the worst flooding happened in the middle of the night.

In the days after the storm, newspapers told horrifying tales of phantomlike houses, still alight with their occupants screaming inside, floating down the swollen, roiling rivers; cows that died at their stanchions in barns; and a crafty soul who lashed together coffin boxes and used this grim raft to rescue people when the villages of Waterbury and Bolton became inundated by floodwaters from the Winooski River.

By the time the water receded, eighty-four people had died in Vermont, including one woman who reportedly "died of fright" in Rutland. And many towns, including Rutland, were cut off because roads and bridges in all directions, as well as railroad tracks and trestles, were washed out. Telephone and telegraph lines across the state were gone. News of flooding in the state capital of Montpelier—where Governor John Weeks and his wife, Hattie, were trapped in the Pavilion Hotel— reached the outside world thanks to a couple of shortwave radio operators, one who reportedly used doorbell batteries to transmit messages after the power went out.

In 137 towns, from Brattleboro to Newport, floodwaters destroyed 1,258 bridges, 264 businesses, 690 farms, 7,056 acres of farmland, 178 farmhouses, 182 barns, 1,704 cattle, and 2,535 cords of wood. The prosperous mill town of Gaysville was virtually washed off the map by the White River. Losses across the state totaled almost $27 million. And recovery changed state politics. For the first time, Vermont sold bonds to pay for repairs.

It's been eighty-four years since Vermonters have experienced such a statewide disaster. The 1938 hurricane also caused devastating flooding, but it was focused on southern Vermont, while the northern parts of the state saw more wind damage. Even that flooding took place seventy-three years before Irene, and in 2011 not many people were still alive who remembered either flood. The word "flood" for most people doesn't conjure up images of debris flows; demolished roads, bridges and buildings; or landslides along stream banks. That type of damage is associated with dams bursting. The word "flood" suggests images of the Mississippi or Missouri rivers spreading vast swaths of water across the countryside. When these waters recede, they leave layers of mud and silt, but flooded roads and houses usually survive. As Irene churned northward, weather forecasters used the term "flash flood" to warn of possible destruction in New England. But flash flooding is difficult for Easterners to comprehend. It's most often associated with the arid West, where monsoon rains in the summer can suddenly fill dry washes.

Then Irene blanketed Vermont's already soaked landscape with five to eight inches of rain, and the state had a quick and painful lesson in flood physics. Unlike rain or runoff hitting the flatter Plain States, Vermont's mountainous topography funneled the prodigious amounts of rainfall into steep mountain valleys. And this funneling effect led to extensive fluvial erosion along the mountain stream banks—which turned the water into roiling flumes of liquid brown earth, trees, and rock, stirred into terrifying Class V and VI rapids as they poured through the steep valleys. Hydrologists studying flood physics employ mathematical formulas to analyze complex fluid flows. But it's common sense that the velocity of water in a stream will increase as the slope increases. Water is heavy (62.4 pounds/cubic foot), and when flowing, the pressure it exerts on objects increases with the square of its velocity. So when more and more rainwater is added to a swift stream that is confined in a narrow valley, the sheer force of the rising flow can move large trees, entire houses, vehicles large and small, and even huge boulders—making the streams as much debris flows as conduits of water.

During Irene, flow rates in Vermont's rivers and streams jumped several orders of magnitude in just a few hours. In Bennington, the Walloomsac River—known locally as the Roaring Branch—hit a peak of 9,420 cfs, the largest flow recorded at the USGS's Walloomsac River Gage since it began operation in 1933. And the river rose to 12.82 feet, five feet above flood stage. Ripping down from the mountains east of

Bennington, the river chewed away at the banks that once confined it, as well as at anything else that sat nearby — such as Barbara Bermudez's blue Plymouth Acclaim, which was safe (she thought) in its riverside garage. The Roaring Branch washed away the land under the garage and sent the blue sedan bobbing down the torrent as if it were a child's plastic boat. The car floated nose-down past a group of flood watchers, including one amateur videographer whose clip was shown over and over on national TV.

On the other side of Vermont, the Saxtons River peaked at 14,700 cfs (more than 5,000 cfs greater than the peak reached in a 1936 flood) and 19.57 feet, almost double the height of flood stage, drowning Route 121 east of the village of Grafton. Jessica Simpson tried to drive home on Route 121 on Sunday during the storm. Her car was so quickly swept away that she did not even have time to open a window and climb out. When the car became lodged against a tree, she managed to open a rear door and climb onto the trunk, where she yelled for help and was eventually rescued.

And cars were some of the smaller items that Irene's floodwaters were about to sweep away.

§   §   §

WHEN SUSIE HAUGHWOUT and Ann Manwaring stepped out of the Wilmington town clerk's office around 10:30 Sunday morning, brown water was flowing over the Main Street Bridge's railing, creating a monstrous, roiling wave. Downstream at the gage in Charlemont, Massachusetts (twenty miles south of Wilmington and below the Harriman Reservoir), the Deerfield's flow was about to peak at 37,100 cfs — up from 2,230 cfs just twelve hours earlier. And flow volume probably went higher. The gage had stopped recording. Johnson and Nutting had left a few minutes earlier, hoping to reach home before water blocked their path, and now Haughwout and Manwaring were trying to get home. But when Haughwout opened the door of her car, still parked in front of the town clerk's office, she realized that she didn't have her car keys. She and Manwaring ran back into the office to look for them. In the shuffle to get the town records to the building's second floor, neither woman could remember where the keys had gone.

With water just feet from the car, the two women gave up the hunt and walked back outside. Manwaring bid Haughwout good luck and left on foot for her house, south of town; she feared that water might be pouring over a bridge that she had to cross and did not want to risk getting stranded downtown. From the sidewalk next to her car, Haughwout called out to a police officer standing across the street. Could he call Greene's Servicenter, a local towing company located east of town? The officer contacted the towing service, but the bridge east of town was already flooded, so they could not get a tow truck into town. Haughwout then asked the officer to call the town road crew. They could get through the high water with the town's bucket loader and haul the Mitsubishi to higher ground. But the road crew was busy using the loader to rescue someone suffering a medical emergency elsewhere in town.

Haughwout sighed and looked down at her rubber Crocs. She was now standing ankle deep in water. Then she looked at the scene in front of her. River water was pouring over the Main Street Bridge's concrete railings, and dumpsters, propane tanks, and even refrigerators were flying by in the torrent. What Haughwout did not know until later was that Ivana Taseva, a twenty-year-old from Macedonia who worked at Dot's, had already drowned about a mile north of downtown Wilmington. Riding in a car with her boyfriend and another friend, she was swept away after the vehicle drove into floodwaters on Route 100. The water was deeper than the driver expected, and as he tried to back up, the car stalled and then began to float, said Wilmington police chief Joe Szarejko. Taseva, her boyfriend, and the friend left the car and tried to walk through the water to higher ground. Unable to get far, they returned to the car. Taseva's boyfriend was able to hold on to the vehicle, but Taseva lost her grip.

Realizing that she could easily be swept into the current, Haughwout turned on her heels and ran up the road toward the town high school. Her white Mitsubishi was about to go for a swim.

On the other side of the Main Street Bridge, Lisa Sullivan and Phil Taylor looked west down Route 9 and noticed that water covered the road. The parking lots across the street from their bookstore were full of water, and the river had crested the Main Street Bridge. They grabbed the bookstore's computers and ran them up to the second floor. Then they moved most of the store's inventory to tabletops and higher shelves. Surely the water would rise only a couple inches more.

When Phil Taylor is not working at the bookstore or on the town school board, he's busy as a building contractor. He looked outside the front windows of Bartleby's, saw that West Main Street had become a river in a matter of minutes, and grew concerned about water pressure on the outside of the building exceeding the pressure inside. Seeing water seeping under the front door, Taylor was worried that the pressure differential would cause the building to collapse. He told his wife that he was going to open the front door and let the water in to equalize the pressure. OK, she said, knowing there was no choice. Taylor opened the door, and the river came rushing into Bartleby's. In a matter of seconds, Sullivan and Taylor were standing in water almost up to their knees. As Taylor tried to prop open the front door, he began to smell propane.

"We'd better get out of here," he said.

They ran out the back door of the bookstore and up a steep embankment to Ray Hill Road, which descends off the ridge and intersects Main Street next to Dot's and the Main Street Bridge. There they joined a small group watching the Deerfield rise higher and higher. It rose so high that brown water was dammed up to the attic window at the back of Dot's.

"We were surprised Dot's stayed there," said Sullivan. "We were waiting for it to break loose."

§   §   §

IN JAMAICA, a village of 1,035 people tucked into a narrow valley in south-central Vermont (and named after the Natick word for beaver, not the Caribbean island), Ed Dorta-Duque could hear the Ball Mountain Brook from the back door of the Three Mountain Inn. The elegant Colonial inn, which Dorta-Duque and his wife, Jennifer, purchased in 2004, sits on Vermont Route 30/100 — a state highway shared by two numbers in Jamaica and known as Main Street in town. The road is above the brook's floodplain, and only during spring runoff had Dorta-Duque ever recalled hearing the brook from the inn's dooryard. With guests still at the inn — a couple from Brooklyn, New York, who had decided to weather Irene in Vermont rather than at home, in what they thought would be the storm's eye — he walked back into the inn and began cooking breakfast.

At 9:30 a.m., Jamaica's fire and rescue chief, Dale West, called the town's volunteer firefighters and Paul Fraser, the emergency management coordinator. The Jamaica firehouse sits on a bank adjacent to the

Ball Mountain Brook, and the fire chief was concerned about flooding. The water in the brook was flowing full speed and was nearing the top of the bank. West wanted to move the town's five fire trucks down the street to the Three Mountain Inn's driveway and parking area. In meetings the previous week, town officials—including Dorta-Duque, who is a volunteer firefighter and the town's emergency shelter coordinator—decided that the inn, not the school, should be the town's emergency command center and shelter; the school building sits in the floodplain, and on the other side of the seventy-two-year-old crumbling concrete Depot Street Bridge spanning Ball Mountain Brook.

As Dorta-Duque and the other volunteer firefighters drove to the station to get the trucks at 9:45 a.m., they couldn't help but notice the Ball Mountain Brook. "Even in spring thaw it's not that high," remarked Dorta-Duque. Also, the sound gave the innkeeper pause. It wasn't just the noise of rushing water that filled the air. He could hear boulders moving.

"It was like thunder all day long," said Jennifer Dorta-Duque.

The volunteer firefighters parked the fire trucks at the inn and immediately joined a few other town officials who were headed to Water Street to evacuate residents. Water Street—known as Back Street to locals—intersects Route 30/100 just west of downtown Jamaica, above where the main road crosses the Ball Mountain Brook. Water/Back Street then parallels the brook for about a half-mile until it Ts at Depot Street near the crumbling Depot Street Bridge, which was constructed in 1939 after the Hurricane of 1938 wiped out the previous bridge. As Irene's rains drenched the countryside, town officials were worried that the residents of the dozen or so homes on Water/Back Street would be isolated from town if the Main Street Bridge on Route 30/100 and Depot Street Bridge washed out. The town was all too familiar with bridge washouts caused by flooding. As Mark Worthen points out in a book on Jamaica's history, "People continually refer to 'hundred-year' storms, but these wild phenomena occur in Jamaica once every ten years or so." Storms in 1788, 1869, 1924, 1927, 1936, 1938, 1948, 1949, and more took out countless bridges, along with mills, homes, and other buildings in town—many of them alongside or spanning the Ball Mountain Brook. In the 1936 flood, Worthen documents one local who watched a building "shut like a pair of scissors and fall into the brook."

As Fraser, Dorta-Duque, and others knocked on doors and told the residents of the Water/Back Street homes to evacuate, they encountered a variety of responses. Brett Morrison was surprised, asking twice if they thought he and his family should leave their well-kept Greek Revival home. Fred Brement, an older gentleman with Alzheimer's disease, refused to leave and said that he planned to climb the steep tree-covered hill behind the house if water threatened his home. The rescuers convinced his wife, Toni, to leave. Neither Karin Hardy nor Tracy Payne was at home.

Payne, who was forty-five when Irene hit, had owned her home for less than a year and had recently finished renovating the lovely 1840 house. Since she had purchased the house on September 1, 2010, Payne had created an open living space on the first floor, a master suite on the second, and built a third floor in the attic, with a large dormer window overlooking the backyard. This would be her mom's room, when her mother could get away from caring for her ailing father in Maryland. Payne had left the outside of the historic house unchanged, with matching porches on the first and second floors overlooking the brook. On warm evenings that summer, she opened the door onto the upstairs porch and listened to the brook as she drifted off to sleep.

As the end of August neared, Payne drove to Boston to help her partner, Kelly Esposito. The two had met the previous spring, and Payne had spent quite a bit of time during the summer in Boston, with weekends in Vermont. Payne had given a key to her friend Kristen Wilson in Jamaica so she could check on the house when Payne wasn't around. On the evening of August 27, as Irene churned up the East Coast, Wilson walked through every room in Payne's house to make sure windows were closed, doors were locked, and nothing remained outside that might blow away. In Boston, Payne and Esposito were packing boxes so Esposito could move to Vermont; she had already given her landlord notice.

After evacuating Water/Back Street, Dorta-Duque and others responded to emergency calls on Route 100, about five miles southeast of downtown Jamaica, where routes 100 and 30 split. But they did not want to drive across the bridge on Route 100. Water from the Wardsboro Brook was splashing over the bridge, and trees and other debris carried along in the flood were slamming into it. As they stood on one end of the bridge, they could feel it strain under the pressure of the torrent. At 10:51 a.m., it collapsed.

Around the same time, a five-foot-wide pavement crack developed on the Main Street Bridge on Route 30/100 in downtown Jamaica. Town officials closed it. Just downstream, the brook was eating away its northern bank and encroaching on Water Street—slowly at first, but inexorably. Instead of flowing in a relatively straight line toward the Depot Street Bridge, the brook was developing a bend. At 11:55 a.m., the northern approach to the Depot Street Bridge washed out. Three minutes later, the Main Street Bridge, just upstream, collapsed.

§   §   §

SHORTLY AFTER 1:00 P.M. in Pittsfield, the Tweed River had nowhere to go but out: out of its banks and over Route 100. The Parmenter Place bridge was clogged with downed trees and remnants of the covered bridge that once had served as a quaint entrance to the Riverside Farm. The West Branch also had nowhere to go. The bridge over Route 100 was dammed with fallen trees and other debris. Between these two bridges sat three homes: a one-story home where Traci Templeton lived with her twelve-year-old daughter, a trailer owned by Evelyn Payette, and the cute, white two-story house rented by Heather Grev and Jack Livesey. Water was already halfway up Templeton's first-floor windows. Through knee-deep water she had managed to escape with only a few mementos—her daughter's baby photos and a few baby clothes. Water was lapping at Payette's front door, but neighbors confirmed that the elderly woman was staying with friends up the road in Rochester.

The water behind the dammed-up bridges rose at an astonishing rate. As shown on time-stamped photos taken by Pittsfield local Barb Woods, the water was halfway up the tires on Grev's and Livesey's Subarus at 1:11 p.m. Seven minutes later, the water had reached the vehicles' undercarriages and was lapping at the front door of the two-story house. Grev and Livesey heard neighbors yelling to them to get out.

By the time Livesey had rescued fourteen-year-old Cody and then waded back into the brown torrent to help Grev with the puppy Irie, it appeared that they might have waited too long. Behind the bridges the water was rising fast and flowing with a force so great it was rocking Greg Martin's heavy Ford pickup. Standing in the back of the pickup, James Marcroft had already twice thrown a length of webbing toward Grev. And twice she had missed it. Martin backed the truck deeper into the flood, the current now rocking it so hard that it felt as if they were within seconds of being washed away.

"We only have one more shot," Martin yelled to Marcroft, as he reeled in the piece of webbing from the last throw.

Marcroft threw the webbed rope again, and this time Grev caught it. She handed Irie to Livesey and held on to the webbing with both hands.

"Grab the rope!" Livesey yelled to Grev.

"I've got the rope!" she screamed back.

"Don't let go!" Livesey warned.

"I'm not letting go of the rope!"

But she couldn't move. The current was just too strong. As she screamed, "I can't do it!" over and over, her friend Beth Philhower, standing in ankle-deep water nearby, was shouting encouragement: "You can do it! You *have* to do it!"

"I can't!" screamed Grev to her friend.

"You're gonna!" Philhower shot back.

Livesey stood in front of Grev to block the force of the water, and step by step she made it to Martin's truck, though she has idea how she did. Marcroft pulled them onto the truck's tailgate as Martin gunned the Ford out of the water. He drove straight to Livesey's mother's house on the other side of the Route 100 bridge. Seconds later, the little white house lifted off its foundation and tipped into the current.

Inside Judy Livesey's house, Grev peeled off her wet shorts and shirt, not because they were drenched but because of the smell. They reeked of propane and soil. She grabbed a towel, sat down in the middle of the living room, and lit a cigarette. Then she found something dry to wear in a bag of cast-off clothes she had given to Judy for a future church rummage sale. But she could not find shoes in the bag, and her flip-flops were long gone, ripped off her feet by the current. As she was searching for shoes, Jack Livesey flew into the house and said they had to leave. In twelve minutes the water had risen two feet, and the flood was nearing his mom's house.

"We have nowhere to go," protested Grev.

But they did. Their friends Matt and Dana, hosts of the would-be hurricane party, took them in, along with Cody and Irie. But Grev doesn't remember how they got there, or what they did when they arrived.

"I think I just shut down," she said.

✍ ✍ ✍

AROUND 2:00 P.M., Rutland City deputy fire chief Brad LaFaso was still on U.S. 4 about a half-mile upstream from the reservoir intake valve when he saw something alarming. As U.S. 4's roadbed cascaded into Mendon Brook, LaFaso could see the Alpine Pipeline, an aqua-colored plastic pipe that brings sewage from Killington and Mendon down to the Rutland Waste Water Treatment Plant. Installed around 1984, the eleven-mile-long pipeline parallels U.S. 4 from the top of Sherburne Pass to Mendon and serves about ten thousand people from the Killington and Pico resorts, as well as homes and businesses along U.S. 4.

LaFaso called Fran Robillard, another deputy fire chief who had been called back to the station. Robillard was at the fire station working the dispatch desk. LaFaso told Robillard to call Mike Garofano. The water treatment manager needed to know that the Alpine Pipeline was broken and raw sewage was now flowing into Mendon Brook above the drinking water intake valve.

"You're sure it's broken?" Robillard asked LaFaso.

"I'm looking at it," LaFaso replied.

Robillard hung up with LaFaso and dialed Young Mike's cell phone. At that point the firefighters were not aware that the intake valve had already been closed.

"I need to talk to your father," said Robillard, who was unable to reach Big Mike's cell phone because his provider does not have service in the tight ravine where Mendon Brook comes out of the mountains. Young Mike handed the phone to his dad, and Robillard relayed the news of the broken sewer line.

"Are you sure it's broken?" hollered Garofano into the phone. Robillard was struck by the roar in the background on Garofano's end but had yet to realize what was making the noise.

Robillard called back LaFaso, who confirmed the damage.

Robillard then redialed Young Mike's cell phone and again asked to talk to Big Mike.

"Yes, the pipeline is definitely broken, Mike," said Robillard, who suddenly realized that the thunderous noise in the background was the sound of the raging brook. "But listen, you'd better get out of there. Call me after you're out of there so I know you're all right. If I don't hear from you, I'll call you back in an hour."

Mendon Brook was raging with an unprecedented amount of swirling, debris-filled water that was undermining the soil and rock of the valley's embankments as the torrent ricocheted down through Mendon Gorge. Embankments were collapsing on both sides of the valley, filling the water with so much debris that the flood was chocolate brown—more like liquid earth than river water. Farther downstream, beyond where the brook merges with East Creek, it was thundering over Patch's Dam, a hydro facility in Rutland that is owned by Central Vermont Public Service Company. Worried about the integrity of the dam and its embankments, cvps had called in Markowski Excavating, a local contractor based just north of Rutland in the tiny town of Florence, and asked them to reinforce the dam with rock from their gravel pit, to the north in Brandon, where they had stockpiled riprap. Sam Markowski, who owns the company along with his three brothers, Marty, Greg, and David, was driving one of the seven dump trucks hauling the riprap. Late the previous evening, he and his wife had returned from North Carolina, where their son-in-law was graduating from a program at Seymour Johnson Air Force Base.

As Sam Markowski dumped a load of rock about fifty feet from the face of the dam, he suddenly realized that he was more terrified than he had ever been in his life.

"I've never seen anything like it," he said. "The water was so high over the top of the spillway and over the top of the dam. It was like the roar of those F15s in North Carolina at the graduation."

It was unfathomable that little mountain brooks could carry this much water and debris—as though the entire world were washing away. Hundred-foot-high river embankments were collapsing into the torrent as if they were anthills of sand.

At the Rutland City fire station, an hour went by and Robillard hadn't heard from either of the Mikes. Around 2:30 p.m. Robillard called Young Mike's cell phone. It went straight to voice mail. He dialed the number again with the same result.

Robillard was uneasy. Still, there was a chance that either of the two Mikes might have shut off the cell phone. Or the battery was dead. Or they had dropped it.

But there was also a chance that Mike Garofano and his youngest son were missing.

๑   ๑   ๑

IN SOUTH ROYALTON, as the White River overflowed onto Geo Honigford's field, he began hauling his farm equipment to higher ground. He had parked most of it—mowers, a hay tedder (a machine for hastening hay drying), hay rakes, manure spreader, and a tiller—on the field near his largest greenhouse. To move the larger equipment, he hooked it up to his tractor and pulled it up to his barn. When he started the process, the field by the greenhouses was high and dry. Twenty minutes later, the water by Honigford's lower greenhouse was two feet deep. He didn't want to stall out his tractor, so he was forced to leave the tedder where it lay.

Honigford didn't worry about the vegetables still in the field, or the onions and tomatoes in the greenhouses. It was just water, after all. He was more concerned about his greenhouses, which cost $9,000 each. Water was hammering the larger one, which sits closer to the river.

By this time, Mark Edsell, his farm manager, had arrived at Hurricane Flats. Worried that the floodwater would sweep away the large greenhouse, the two men decided to open the front door and slash the plastic on the back side to let the river water flow through. But they soon realized that they should slash the plastic on the front too. Wielding knives, Honigford and Edsell waded out into the waist-deep water and began cutting at the plastic. Then they rolled up the sides. As they worked, a gazebo floated by. Shaped like a covered bridge, the gazebo had sat on the grounds of the Vermont Law School, about a mile upstream, and was often the subject of ridicule. Honigford's neighbor pointed at it and chuckled. It was the only time they laughed all afternoon.

By the time they had finished slashing the plastic, the water had risen to chest height. To maneuver, the men grabbed the greenhouse posts, leaping and floating from one to another. Edsell began to fear that he might be swept away, but both men managed to work their way to higher ground. Suddenly they heard a huge crunch. A submerged tree trunk had smashed in the greenhouse's sliding barn-style door. Edsell had been standing in that exact spot just two minutes earlier. Not too long afterward, the water reached the greenhouse roofs.

"At that point, there was nothing else we could do," said Honigford. "We just watched."

§ § §

AS MUDDY BROWN WATER and debris poured down the Ball Mountain Brook—as if a dam had burst upstream—the brook now came perilously close to Water Street in Jamaica. As the brook ate at its northern bank, a shed on Tracy Payne's land collapsed into the roiling flume. The shed had sat across Water Street from her house; inside it, she stored amplifiers for her electric guitars, a massage table, and several items she was selling on eBay.

Shortly before 2:30 p.m., the Ball Mountain Brook surrounded four houses on Water Street near the Depot Street Bridge. The large maple tree that had shaded Payne's front yard fell into the swirling waters. A few minutes later, as townspeople watched from the opposite bank, Dave Kaneshiro's house tore away from its back room and slipped into the torrent. Half submerged in the roiling brown water, with only the shingled roof visible in the rapids, his house floated about one hundred yards until it hit the Depot Street Bridge. Almost instantly it disintegrated, as if a bomb inside had detonated. The back room remained on his land, looking like a mangled limb torn from its body.

Karin Hardy's house was the next to go, then Payne's. Brett Morrison's house was the last of the Water Street houses to float off, its red metal roof bobbing in the rapids. Within twenty minutes, all of them had lifted whole—or almost whole—from their foundations and washed away in the angry current until they hit the bridge. There, they shattered.

With the houses now gone, the brook continued to eat away property on Water Street, gobbling up topsoil, gardens, trees, and shrubs. The only structure that the brook spared on Payne's property was a small barn. She had used the barn to store building supplies, such as paint, the house's old windows, and a ladder. Everything else she had owned was in the house, including a safe in which she stored cash, jewelry, and her grandmother's pictures. The only item she had brought with her to Boston, besides a suitcase of clothes and bag of toiletries, was her mother's violin.

AT THE RUTLAND CITY Fire Station, deputy chief Fran Robillard was still at the dispatch desk around 3:30 p.m. when Brad LaFaso returned to the station. Along with the Vermont State Police, he had stayed on U.S. 4 in Mendon trying to keep people off the highway, as well as off Meadow Lake Bridge, which crosses Mendon Brook near the bottom of Mendon Gorge just above the Rutland City Reservoir water intake building. The raging brook was almost up to the bridge, and trees were smashing into it. All around, power lines were coming down, "arcing and sparking," in LaFaso's words. Several onlookers were walking from U.S. 4 down Meadow Lake Drive to the bridge to take pictures. LaFaso left the state police to corral the onlookers back to a safer location. He returned to the fire station to answer emergency calls, which were coming in fast.

LaFaso walked into the station and touched base with Robillard, who was still at the dispatch desk. Robillard explained that he had talked to Garofano around 1:30 p.m. but hadn't heard back from the water department chief since then, nor had Young Mike answered his cell phone when he'd called around 2:30. LaFaso turned on his heels and walked back to the fire truck, along with three firefighters. They drove straight to the reservoir to look for the two Mikes. The state police also responded and brought a search dog.

They found Garofano's truck parked in a pullout on the access road about a quarter-mile beyond the reservoir. They also ran into a home-owner, who lives near the reservoir and often walks on the road through the peaceful, well-kept property. The homeowner confirmed that he had seen the Garofanos near their truck around 1:30 p.m., and that they were walking on the embankment toward the intake valve.

The search party observed Mendon Brook from the place where the Garofano's truck was parked. The steep banks that line the brook had collapsed, and "water and trees were just smashing into everything and water was everywhere," said LaFaso. "It was a big gigantic roar, a roar and snapping."

From the pullout where the truck was parked, the search dog followed a scent up the nearby embankment, then upstream along the hillside to-ward the valve. About twenty yards from the intake valve housing, the dog stopped. Below, the embankment had given way in a landslide. Now an almost vertical scar of fresh dirt, the embankment dropped straight into the raging water below. What had recently been a wooded hillside above Mendon Brook was gone. The search party was just downstream of the intake building.

But LaFaso and the rest of the group did not give up. Unable to shout above the roar, they threw rocks at the intake building's door. The building was surrounded by raging waters, but LaFaso thought that the Garofanos could have made it inside and might now be trapped there. If the Garofanos responded, or if LaFaso or any of his men saw anything to indicate that the men might be inside, they were going to attempt to reach the building's roof and cut through it.

They heard and saw nothing from inside the building. It was too dangerous to try to reach the building if there were no definite signs of life. So LaFaso temporarily terminated the search. He held on to the hope that the water treatment supervisor and his twenty-four-year-old son were inside the intake building and unable to hear anything above the jet-engine roar of the waters and the thunder of the moving boulders.

5

UNHERALDED DEVASTATION

You understand being flooded. You don't understand being washed away.

⚓ Jennifer Dorta-Duque, Jamaica town lister, Jamaica
 Memorial Library board chair, Jamaica Old Home Day
 committee member, emergency shelter co-coordinator,
 innkeeper

AS IRENE PUMMELED VERMONT, TOWNS from Bennington and Brattleboro in the south to Waterbury in the north saw their worst flooding since 1927—or in southeastern Vermont, since 1938. Throughout the state, official reports showed that Irene had unleashed more than seven inches of rain, particularly in Ludlow, Cavendish, Woodstock, and Randolph—though unofficial reports often showed much higher totals (in Pittsfield, Peter Borden's two sons measured sixteen inches of rain in a jar they had left on their porch). Irene's wake of destruction left Vermonters shocked. Normally placid streams tore out their banks, and whole embankments collapsed, carrying the load of dirt, rocks, boulders, trees, and anything else that sat in the way downstream. In geologic terms, Irene created mass wasting. And most of the flood damage was caused not by the state's larger rivers, but by smaller mountain tributaries. Even rivulets.

In Newfane, just north of Brattleboro along Route 30, the Rock River demolished parts of the Dover Road, and the Smith Brook took out sections of South Wardsboro Road. Two houses were destroyed, including the second home of a Scottish family still overseas. The Mill Brook in Danby threatened to inundate that small southern Vermont village along U.S. Route 7 after a house once owned by Nobel Prize–winning author

Pearl Buck collapsed into the brook. As the house jammed against the village bridge, Tommy Fuller, who was working his excavator to try to fortify the town bridge, smashed the house with the excavator's shovel. Had he not acted quickly, the brook would have overflowed the bridge and flooded the entire village. Less than twenty-four hours earlier, the town had celebrated its 250th anniversary. In tiny Plymouth, on Route 100 between Ludlow and Killington in central Vermont, a rivulet tumbling down a steep mountainside left four to five feet of rock piled on the road and nearly took out a nearby sugarhouse. Ten miles south of Montpelier in Northfield, thirteen homes on the east side of Water Street were destroyed beyond repair by the Dog River.

In Cavendish, near Ludlow in central Vermont, the Black River cut a new path when the town's hydroelectric dam overflowed. The "new" river carved a hole eighty feet deep in Route 131 just east of this lovely village of stately stone buildings. The hydrodam, built in 1907–8 by the Claremont (NH) Power Company, harnesses power generated from the water losing 120 feet of elevation through the narrow, boulder-strewn Cavendish Gorge. But the river didn't always flow through the gorge. Sometime in the geologic past it had flowed through the valley where Route 131 now sits. When Irene's floodwaters topped the hydrodam, the water found its former route — and in the process tore out the road, leaving what locals referred to as the "Cavendish Canyon." The torrent also took out the town's water and sewer line (the wastewater treatment facility sits adjacent to Route 131, just below the "canyon"). The river had found the same path during the 1927 flood and had overtaken several of the village's lovely stone homes.

Farther north, in Bethel, Lang Durfee thought he could hold back the Third Branch of the White River from his family's lumber business with two rows of concrete jersey barriers and hundreds of forty-pound sandbags. Throughout the day, Bethel Mills employees fortified the 230-year-old business (believed to be the oldest continuously run company in the state) with barriers, drained the torrential rain pouring off the acre of metal roofs, and moved inventory to higher ground. But by 6:00 p.m., the crews exhausted, Durfee sent them home, then watched helplessly as the sky grew darker and the water deeper, topping the jersey barriers. With the Third Branch draining mountains farther north, where Irene continued to unload rain into the night, the flood in Bethel would not crest until close to midnight. Late that evening, from his second-story office, Durfee reached outside the window and touched the water as it rose up the building's sides. With generator-powered lights still ablaze in the mill, their beams reflected in the rising water, Bethel Mills looked like the *Titanic* as she sank in the North Atlantic.

Devastation to the state's infrastructure, homes, and businesses was not all that Irene's floodwaters brought. Just downstream from Bethel on the White River, eighty-one-year-old Harland "Duke" Perley watched twenty-five of his milking herd get washed downstream. Perley had recently suffered a heart attack and had had a pacemaker installed. As he sat on a stalled tractor and watched his cattle swept away in the torrent, he feared he would have another heart attack, reported the *Valley News*. A boat rescued him.

In Rochester—a town of 1,171 people and one of the worst hit in central Vermont—the raging Nason Brook ripped through Woodlawn Cemetery. The erosion caused by the flooding unearthed some twenty-five caskets and left the remains of residents' loved ones strewn downstream. The cemetery sits on a hill across Route 100 from the White River, and flooding in 1927 and 1938 had never threatened any of the burial plots. The Nason Brook is normally so small that many people were not even aware that a stream flowed near the cemetery. Another small brook north of downtown Rochester undermined Jon Graham's home. As he reached to grab a few last items (important papers and his laptop), the house collapsed on top of him. Neighbors pulled him to safety.

North in Waterbury—one of the hardest hit towns during the 1927 flood—Vermont Emergency Management had to evacuate its offices midstorm when floodwaters from the Winooski River reached the state office complex. Nearby, the state hospital's 51 patients were moved to higher floors. It was a scenario similar to the one that played out during the Flood of 1927, except with far fewer patients. Back then, the state hospital housed 872 patients, one of whom died in the flood—a tuberculosis patient who had remained behind when others moved to the second, then third, floor of the tubercular ward (other reports state that he died from the exertion of climbing stairs to the third floor). Floodwaters inundated the hospital's boilers, so those trapped inside were left with no heat or water—which was a problem during the November 1927 flood, when temperatures were far colder than in August. "With heat, water and lights gone and only a few cans of milk available for food, prospects were not too bright at first," wrote Luther B. Johnson in *Vermont in Floodtime*, published in 1928, "but the townspeople exerted every effort and on Friday more milk and bread came and by degrees other articles of diet."

During Irene, a big concern at the Waterbury facility was the state of the Marshfield Dam, thirty miles upstream. As the storm dumped inches of rain on the state, Green Mountain Power reported that the earthen dam was in danger of overflowing, endangering the downstream towns of Marshfield, Plainfield, Montpelier, Waterbury, and so on down river. To prevent such a calamity, the power company considered releasing water from Molly's Falls Pond behind the dam. That water release would reduce the chance of a sudden catastrophic deluge, but still meant that the downstream towns would likely flood. With water already up to the ceiling of the state hospital's first floor, more flooding would be most unwelcome. Fortunately, the rain stopped before the power company released any water.

As disaster unfolded, many people both in state and out of state remained astonishingly unaware of what was happening. On Sunday afternoon, those on high ground and not in the heat of battle still thought Irene was just a rainstorm. Those who had power—and many did—watched storm updates on the Weather Channel and CNN, and from those news accounts, it appeared that the storm had wound down. Throughout Sunday afternoon, reporters and commentators were expressing relief that Irene had mostly spared New York City and vicinity.

For many, the storm came alive on Facebook and in blogs. At 2:52 p.m., Vyto Starinskas, head photographer for the *Rutland Herald*, Vermont's second-largest daily newspaper, posted a photo on the *Herald's* Facebook page of U.S. 4 collapsing into Mendon Brook.

"I am sitting in my car watching Route 4 in Mendon fall into the roaring river," Starinskas wrote on Facebook. "Telephone poles and lines are also falling in the water. . . . Cops just told me to leave."

In the coming days, this photo would end up on websites and in newspapers around the world, including the *New York Times*.

Others around the state began posting photos of similar devastation. Between 3:00 and 4:00 p.m., someone reported that the House of Pizza in downtown Brandon had floated off its foundation and was sitting in the middle of U.S. 7. But it didn't really matter, since the Neshobe Creek had already rendered impassable that section of western Vermont's major north-south corridor.

At 4:10 p.m., another Vermonter reported that a bridge on U.S. 7 had collapsed south of Rutland. Not just flooded, but collapsed. Bruce Nichols, the Vermont Department of Transportation's District 3 general manager, had just driven over the bridge and noticed a kink in what should have been a straight guardrail. He stopped his pickup truck in the breakdown lane, saw the river slamming into the bank, and knew he had to close the road. He pulled his truck across U.S. 7 just as six cars were approaching the bridge. As he was getting out of his truck to tell the drivers the road was closed, the bridge and breakdown lane where he had parked just two minutes earlier disappeared.

At 5:12 p.m., Susan Hammond uploaded a video showing the Lower Bartonsville Bridge—a nineteenth-century one-lane covered bridge—being wrenched from its abutments by the Williams River near Chester, Vermont. It slipped beneath the riverbank as Hammond cried, "Oh my god . . . shit." She wasn't the only one who cried. Or swore. This video soon went viral, with almost a half-million people watching it online. News stations played the video over and over.

A series of photos showed the Woodstock Farmers' Market, a favorite stop for foodies along the Ottauquechee River, almost up to its eaves in floodwater. Next door, the offices of the *Vermont Standard*, a weekly newspaper, were under water, with the front of the building tilting at an odd angle. The newspaper has not missed publishing a single issue in its 158-year history. Nearby, the White Cottage, a popular summertime snack bar, was under water as well.

Another series of photos shared on Facebook showed the Simon Pearce glass blowing factory, showroom, and restaurant in Quechee and its neighboring covered bridge being pounded by raging brown water—as well as hundreds of white propane tanks (mostly empty) picked up from the Dead River Company in Woodstock and from homes and trailer parks upstream. As these tanks hurtled down the Ottauquechee, they slammed into a new concrete bridge in Woodstock. The ones that still contained natural gas began leaking, with a menacing hiss, as the big white tanks continued their roller-coaster ride downstream. When they reached Quechee, many of them circled in an eddy below the covered bridge.

Another mile downstream, the 165-foot-deep Quechee Gorge was almost half full of water (the U.S. Army Corps of Engineers does not measure water depth in the gorge, but a few miles downstream the North Hartland Lake rose 81 feet). The water through the gorge was so high and moving so fast that Rob Greenwald, a New Jersey hydrogeologist visiting his parents in Quechee, thought it looked like a "made-for-TV-movie of when the dam breaks." Fearing that the bridge over the gorge, a 285-foot-long steel arch bridge built in 1911 and converted from a railroad bridge to an automobile bridge in 1933, wasn't designed for a flow rate that high or that fast, Greenwald floored the family minivan and flew over it, with his mother in the backseat hollering for him to slow down.

In Killington, photos posted on Facebook showed the Roaring Brook living up to its name. Near its headwaters on Killington Mountain the brook tore through the ski resort's K-1 Lodge and dislodged the main support for the Superstar Pub, causing it to collapse into the ever-widening streambed. Farther down the mountain, the brook washed out the large parking lot at Ramshead, where many of the ski resort's children's programs are based. Then the brook's angry torrent ripped a huge gash through Ravine Road above the Wobbly Barn, a popular steakhouse and nightclub.

As the brook's floodwaters tore down the valley toward the Ottauquechee River, the brook removed a nineteenth-century white farmhouse that had sat next to U.S. 4 near a quaint white church in what might be considered "old" Killington—or Sherburne, as the town was called from 1800 to 1999. Floating downstream, the house smashed against a bridge on U.S. 4 and disintegrated. The brook then cut itself a new path, ripping up central Vermont's main east-west artery and depositing tons of mud and debris on the valley floor below—as well as in the yard of Goodro Lumber. Killington Resort president Chris Nyberg could not reach his home in Pittsfield on Sunday evening—or for days to come—and hundreds of tourists were trapped in the resort community as well, including a few people who had just been passing through on U.S. 4 on Sunday afternoon. They became stranded when U.S. 4 washed away on either side of town.

It felt as if the entire state were under attack—Irene dropping bomb after bomb. On Facebook, the predominant comments under photos of angry, turbid streams, demolished roads and bridges, and submerged homes and businesses were "OMG" (vernacular for "oh my god") and "holy shit."

By evening, the national news networks finally clued in to what Irene was doing in Vermont. One of the first national broadcasters to recognize the disaster unfolding in the state was the Weather Channel's intrepid Jim Cantore. Raised in White River Junction, with a meteorology degree from Lyndon State College in Vermont's Northeast Kingdom, Cantore was on camera Sunday evening talking about how New York had escaped major storm damage. As he stood harborside in Lower Manhattan, he suddenly could no longer go on with the scripted program.

"I've got to just stop right here for a second and throw this in," he said, looking close to tears. "I am absolutely heartbroken at what I'm seeing right now coming in out of Vermont. I can't believe these pictures. This entire state is almost under water." For more than two minutes, Cantore, a veteran Weather Channel forecaster who has made a career standing on-camera in hurricane-force winds and sideways-blowing snowstorms, kept repeating, "I just can't believe what I'm seeing."

Shortly thereafter, CNN aired the amateur video of Barbara Bermudez's blue Plymouth Acclaim bobbing down the raging Roaring Branch in Bennington. And most national news broadcasts repeatedly showed downtown Brattleboro under three to four feet of water from the Whetstone Brook. This scene aired so frequently that outsiders might have thought that this southeastern Vermont town was the only place suffering flood damage from Irene. In truth, it was the only place that the national news media, coming up from Boston and New York, could reach. Most of the roads that traveled deeper into Vermont were washed out.

§   §   §

WITH WATER POURING over the railings of the Main Street Bridge, Susie Haughwout headed for the town high school, which sits on a hill overlooking the village. On the way, she encountered her husband, a volunteer firefighter.

"What are you doing?" she asked.

"Heading to the high school," he responded. The firehouse was flooded with two feet of water, and the Wilmington Police Department was soon to go under. Both departments had set up operations at the high school.

Haughwout and her husband found almost forty people already at the school, including most of the town's police officers. There was no water or power, and no functioning toilets, but the school building had been transformed into an emergency center by firefighter Brian Johnson's wife, Monique. He had begged her to come into town with him that morning. Sam Hall, another firefighter, is also the school janitor, and he had the keys to the school cafeteria, which was already fully stocked with food. School had been scheduled to start the next day.

Sometime during the afternoon, the Vermont Army National Guard dispatched soldiers to Wilmington. They drove light-medium tactical vehicles that can make it through two to three feet of water and arrived in town to assist with rescues. A woman was in labor about ten miles north of Wilmington in Dover, reported the *Burlington Free Press* at 2:45 p.m., but even with the tactical vehicles the Guardsmen and other first responders were having trouble reaching her.

On West Main Street in Wilmington, Lisa Sullivan and Phil Taylor returned to Bartleby's in the early afternoon to check on the damage — by scrambling back down the embankment from Ray Hill Road and entering the bookstore's back door. But one look at the four feet of water inside their bookstore made them turn their backs. Most of the shelves that weren't nailed to the wall had tipped over into the flooded store. Books floated by the stairwell. They walked out of the store and climbed back up the steep embankment. Disaster had struck twice. But what could they do?

Back on Ray Hill Road they met a couple who had had to flee their Main Street home. Sullivan invited the couple to stay with them, and they all walked down the road to Sullivan's and Taylor's home.

ʕ ʕ ʕ

IN JAMAICA, calls were pouring in to the emergency command center at the Three Mountain Inn. People would call to report information on their neighbors, or ask if someone had heard from their neighbors. Pikes Falls and West Jamaica Roads, which rise steeply out of town along the Ball Mountain Brook and North Branch Brook, were completely washed out in places. By the time Irene blew off to Canada, more than a dozen homes in Jamaica had been severely damaged, with five completely obliterated — their property gone as well. A few refugees who either could not go back to their homes, or were afraid to, stayed at the inn that night.

As the Ball Mountain Brook receded, boulders and gravel were all that was left along the lower half of Water/Back Street — a moonlike surface that lay several feet below where Dave Kaneshiro's, Karin Hardy's, Tracy Payne's, and Brett Morrison's homes had once stood.

Sometime during the afternoon, Tracy Payne's cell phone rang. She thought it might be Kristen Wilson, the friend who had promised to check her house and, if need be, turn on the sump pump to drain the basement. As Payne watched news channel coverage of the storm, she wondered why Wilson hadn't yet called, but she figured her friend was busy, perhaps pumping out her own basement.

The call wasn't from Wilson. It was Ed Dorta-Duque.

"Everybody on Water Street has been evacuated," Payne remembers Dorta-Duque telling her. "It's not good. The houses on Water Street are in bad shape, and I'm really, really sad to report to you that your house is gone."

Payne asked what "gone" meant. She thought Dorta-Duque was telling her that the brook had flooded her first floor, submerging her beautifully renovated living room and kitchen in muck.

"I'll come back as soon as I can get there and get what I can off the second and third floors," she remembers saying into her phone. The word "gone" hadn't registered. She couldn't imagine her house gone. Nobody's house just up and leaves, she thought.

"No, Tracy," Dorta-Duque repeated. "Your house is gone, it went down the river."

Payne was speechless. Overcome by a sick feeling, her first thought was, "Oh, thank god I have home owner's insurance! Thank god!"

But she did not have flood insurance. Nor did her neighbors.

§ § §

IN SOUTH ROYALTON, Geo Honigford had moved all the farm equipment that he could from his flooded field. And he and Mark Edsell had done all they could to save his two greenhouses. There was nothing more they could do now to save his farm. So Honigford, his wife and two daughters, along with Edsell and his wife, Liz, drove a mile up the road to see how the village of South Royalton was faring. Watching the White

River lap at the iron girders supporting the town's new bridge, Honigford's eyes suddenly grew wide.

"Crap, what about my neighbors?" he thought.

South of Honigford's field sit five modern ranch houses, all on the White River's floodplain. They drove down to the little housing development. The river was flowing through every house. One neighbor, Paul Babcock, was standing near his house looking shell-shocked. He said he was planning to sleep in his truck. So Honigford and O'Connor invited him back to their house for the night.

ᛋ   ᛋ   ᛋ

AS EVENING CAME in Pittsfield and the rain wound down, townspeople in yellow raingear leaned over the bridge railing on Route 100 and chain-sawed the trees that clogged it. Nearby, the cute little white house that had once been home to Heather Grev and Jack Livesey sat behind its foundation, tipped forward on one corner. Part of its north side was ripped off, and the first floor was buckled. Like a scene from the *Wizard of Oz*, the house looked as if a tornado had picked it up and dropped it into a pool of brown water.

Next door, Evelyn Payette's mobile home drooped with a broken back, and Traci Templeton's house, upstream from the trailer, was buried in muck and debris. But Templeton wasn't sitting around and contemplating her fate. She headed up to Doug and Kathianne Mianulli's house on a steep hillside above Pittsfield. Water was pouring down the hill and threatening their home. Pittsfield's mustachioed second constable, who also works as a bartender at the Clear River Tavern, Doug Mianulli had been out during the storm checking on residents who might need help. Little did he know that his own house was one of the many in trouble that afternoon. So Templeton, along with Greg Martin and others, headed to the Mianulli's and helped Kathianne redirect the water away from the house.

About a half-mile farther upstream of Templeton's destroyed home, the Tweed cut itself a new channel through Brian Halligan's living room. At the other end of town, Gary and Janice Stumpf had also been made homeless. The Stumpfs had rebuilt their house after a fire destroyed their previous home twenty years before. During Irene, as the Stumpfs moved their cars to higher ground, the Guernsey Brook—usually a little backyard landscape feature — swept their house off its foundation and deposited it almost upside down against a culvert under Route 100. The Stumpfs had only what they were wearing — for Gary, a Hawaiian shirt and shorts.

Even on a good day, cell phone coverage in Pittsfield is spotty, with only a few bars if you stand on the town green. By nightfall, there was no coverage at all. Townsfolk knew that Route 100 was washed out both north and south of the village, but they were unaware that much of the state had also suffered significant damage. Word spread that a town meeting would be held the following morning at 7:30 a.m. Trapped in town, Marc and Janina Leibowitz's wedding guests hunkered down at a few inns in town.

"It slowly became clear to me that we were not driving out of here tomorrow," wrote wedding guest Brian Mitchell in a memoir submitted to the town archive. "How long does it take to build a bridge?"

Peter Borden, Pittsfield's emergency management coordinator, put his kids to bed Sunday night, then sat down in his favorite chair. By candlelight, he read Pittsfield's emergency plan cover to cover. Twice.

§   §   §

MOST OF RUTLAND COUNTY received over five inches of rain, and flooding approached that seen in 1927. In fact, as Irene's floodwaters rose on Sunday, Fire Chief Robert Schlacter grabbed a FEMA-created flood zone map off the wall in city hall and brought it to the city's emergency operations center at the police station. The map showed the hundred-year floodplain, five-hundred-year floodplain, and a line indicating how far the 1927 flood had reached. The chief used the map to help the city evacuate streets in anticipation of flooding.

Down in the floodplain near East Creek and Otter Creek, Doug Casella managed to keep the Casella Customer Care Center free of water, thanks to constant pumping. He and his son Joe returned home to Mendon briefly for dinner with Maureen and Joe's twenty-five-year-old sister, Kristen, their cousin John Casella, Jr. (known as "Little John"), and Brad Matteson, a friend. Dinner conversation revolved around the desperate news that the Garofanos were missing, and they discussed bringing an excavator to the Rutland City Reservoir early the next morning to help search for the men. So far, only one Irene-related death had been reported in Vermont. At 5:30 p.m., Ivana Taseva's body had been found, in a ballfield about 175 yards from where she had lost her grip on the car on Route 100 north of Wilmington.

After dinner, Doug Casella headed back to the Customer Care Center to make sure it was still dry. But when he tried to drive back to downtown Rutland, he found the bridge on Meadow Lake Drive impassable. Water was flowing over the bridge. He turned around and drove a circuitous path to town.

Casella didn't return home again until 1:00 a.m. So he wouldn't wake his wife, he lay down on the couch and fell asleep there. He would get four hours' sleep that night—more than he was going to get at any one stretch during the coming month.

PART II

THE RESCUE

6

YOU CAN'T GET THERE
FROM HERE

I was standing outside Sutherland's IGA store one morning, when
I heard a flivver approaching down the street toward me.... Which
way to Millinocket? ... Well, you can go west to the next intersection,
get onto the turnpike, go north through the toll gate at Augusta, 'til
you come to that intersection ... well, no. You keep right on this tar
road; it changes to dirt now and again. Just keep the river on your
left. You'll come to a crossroads and ... let me see. Then again, you
can take that scenic coastal route that the tourists use. And after
you get to Bucksport ... well, let me see now. Millinocket. Come to
think of it, you can't get there from here (pronounced "cahn't get
they-ah from hee-ah").

   § Bert & I, *"Which Way to Millinocket"*

VERMONTERS AWOKE MONDAY MORNING — if they had slept at all —
to a calm blue sky. It was as if Mother Nature were trying to make up for
her foul temper the previous day when, in a full-on rage, she had gouged
her nails into the landscape and swiped her arms across the furnishings.
The weather Monday morning was such a contrast to Sunday's tempest
that Irene felt like a bad dream. Until Vermonters began surveying the
damage. Or tried to drive to work.

The carnage she left in her wake was a nightmare. Across two-thirds
of the state, the infrastructure damage was mind-boggling. Everywhere
Vermonters turned, roads had washed out, bridges collapsed, and culverts blown out; pavement was undermined, and highways were still
covered with floodwater or mud. So many roads were damaged that the
Vermont Agency of Transportation (also known as VTrans) ran out of

"Road Closed" signs. And many of those signs, along with orange traffic cones and barrels, were available only because Bruce Nichols and a few other VTrans employees had pulled them out of VTrans's District 3 garage in Rutland with a bucket loader after East Creek had poured into the agency's parking lot and threatened to flood its district headquarters.

Questions abounded about which roads were open and which closed, and phones at VTrans headquarters were ringing off the hook. Could you get from Rutland to Burlington? Dorset to Rutland? Bethel to Woodstock? Brattleboro to Wilmington? Waitsfield to Montpelier? Rutland to White River Junction? In fact, could you drive east-west across the state anywhere in southern or central Vermont? Mostly, the answer was no. And if you *had* to travel around the state on Monday morning, it was by a series of circuitous back roads, many pocked with their own washouts.

It was also quickly apparent that there was no way in or out of many Vermont towns. In the mountain resort town of Killington, about four hundred tourists who had been visiting for a summer break were now marooned. When asked by a reporter what would happen if an emergency arose requiring outside help, Killington town manager Kathleen Ramsay paused, then responded, "I don't know."

Washed-out roads were only one of the many catastrophes most Vermont towns faced on Monday morning. In southern Vermont, the downtown business districts in Brattleboro and Wilmington, which had been inundated by floodwaters on Sunday, were now deep in wet mud and silt. On the corner of Flat and Main streets in Brattleboro, the historic Latchis Theater, built in 1938 as a model of Art Deco and Greek Revival design, lost its mechanical and electrical equipment to seven feet of water in the basement from the Whetstone Brook. Nearby, the Boys & Girls Club and several stores were buried in almost a foot of mud and silt, left from two- to three-foot-deep floodwaters. The Whetstone also took out a sewer line. And a seventeen-year-old teen, Marble Arvidson, was reported missing.

State Route 9, the primary east-west thoroughfare in far southern Vermont from Brattleboro through Wilmington to Bennington, was eroded down to one lane in several places, with at least one bridge washed out. Residents and emergency workers could make it from one town to the next, but only via a maze of back roads. In Bennington, the Roaring Branch had destroyed the city's drinking water intake, severed the water main, and taken out bridges and culverts. Three miles of the Roaring Branch's riverbank through Bennington were eroded, and a levee protecting Mount Anthony Union High School was undermined.

In Wardsboro, a hamlet nestled in a tight mountain valley eighteen miles north of Wilmington on Vermont Route 100, residents were cut off, severed from the outside world. The Smith Brook had washed out South Wardsboro Road leading east to Newfane, and Wardsboro Brook had devoured Route 100 so badly that town officials were told it would take three months before the road could reopen. And Wardsboro was just one of many towns along Route 100 that were in trouble. Vermont's signature scenic road, Route 100 winds about two hundred miles from the Massachusetts line to the Canadian border along the spine of the Green Mountains, crossing countless small mountain streams and larger rivers. From Readsboro in the south to Moretown in northern Vermont, Route 100 was riddled with countless washouts and chasms, some fifty feet deep.

A few miles north of Wardsboro in Jamaica, the Ball Mountain Brook took out the Main Street Bridge on Route 100 (shared there by Route 30). Up the road, the West River inundated Route 100 in the towns of Londonderry and Weston, covering the road in mud in some places, washing it out in others. In Londonderry, water rose three feet on Main Street; in Weston, five feet of floodwater drowned the Weston Playhouse, renowned for its summer stock theater, and interrupted the premiere of the musical *Saint-Ex*, with a cast of Broadway veterans.

Still farther north in Ludlow—where Route 100 intersects 103, a primary east-west road cutting across south-central Vermont—the Black River flooded half of the downtown shopping district, including the town's only major grocery store. Tragically, Ludlow realtor Kevin Davis, fifty, was discovered on Monday morning floating in the water by his boat dock. He appeared to have drowned in what is ironically called Lake Rescue, a few miles north of town. But no one witnessed the accident. He would be Irene's fourth victim in Vermont (fifth, if the Brattleboro teen were never found).

Lake Rescue and Echo Lake, two lovely lakes in a chain along Route 100 north of Ludlow, were opaque brown with suspended silt—a clue to the devastation farther upstream. From there north to Granville—a distance of forty-two miles through the heart of the Green Mountains in central

Vermont—Route 100 and the homes and businesses along it looked as if they had been bombed. Streams that you could normally jump across, and even small rivulets usually no wider than a foot or two, had poured out of the mountains like high-pressure fire hoses. Route 100 was either washed away or covered in mud, rocks, and silt in more places than not. Although President Calvin Coolidge's homestead, where he grew up and took the oath of office on August 3, 1923, remained undamaged (it sits on a hill in a hamlet called Plymouth Notch), Route 100A was destroyed in too many places to count, as a result of run-off using the seven-and-a-half-mile-long road through a tight mountain valley as a funnel. Two homes and a motel in Plymouth were completely destroyed.

North of the Route 100 damage in Killington and Pittsfield, Rochester sat cut off from the outside world. Route 100 south of town was submerged, the White River having filled the wide valley floor with more than eight feet of water. The electrical substation in town was ripped out, and the east side of the Route 73 bridge had fallen into the White River, lying like a boat ramp in the river and cutting off the town from the west. Even if the bridge had not collapsed, the town still would have been cut off. Route 73 over the 2,185-foot Brandon Gap was completely washed out in multiple places on both sides of the Green Mountain Range, with nothing but boulders where the road once traveled.

Up Route 100 in the hamlet of Granville, population 303, a couple of houses were inundated by floodwaters, and the road damage was severe. North of Granville in Granville Gulf, Route 100 shares the tight notch with the headwaters of the White River on the south side and the Mad River on the north. With the steep notch serving as a sluice in both directions, Route 100 didn't stand a chance.

At the northern end of Route 100 in Waitsfield, Bridge Street in downtown was the hardest hit by the raging Mad River. The Green Cup and Mint restaurants were wiped out, as were several other businesses. Flowing north to Moretown, the Mad River also gobbled up sections of Route 100B and its bridges.

Then there was Waterbury, where Route 100 intersects U.S. Route 2 and I-89 and crosses over the Winooski River. With tributaries like the Dog and Mad River pouring from the hills, the Winooski rose rapidly and inundated more than two hundred homes and businesses, as well as the state hospital—nearly a third of the properties in town. On Monday morning, fifteen hundred state workers flooded out of their offices could not return to work in Waterbury.

Although Route 100 was pocked with destruction for 150 miles, the road was not the most damaged in the state. That honor would be bestowed on Route 107, a ten-mile stretch of pavement from Route 100 north of Pittsfield east to Bethel. Route 107 is regularly traveled by people in southwestern Vermont trying to reach the state capital of Montpelier, about thirty miles north of Bethel on I-89. It follows the tight White River Valley and in places is literally carved into the valley wall. Though "Refrigerator Flats," a straight section of 107 along the White River in Stockbridge, fared remarkably well, with only portions of the west-bound lane cracked and sagging into the river, Route 107 was completely gone for two long stretches between Gaysville and Bethel. Where the road had once sat, the river now flowed lazily through bigger bends. A few patches of asphalt clinging almost vertically to the mountainside were the only indication that a road had once been there. This area had faced even worse devastation in 1927, when floodwaters eradicated most of Gaysville, a bustling mill town on the White River.

At 107's eastern terminus in Bethel, where the White River and Third Branch meet, the rickety River Street Bridge miraculously still stood. This ancient iron bridge was constructed after the 1927 flood had taken out its predecessor. But houses near the bridge lay in ruins. Mike and Leslie Piela's home lay decapitated in the muck, its roof, dormer, and cupola lying intact behind the foundation but the lower floor gone. Around Bethel, seventy miles of roads and nine bridges were damaged, along with the town water and sewer systems. The silt was so deep in the Bethel Mills yard that it almost buried the four-foot-high wall of jersey barriers. The mill had also been wiped out in the 1927 flood (and been rebuilt a quarter-mile upstream, at the current location). After watching the sun rise over his family's demolished business and surveying the destroyed inventory, Lang Durfee looked at a jack-o-lantern that a local had given him the previous week. Carved into the pumpkin was: "Bethel Mills, 1781–2011." Durfee wondered if it was a sign of the business's impending demise, an orange gravestone foretelling doom.

Farther south, the U.S. 4 corridor suffered almost as badly as Route 107. In West Bridgewater, east of the washout in Killington, the Ottauquechee ripped up Blackie's, a deli and gas station at the intersection of

U.S. 4 and Route 100 in West Bridgewater. Although the two-story blue clapboard building somehow held its ground during the storm (with at least two people inside), floodwaters tore parts of the building away from the main structure. A side wing had separated from the west wall of the main building and lay tipped at an odd angle, and the parking lot looked as if it had melted. Farther east on U.S. 4, the Long Trail Brewery, located on the banks of the Ottauquechee in Bridgewater Corners, took on water, but not as severely as the homes and properties around it. Route 100A intersects U.S. 4 in Bridgewater Corners, and the devastation up the 100A valley was astounding. Homes either lay in heaps or in muddy ruins, fields were feet deep in silt, the road full of chasms and crevasses — devastation wrought by the Broad Brook. Seven homes in this rural valley were destroyed beyond repair.

East of Bridgewater in Woodstock, the Woodstock Farmers' Market still stood beside the Ottauquechee, but the popular gourmet food store was buried up to eight feet in mud. A few yards down the road, the iconic White Cottage Snack Bar lay in a pile of rubble, its broad porch roof sagging, the parking lot gouged out. Behind it, the river was now closer than ever to the popular summer eatery. Between these two Woodstock mainstays, the *Vermont Standard* building still stood, though its entire front was pulled from the structure. Inside, computers, files, photos, and office furniture lay buried in mud. Still, publisher Phil Camp, who grew up in Woodstock and was Killington Resort's first marketing director (the first marketing director in the ski industry), was determined to get the weekly newspaper out on schedule.

"After 158-plus years, this newspaper has never ever missed a week of publication," he said, "and on my watch, it wasn't going to be the first."

George Helmer, who owns a small office building complex about two miles west of Woodstock, offered Camp a vacant office. Seven of the newspaper's eight employees showed up Monday morning (the eighth was unable to reach town). They sat on the floor, porch furniture, and at a picnic table that Camp had brought from his home. With no computers, phones, electricity, or water, they made plans to get the paper out that week.

In Quechee — an upscale village in the town of Hartford — the Simon Pearce glassblowing factory, gallery, and restaurant visited annually by more than 300,000 people looked like a battered warrior. A former woolen mill that sits on the Ottauquechee, the building had taken a direct hit from the floodwaters. The glass melting furnace, six "glory holes" where the glassblowers reheat the glass, a hydroelectric turbine, and the restaurant's prep kitchen were destroyed, the entire lower floor having been submerged in the Ottauquechee's brown floodwaters. Glassware lay in piles amid the muck, yet oddly most was not broken. And hundreds of bottles of wine from the restaurant's collection were long gone. Upstairs, water grazed the retail space's floor but somehow stayed out of the restaurant, part of which is cantilevered over the river. It was the second devastating blow for Simon Pearce in less than two years. On December 31, 2009, his son Kevin suffered severe brain trauma while snowboarding, training to make the 2010 U.S. Olympic team in the halfpipe.

Just downstream from Simon Pearce, the Quechee covered bridge had somehow withstood the barrage of water and debris. But a gaping cavern separated its northern end from the road, and the water and sewer line that had been anchored to the bridge were severed.

Quechee was not the only village in the town of Hartford that was hit hard by flooding. The hamlet of West Hartford along the White River, near its terminus at the Connecticut River, was overwhelmed by water. And silt.

"Stunned-looking residents wandered the dirty streets, surveying devastation and snapping pictures of wreckage—a bridge, built just a few years ago, rendered impassable; power lines down in the streets; a once vibrant waterfront park hidden beneath mounds of stinking silt; and a library flooded and muddy," wrote Gregory Trotter for the *Valley News*. "One home stood agape with its front face ripped off, the structure yawning over water pooled in the front yard, allowing passers-by an unsettling look at the paintings and diplomas on the living room wall."

Below where the White River emptied into the Connecticut River, the larger river could not handle the volume of water and had overflowed its banks near West Lebanon, New Hampshire. The massive flooding in West Leb's strip of shopping centers on Route 12A was the only indication to people on the New Hampshire side of the river that anything catastrophic had happened in Vermont.

On Monday morning, questions also abounded about the state's historic covered bridges. Had the Taftsville Bridge across the Ottauquechee between Woodstock and Quechee survived? Would the recently refurbished Gorham Bridge in Proctor be passable after the Otter Creek's floodwaters receded? What about the double-span West Dummerston covered bridge over the West River? Sadly, many already knew that the 151-foot-long Bartonsville Covered Bridge—four miles southeast of Chester—was gone. Built in 1870, the bridge fell victim to the Williams River, its demise immortalized on YouTube.

Vermont governor Peter Shumlin took to the air Monday morning in a Vermont Army National Guard helicopter, along with U.S. senator Patrick Leahy and Adjutant General Michael Dubie, head of the Vermont Army National Guard. It was the only way the state's leaders could move around the state and assess the damage. They dropped down into one community after another, setting the chopper down wherever they could—far from downed power lines, sometimes next to cemeteries.

"It was absolutely heartbreaking to see people who had lost everything, their belongings, their homes, the photographs of their family, everything gone," said the governor. "The enormity of the devastation was overwhelming."

As the chopper flew into one devastated area after another, the governor began to worry about the state's businesses that rely on tourism. "My God," he thought, "we're not going to be open for leaf-peeping season, let alone ski season."

With arteries severed, people trapped in towns—some without homes, some far from home—tens of thousands without power, some of the state's historic landmarks in ruins, Vermont looked as if Irene had inflicted mortal wounds. How could a state that has only 626,431 people—the second least populated state in the United States after Wyoming, with 1.6 percent the population of California (America's most populated state)—and a relatively austere budget recover from this? The state's revenue is only 4 percent of California's—and one-thirteenth Microsoft Corporation's annual revenue. And what about the people who had lost far more than just the roads and bridges leading to their towns? For those people, the nightmare was just beginning.

֍ ֍ ֍

AROUND 5:30 A.M. on Monday, Kristen Casella called her dad. He was still asleep on the couch, where he had lain down just a few hours earlier.

"Dad," she said into her cell phone, "can you come to the reservoir and run an excavator?"

A crew from Casella Construction had hauled one of the company's excavators to the Rutland Reservoir in the wee hours of Monday morning. The plan—hatched over dinner the previous evening—was to use the excavator's arm to reach over Mendon Brook's raging floodwaters and confirm if Big Mike and Young Mike Garofano had reached the city reservoir's intake building during the storm. If they had made it to the building before the raging brook completely surrounded it, there was a chance that they might still be trapped inside. No one had heard from the Garofanos since 1:30 the previous afternoon.

When Kristen, Joe, Little John, Brad Matteson, and the rest of the Casella crew arrived at the reservoir before dawn, they found Rutland deputy fire chief Fran Robillard already at the scene, with a thirty-person search party. Robillard, who had known Big Mike Garofano for so long that he didn't remember ever not knowing him, had begun organizing the search party the previous evening. Most members were off-duty firefighters, Big Mike's coworkers from Public Works, and friends and family of the missing men. When Robillard had arrived at the scene, he'd been stunned at "the absolute destruction" that Mendon Brook had caused as it tore out of the mountains and past the Rutland City Reservoir's intake valve. Hundred-foot-high embankments were gone, stripped down to dirt. About a thousand feet of pipe that carried water from the brook to the reservoir were utterly destroyed, with whole sections of the twenty-inch iron pipe ripped from the ground. And Mendon Brook was still roaring in the predawn light, lapping at the girders of the Meadow Lake Drive Bridge and still surrounding the intake house.

A quiet, contemplative man, Robillard knew the search had to be organized with the safety of the search party as the top priority. Robillard asked Kristen and Joe to call their dad. Although Joe has run heavy equipment since he was a kid, Robillard understood that experience would be key in maneuvering an excavator on the banks of a raging brook. One misstep could be fatal.

Doug Casella hung up the phone with his daughter and stood up from the couch. He made coffee, put on his boots, and climbed into his truck. He was at the reservoir by 6:00 a.m.

As the sun rose over East Ridge in Mendon, Doug Casella delicately worked the excavator's arm toward the intake building. But the searchers could find no sign of the Garofanos inside it.

With heavy hearts, everyone looked downstream. Below the intake valve, Mendon Brook was lined with twenty- to thirty-foot-high piles of tangled trees, root balls, boulders, and other debris that the floodwaters had swept downstream, then deposited into huge knotted piles along the banks. The search would now have to focus on those piles.

Robillard divided the searchers into teams, and each team began examining a different part of each debris pile. New England K-9 Search & Rescue responded with two dogs and their handlers, but conditions were tough. The piles were impenetrable tangles, and it was difficult for the dogs to walk on them, let alone find a scent. And human eyes could see only so far into each pile. Casella had to pick delicately at the debris with the excavator, removing branches and logs one at a time. It was nerve-racking work.

"It seems like everything you see looks like a leg or an arm," Casella said. "A barked-up tree looks like an arm."

ริ   ริ   ริ

JUST UPSTREAM from the Meadow Lake Bridge, Joe Kraus arrived at Mendon Gorge early Monday morning. The senior vice president for engineering, operations, and customer service for Central Vermont Public Service, Kraus knew the damage along U.S. 4 in Mendon was bad. Chris Gandin, CVPS's operations supervisor, had given him the news. Gandin couldn't sleep during the storm. So at 1:30 a.m. he had driven around Rutland County to assess the road damage. He wanted to know what roads would be passable for utility crews on Monday morning. More than 55,000 CVPS customers had lost power during the storm, and as of early Monday morning, 37,500 were still in the dark. To reach many of the downed lines serving those customers, CVPS needed trucks to replace the 450 or so utility poles that had been either broken or simply wiped out by floodwaters (in a typical major storm, the utility loses only 25 to 30 poles, most broken by downed trees). But it was going to be hard to get anywhere from the power company's headquarters in Rutland. The bridge on U.S. 7 over the Cold River south of Rutland had collapsed, the span falling at a slant into the river, bringing to mind California's Bay Bridge after the 1989 Loma Prieta earthquake. North of Rutland,

East Creek's floodwaters had receded, but a thick layer of muck covered a two-hundred-yard stretch of U.S. 7 where the brook had flooded the previous day. Farther north in Brandon, U.S. 7 through the village was closed, undermined in places by the Neshobe River and with the House of Pizza—pushed off its foundation by the river—sitting on the tarmac.

Vermont is crisscrossed by back roads, and with a map and some creativity, CVPS crews would be able to get around some of the damage. But not U.S. 4. The mile-long stretch through Mendon Gorge leading up to Killington was gone, eaten away by the Mendon Brook as it ricocheted down the narrow gorge. In some places, not even a tire's width of road remained between the brook and the steep hillside. Gandin knew there was no way to get a truck up U.S. 4. Wheelerville Road, a seven-mile-long dirt road that runs from the southeastern side of Rutland to U.S. 4 above Mendon Gorge, was also impassable. Mendon Brook had turned five of the road's seven miles into a boulder-strewn streambed and left several bridges standing like statues, the road washed away on either side. Wheelerville was in worse shape than U.S. 4.

Gandin relayed his findings to Kraus, who drove up to U.S. 4 to see the damage for himself. He was overwhelmed by the destruction. The utility had never faced damage on this scale. Kraus estimated that it would take weeks to restore power to most CVPS customers in Vermont's mountains. They were in uncharted territory—how do you restore power to a town when you can't get there? He called VTrans headquarters in Montpelier and asked if the agency could send someone to rebuild U.S. 4, the primary gateway to at least nine mountain towns currently without power. Everyone he talked to at VTrans told him to take a number. The agency was tapped out.

About the same time, Kent Belden arrived at the blowout on U.S. 4 in Mendon. Owner of Belden Construction, Kent had received a call that morning from the Alpine Pipeline's treasurer telling him that the sewer line coming off the mountain was broken at Cream Hill Road where it intersects U.S. 4 (about a mile uphill of the destruction in Mendon Gorge). Kent's father, Bruce Belden—who owned Pico Ski Area from 1964 to 1987—had been instrumental in the Alpine Pipeline's construction in the mid-1980s, and the family construction company had worked to maintain the pipeline ever since. The pipeline carried sewage from properties along U.S. 4 in Mendon, as well as part of Killington, in an eleven-mile pipe that paralleled U.S. 4 from Pico to the Rutland Wastewater Treatment Facility.

Kent Belden drove his truck around the sweeping corner of U.S. 4 past Sugar & Spice in Mendon and immediately saw that the damage to the sewer line was far more extensive than just a break at Cream Hill Road — which he couldn't even reach. The pipeline in the gorge was completely gone, swept away, along with the road. Belden parked his truck, then walked about a half-mile up U.S. 4 — or what remained of it. The pipeline in the gorge was wiped out — three thousand feet of pipe, thirty-five to forty manholes, everything — and sewage was flowing into the brook. Only fractured bits of the aqua-colored pipe remained, sticking up at odd angles through the debris. Belden called his project manager, Kevin Creed, and asked him to order temporary pipe and pull together a crew. He wasn't sure where he was going to put a temporary sewer line in this mess, but he and his crew would figure it out.

With Belden back from his hike up the destroyed road, Kraus asked the contractor if his company could build a temporary road through the gorge so the utility could get its bucket trucks up the mountain. CVPS had sent a couple of utility workers up the damaged road on ATVs that morning to do what they could to restore power in Killington and Pittsfield. But to replace the downed power poles they needed multi-ton bucket trucks up there. A quiet unassuming guy who still looks fit enough to ski race on the Pro Tour, as he did briefly in the late 1970s, Kent Belden agreed to do the work, then called Creed again — there was more to do than just a pipeline rebuild. Creed immediately phoned Bruce Nichols, VTrans's District 3 general manager (the district is one of nine in Vermont and comprises all of Rutland County and a few outlying towns). If VTrans couldn't rebuild the road, could Belden have permission to build a temporary road where this section of U.S. 4 once sat?

"By all means," replied Nichols, who was dealing with more washed-out roads than he ever thought imaginable. Help from a reputable contractor was welcome.

When Nichols arrived at the U.S. 4 washout shortly after hanging up the phone, he asked Creed, "When you get done building [the temporary road], can you guys just stay here and start rebuilding Route 4?"

ᕼ ᕼ ᕼ

ON THE OTHER SIDE of Sherburne Pass in Killington, Craig Mosher
walked out of his house in the gray light of dawn and knew he had work
to do. The Ottauquechee River had left rocks, trees, and other debris all
over his property — including what was left of the pasture where his Scottish Highlanders Big and Rob, ornery donkey Pedro, and his two sheep
grazed. Mosher figured that the river had left a similar amount of debris along U.S. 4 as it tore east through a narrow, winding valley toward
Bridgewater, Woodstock, and Quechee. He knows the area well, having grown up in neighboring Bridgewater, where his mom was the post-
mistress. And he knows his way around heavy equipment. He learned
to ski in the area, just like his Aunt Becky Fraser, a 1948 Olympian, and
his first construction job in 1979 was building ski trails — the steeper,
the better. When nearby Killington Mountain Resort constructed trails
on Bear Mountain, including Outer Limits, which the resort touts as the
longest, steepest mogul run in the East, Mosher drove the last bulldozer
down the perilously steep trail. At Sunday River in Maine, he built ski
trails like White Heat, known as one of the scarier trails in the East,
and its even steeper neighbor, Shockwave, to name a few. He still skis
(though knee surgery has slowed him down, he says), and his healthy
good looks and full head of hair make him look at least a decade younger
than his real age — fifty-seven at the time Irene hit. For a guy like Mosher,
scooping up mud and rock from a flat road sounded relatively easy. Until
he saw the extent of the destruction.

Mosher walked to his garage, fired up his rubber-tired front loader,
and turned east onto U.S. 4. The little development where U.S. 4 and
Route 100 intersect in West Bridgewater was in shambles. The First Stop
Ski Shop and Board Barn, which he had tried to help save from flooding on Sunday morning, hadn't been washed away. But the property
around the store had been scoured in places and strewn with mud and
rock. Next door, the Back Behind Restaurant & BBQ Smokehouse sat
in a lake of brown water that came up to its windows. And a handful of
cars parked in front of Blackie's Deli were miraculously still there. But in
front of the gas pumps by the road, a pickup truck sat nose down in the
broken pavement, with grass hanging from its rear bumper.

Mosher could do little here at the moment to help his neighbors, and he figured it was more important to get the road open. So he began clearing gravel and mud off the road. Miraculously, the bridge over the Ottauquechee just east of the Route 100 intersection was intact, the river having flowed over and around it. He rumbled over it and kept clearing the road, which the previous day had become the riverbed. On this relatively flat, straight stretch of river (and road), the velocity of the water must have been slow enough that it did not rip up the pavement or roadbed. At least not here.

But at the first bend in the tight valley that U.S. 4 shares with the Ottauquechee, the river had chewed the road down to one lane. And wherever a small mountain tributary tumbled down the valley walls and crossed under U.S. 4 in a culvert, floodwaters had left mounds of gravel and dirt on the road. Using the loader's bucket, Mosher scooped up the mess and opened up one lane. Along the way, he found dumpsters, gas tanks, and at least one sailboat littering the pavement. As long as traffic could get around the clutter, he left it. Just under six miles east of his house, he turned around and headed back to West Bridgewater. He had reached Bridgewater Corners and knew there were enough people with heavy equipment in town to dig out the road there.

Back in West Bridgewater, Mosher turned south on Route 100 and scooped up more gravel deposited by the flooded Ottauquechee. A couple of miles farther south, one of Markowski Excavating's employees had walked into the company's gravel pit and was singlehandedly loading a giant off-road truck with gravel, then driving the truck to washouts along Route 100 in Plymouth, south of West Bridgewater. After dumping big loads of gravel, he returned to the pit to get the loader so he could push around the material and make a passable lane for the stranded residents of Plymouth. He worked all day Monday by himself, a one-man road rebuilding crew. Mosher had no idea he was there.

After doing what he could to clear this section of Route 100, Mosher headed north on U.S. 4 toward Killington. He knew he would find a mess of mud and gravel by the Killington Skye Ship gondola base. He had driven that far during the storm and had seen the Ottauquechee's floodwaters spread over the road—a lake waiting to funnel into a tight mountain gorge that would drop the river down to Mosher's property a mile farther east. He scooped up the layer of muck across U.S. 4, then dug through a six-to-eight-foot-deep fan of gravel left when a stream

Overleaf: The Ball Mountain Brook washes away both land and houses in Jamaica, Vermont. FRAN JANIK

Top: The Ottauquechee River surrounds Blackie's Deli on U.S. 4 in West Bridgewater near Killington after Tropical Storm Irene hits Vermont. NICOLE KESSELRING

Bottom: The Deerfield River tops the Main Street Bridge in downtown Wilmington on Sunday morning as Tropical Storm Irene dumps heavy rain in Vermont.

ANN MANWARING

Top: Hurricane Flats resembles a sandy beach after the White River floods the field with up to eight feet of water. MARK EDSELL

Bottom: Tomatoes still cling to the vines after the White River floods Hurricane Flats' greenhouses to the eaves. MARK EDSELL

Above: The northern access to the Royalton Bridge, washed away by the White River. GREG RUSS

Opposite page, top: For months afterward, Heather Grev's and Jack Livesey's rented house sat tipped in the mud behind its foundation in Pittsfield. PEGGY SHINN

Opposite page, bottom: The ruined home of Traci Templeton in Pittsfield. On the door are the words "Irene You Bitch." PEGGY SHINN

Above: Dot's Restaurant in Wilmington, still cantilevered over the Deerfield River, is a battered warrior illustrating what the town went through. PEGGY SHINN
Right: Work begins to repair U.S. 4 in Mendon.

LARS GANGE & MANSFIELD HELIFLIGHT

Top: In Rochester, Jon Graham's house lies collapsed on its back after being undermined by floodwater. LARS GANGE & MANSFIELD HELIFLIGHT

Bottom: The Roaring Brook in Killington trashes U.S. 4, Goodro Lumber, and the Kokopelli Inn. Craig Mosher began rebuilding this section of road the day after Irene hit Vermont. NICOLE KESSELRING

Left: Quechee Gorge at its normal water level. DAVID COREY

Right: Quechee Gorge the day after the flood. DAVID COREY

Top: Volunteers help Lisa Sullivan and Phil Taylor clean out sodden inventory and mud from Bartleby's Books. ANN MANWARING

Bottom: High-water marks for the 1938 and 2011 floods, painted on the side of the Wilmington Police Department next to the town office. SHELLEY LUTZ

Top: A Pittsfielder shares food from the garden with neighbors and townspeople in the stranded village. PEGGY SHINN

Bottom: The Army National Guard flies water, MREs, and other supplies into Pittsfield on Chinook helicopters. PEGGY SHINN

Top: In Rochester, a temporary footbridge crosses the White River after the collapse of the Route 73 bridge. LARS GANGE & MANSFIELD HELIFLIGHT

Bottom: Local contractors in Jamaica rebuild Water Street along the Ball Mountain Brook where four houses once sat. KRISTEN WILSON

Opposite page, top: Craig Mosher works hard to rebuild U.S. 4 in Killington.
CRAIG MOSHER / MOSHER EXCAVATING, INC.

Opposite page, bottom: Craig Mosher has one lane of U.S. 4 in Killington ready for traffic within thirty-six hours of the end of the storm. PEGGY SHINN

Above: Eighteen days after the Roaring Brook washes out U.S. 4 in Killington, Craig Mosher has rebuilt the entire road. PEGGY SHINN

Top: Two long sections of Route 107 disappear, completely obliterated by the White River. To rebuild the road, Casella Construction must begin at the riverbed.
PEGGY SHINN

Bottom: Contractors and members of the Army National Guard who helped rebuild U.S. 4 gather with Governor Shumlin in front of a Casella Euclid off-road truck to celebrate the reopening of the road on September 16, 2011. PEGGY SHINN

Left: The reconstructed section of U.S. 4 in Mendon as seen from the air during foliage season, 2011. LARS GANGE & MANSFIELD HELIFLIGHT

Below: Local residents ride a golf cart along the Woodchip Parkway in Mendon. Until U.S. 4 was reconstructed in Mendon, this trail through the woods was the only route into Rutland from mountain towns to the east. PEGGY SHINN

The remains of a sugaring house near Cavendish, more than six months after the flood. FRAN JANIK

tumbling down the steep hillside just north of the gondola station had poured across the road. He has no idea how long it took to free up one lane of U.S. 4 in that area.

"I was just going like hell," he said.

Once through the muck around the gondola base, Mosher rumbled across "the flats," a three-mile-long straight stretch of U.S. 4 between West Bridgewater and Killington that borders a long marsh. It's the headwaters of the Ottauquechee, and dozens of mountain streams drain into the marsh. Widened and straightened between 1961 and 1963, U.S. 4 across the flats is often a speedway for cars and trucks trying to make up time on an otherwise curvy road. At the western end of the flats sits "old" Killington—a few houses, the quaint Our Lady of the Mountains white clapboard church, the Kokopelli Inn, and Goodro Lumber. Across from the church, the Roaring Brook tumbles out of a steep mountain ravine and crosses under U.S. 4, then under River Road, which travels farther north into the valley and leads to the Killington Town Office, garage, library, and recreation center, along with several houses.

From this little section of "old" Killington, U.S. 4 widens to three lanes and climbs steeply for another couple of miles to what most people now know as Killington—a series of ski shops and gift stores that line both U.S. 4 and Killington Road (referred to by locals as the Access Road, since it winds up to the main part of Killington Mountain Resort). The section of U.S. 4 above "old" Killington is one of the steepest grades along the entire road. A highway sign labels it as a 7 percent grade, but anyone who has ridden a bicycle along this stretch of road knows that it's closer to 10. Before the road was widened to three lanes in the 1960s, this section was called the "dugway," meaning that the road had been literally blasted into the mountainside.

Driving west across the flats, Mosher found little damage to U.S. 4. But when he hit Goodro Lumber, just before U.S. 4 begins its climb up the old dugway, he stopped and stared. The road disappeared into a lunar landscape of mud and rock stretching from where the Roaring Brook came out of the mountain well into the valley. A 50 mph speed limit sign stood alone in the debris. It was the only indication that a road had once sat here. In its place was the Roaring Brook, and all the rock, trees, and debris it had carried down from Killington Peak. The yellow-clapboard Kokopelli Inn and Goodro Lumber were buried under feet of rubble.

Mosher took a deep breath and turned the loader around. A loader, with its shovel-like bucket, could do nothing here. Mosher knew that the river needed to be put back in its channel before the road could be rebuilt. And the only machine for that job was an excavator. Its tank-like tracks would hold it in place while Mosher maneuvered the arm and bucket to scoop up piles of rock and gravel and rebuild the brook's banks. He rumbled four miles back to his garage, parked the machine, and began loading the excavator onto a flatbed truck. Suddenly, he heard someone outside.

"Man, how'd you get here?" Mosher asked, as Mark Bourassa walked up to the truck.

One of Mosher's employees, Bourassa lives in Rutland. He had left his house early that morning and found that he couldn't get to work via his usual route — by driving east on U.S. 4 in Mendon. So he headed south to Vermont Route 103, a main road that crosses the state in a southeasterly direction from Clarendon (just south of Rutland) to I-91 in Rockingham. This route was also damaged, but Bourassa managed to drive his truck around the washouts. Near Ludlow he turned north on Route 100 and drove until the first washout south of Plymouth. He left his truck there and started to walk the remaining six or so miles to Mosher's business. He hiked across the first washout, then found a truck on the other side with the keys still in it. He had no idea who owned the truck, but he knew he had to get to work. So he climbed in, turned the ignition, and drove the borrowed truck another mile or so until he reached the next washout. He parked the truck there, left the keys where he had found them, and kept walking. He arrived at Mosher's sometime between 11:00 and noon.

Mosher and Bourassa ferried the excavator across the flats to the Roaring Brook washout on U.S. 4, then Bourassa headed back to the garage to get a bulldozer. Before Mosher fired up the excavator, he called the VTrans district office in Rutland and was patched through to headquarters in Montpelier. When he gave his name to the person who answered, she informed Mosher that he was not an approved state contractor on her list.

"I'm not asking for permission," Mosher told her. "I'm telling you what I'm doing."

Then he hung up and began rebuilding U.S. 4.

So many contractors telephoned VTrans and offered their services and equipment to rebuild the roads that day that the agency set up a separate 1-800 number to handle the volume of incoming phone calls.

ဖ   ဖ   ဖ

DOWN IN WILMINGTON, Lisa Sullivan and Phil Taylor pulled together breakfast for their two children and the couple who had stayed with them during the storm and then set off on foot to downtown Wilmington. They knew that they had a mess on their hands. At least four feet of water had flowed into Bartleby's Books on Sunday; they had seen books swimming in the mire the previous afternoon when they slid down the hillside behind their business in the rain and scrambled in the back door. At the time, the river pouring through the bookstore was still at flood stage. There was nothing they could do. They had moved their inventory onto higher shelves, but they'd had no idea the water would reach as high as it did.

It was the second time in five months that water had ruined Lisa Sullivan's livelihood. She had been on vacation when a fire had destroyed the Brooks House in Brattleboro, along with her bookstore, the Book Cellar, a downtown institution that had been there for decades. But she hadn't cut her trip short. What could she do? The fire department had poured 1.5 million gallons of water onto the building to douse the flames. Books don't do well in water. Her inventory was destroyed. She had no plans to reopen the Book Cellar.

Now she had to see what sort of damage Bartleby's had sustained. Maybe a few books had survived the flood, she thought. She needed to get into the building to see what, if anything, was still high and dry. And Taylor was concerned about the building's integrity. Although Sullivan and Taylor had become the sole proprietors of Bartleby's seven years before Irene, they had purchased the three-story building on West Main Street only two years prior to the storm, almost to the day.

Ray Hill Road intersects Main Street by Dot's Restaurant, and as Sullivan and Taylor descended into town, they noticed that the restaurant was sitting in an island of rubble. The river had pounded the back of Dot's and carved a path from behind the building to the street, ripping out the restaurant's small parking area and gouging the earth beneath it. The wing of the building overhanging the Deerfield River was in shreds, the siding ripped off down to the framing, and the building had shifted on its stone foundation. Miraculously, the floodwaters that had topped the Main Street Bridge the day before had not completely torn the building from its foundation. It still stood, like the battered stars-and-stripes flag over an American garrison in wartime.

From what Sullivan could see from the bottom of Ray Hill Road, the rest of downtown Wilmington was in equally rough shape. The Mount Snow Valley Chamber of Commerce building had lost all its windows, and its front door was torn from its hinges. On South Main Street, a gallery had a large hole in one wall, torn open by both the raging torrent and the debris it carried. On West Main Street, bottles of vodka, scotch, and gin lay strewn under toppled coolers and shelves at Robinson's Liquor Store, the name recently changed from McBrearity's Marketplace. Much of the liquor had no doubt been carried downstream. And Ann Coleman's gallery was completely gone.

"The floodwaters pushed the whole building, including its slab foundation, into the middle of Route 9," wrote Mike Eldred in the *Deerfield Valley News* (Route 9 is West Main Street in Wilmington). "From there, the torrent that raged down West Main Street tore the recently renovated building off its foundation and it disappeared downriver. Except for the slab, which remained across Route 9, no trace of the building is left in the village, not even a splinter."

The Vermont Army National Guard had arrived in Wilmington during the storm on Sunday. By Monday morning they had barricaded the streets leading to downtown. No one was allowed entry, not even business owners. The president of the Mount Snow Valley Chamber of Commerce at the time, Sullivan was stunned. Business owners *had* to be allowed access so they could salvage what they could of their livelihoods. Where were the town police? They would surely allow business owners access to their property. Sullivan and the chamber's executive director, Laura Sibilia, started making phone calls.

The police, as well as other town officials, had problems of their own. Both the police and fire departments were flooded out, as was the town office. A command post was set up at the Twin Valley High School in Wilmington, which was also serving as the town's emergency shelter (without a functioning sewer system, volunteer fire fighters drove to the nearby Harriman Reservoir recreation area and, without asking anyone, expropriated a row of portable toilets). Town officials called an emergency management meeting. Among other topics, both the fire chief and police chief suggested to the select board that the town move both departments out of the floodplain.

"We all agreed, at least theoretically, that the first responders and the town records probably shouldn't be in the floodplain," said town clerk Susie Haughwout. "It really seems not bright."

Haughwout then went to the town office. Her Mitsubishi was still parked out front, but water had risen over the hood and destroyed the engine. Inside the office, she found a toxic environment. Fumes from a tipped-over heating oil tank in the basement mixed with the smell of muck and stale water in the closed, locked building. An oily film coated everything on the first floor. The vault was full of muck, but the books and records that they had left behind the previous day—the ones that sat above eye-level—were undamaged.

"We knew that we didn't have a lot of time to leave those documents in that environment," she said.

Haughwout and assistant town clerk Pat Johnson made a plan. They would move all the documents left in the vault to Johnson's barn. The barn was not an ideal location for sensitive legal records, but they couldn't think of anywhere else to take them.

ᔕ   ᔕ   ᔕ

TWENTY-SEVEN MILES north of Wilmington in Jamaica, the select board, fire department, rescue workers, emergency management coordinator, and other town officials convened at the plush Three Mountain Inn, offered as the emergency shelter and command center by its owners, the Dorta-Duques. Jamaica was in rough shape. In the village alone, four houses on Water/Back Street were gone, the Main Street Bridge on Route 30/100 had collapsed just north of the village, and the river had gouged a chasm at the north end of the Depot Street Bridge—though surprisingly, the crumbling concrete bridge still stood. People on the north side of Jamaica had no way of reaching town. To the south, Route 30 was open, allowing the Brooklyn couple who had stayed at the Three Mountain Inn during the storm a passage home. But officials soon closed it after the stability of the bridges came into question.

Outside the village, town officials knew that Pikes Falls and West

Jamaica roads, two tertiary roads leading up into the mountains west of town, were in bad shape, with several complete washouts. But no one knew the exact extent of the damage.

The Dorta-Duques made a pot of coffee (surprisingly and ironically, given the size of their generator, the inn lost power for only about ten minutes during the storm), and everyone sat down on the two couches and assorted chairs in the inn's lovely wood-paneled, eighteenth-century living room in front of the fireplace. Their first mission was to make sure that everyone in town was safe—all 1,035 residents. But many of Jamaica's homes are second homes for flatlanders (the name Vermonters give to anyone who lives outside of northern New England).

"It made it difficult," said Ed Dorta-Duque. "No one knew who was here."

He ran over to the town hall and pulled property listings so they would have the names of people who owned homes on Pikes Falls and West Jamaica roads. Some of the select board members then organized a search. After the meeting, Stewart Barker and town road commissioner, Brian Chapin, would drive ATVs up Pikes Falls and West Jamaica roads on a reconnaissance mission.

Town officials also knew that they had to address the road and bridge washouts, so residents on the north side of town would not be stranded. As a temporary fix, local residents Andy Coyne (whose house on Water Street next to the bridge miraculously did not wash away) and Ray Ballentine both brought tall extension ladders to the chasm by the Depot Street Bridge. The ladders allowed people to reach town by climbing down one side of the washed-out embankment, then up the other side to the bridge. It wasn't a route for the weak and feeble, or for those afraid of heights. Or for anyone carrying supplies, food, or water. And rescuers and supply trucks approaching from the south on Route 30 needed a route through town.

A small group walked down to the Depot Street Bridge to look at Water Street. Or at least to look at where Water Street used to be. The tree-lined street used to lead directly from Route 30/100, just north of the collapsed Main Street Bridge, to the Depot Street Bridge. But now the eastern end of the street was gone, consumed by the Ball Mountain Brook. And the brook now flowed where the street and four Water Street houses had once stood. The idea of rebuilding the road in its former location seemed impossible. There was no land left, just a river channel. Select board member Lou Bruso suggested that they rebuild the road behind where the four houses had sat. But that would tear up what little of their property remained. Plus, their septic tanks most likely sat behind their former homes.

Wesley Ameden had another idea. Ameden owns Ameden Construction and had called the select board the night before to see what he could do to help. They told him to show up at the morning meeting, where they would figure out how to proceed.

"I can build you a road back through there," said Ameden, pointing to where the river now sat. The contractor then explained that if he redirected the river to its previous channel, he could rebuild Water/Back Street, not where it had been but where the four houses had stood. Stewart Barker liked the confidence in Ameden's voice.

"Since we were overwhelmed and he was full of confidence, we gave him the green light to go ahead with his idea," recalled Barker.

Ameden returned with his heavy equipment and shortly after 7:00 a.m. began building a road.

§ § §

THE TOWN OF PITTSFIELD is a triangle of land located almost on the spine of the Green Mountain Range in central Vermont. The village itself sits in a narrow valley. But the rest of the town is so mountainous that a nineteenth-century humorist supposedly claimed that the good people of Pittsfield were forced to invent the one-legged milking stool because the ground was too uneven for the traditional three-legged variety. Bordered by Chittenden to the west, Stockbridge to the east, and Rochester to the north, Pittsfield has only one main road passing through it— Route 100. Several dirt roads lead out of town, but those are either dead ends or become rough trails deep in the mountains.

With Irene's floodwaters creating a fifty-foot-deep chasm on Route 100 north of Pittsfield and the bridge washed out south of the village, Pittsfield was isolated. Town officials gathered at 7:00 a.m. on Monday morning to figure out a plan to present at a townwide meeting at 7:30. They knew that they had to fix Route 100. But meanwhile, the townspeople would have questions—such as where could they get food, water, and medicine. And how long would they be without power?

Once assembled at the town hall that morning, the officials broke into five groups: road crew, medical, security, food, and administration, with emergency management coordinator Peter Borden serving as ringleader. The road crew, led by town road commissioner George Deblon, would focus first on rebuilding Route 100 in both directions. And he knew who would do the work. Local contractors, such as David Colton and his eighty-three-year-old father, Mel, who run the family-owned Colton Enterprises in town, showed up that morning without being asked. Deblon assigned them to the various washouts on Route 100. Connie Martin, a nurse, would coordinate a medical team, find supplies, and set up a clinic in the town library. Constables Tim Hunt and Doug Mianulli would enforce a speed limit in town, a gun law prohibiting the carrying of weapons, and a curfew, among other measures. And town clerk Patty Haskins would focus on the town's administrative needs, such as filing a disaster declaration order with the state.

Armed with a plan, the officials waited for the townspeople to arrive. Word of the meeting had quickly spread through the village of 546, and as the sun worked its way over the mountains east of town, residents walked or rode bikes and ATVs from all parts of town. The smell of up-turned earth hung heavy in the clear morning air.

No one had to look far to see the destruction caused by Irene. En route to the town hall, residents on the south side of town passed the little white house where Heather Grev and Jack Livesey had been rescued the day before. It sat tipped forward in the brown muck, the kitchen wall gone. Next door was Evelyn Payette's mobile home, looking as if it had been dropped to earth from a thousand feet. And at Traci Templeton's home, the frame was bent and sagging, with the siding peeled off. In front of these homes, Route 100's pavement was broken into jagged pieces, as if it were a giant puzzle waiting for someone to put it back together. Farther south, some of the wedding guests had climbed a ladder down from a washed-out bridge separating Riverside Farm from Route 100.

The town hall was soon packed, with people standing in the vestibule. At real town meetings, held annually the first Tuesday in March throughout the state, Vermonters have—for 259 years—elected local officials, voted on town and school budgets and other legislation, discussed civic issues, aired their grievances, and said hello to fellow residents they otherwise rarely see. Town meetings are usually informal affairs, with most of the voting done by saying "aye" or "no," not by written ballot. This town meeting was equally informal, but voting was far from people's minds. They were here for information. And to see if there was a plan to straighten out this mess. As they waited for the town hall meeting to start, most of the people stood wide-eyed, sharing their experiences with their neighbors.

"Everybody in town was shocked that we just went through what we went though," said Peter Borden, a gregarious and fit forty-two-year-old who works as the retail manager for the *Times Argus* newspaper an hour north in Barre.

It was also the first time that many people in town realized that Pittsfield was totally cut off from the outside world, that Route 100 was gone in both directions. And if the tiny Guernsey Brook could cut a fifty-foot-deep chasm through the road and carry a house off its foundation just north of town, then surely there was more road damage beyond what the villagers could see. Pittsfield was an island, and no one really knew how far it was to safety.

But no one considered sending an sos—except for a few of the wedding guests who were frantic to return to children, pets, and businesses left at home for what they had assumed was a weekend, and at least one guest who was running out of medication. Not that anyone could call for help. With power, phone lines, and cell service out, the town had no ability to communicate with anyone on the outside. They had no idea what Irene had done to the rest of southern and central Vermont. Like miners trapped by a cave-in, they only knew that they couldn't get out. And that no one could get in.

After the pastor led a prayer, George Deblon was the first official to address the shocked townspeople. A tall, soft-spoken man who is quick to smile, Deblon looks more like a kindly college professor than a road commissioner. But he has been at his post for twenty-one years and has lived in Pittsfield since he was ten years old. He knew the roads as well as he knew the audience.

Standing in front of the town hall that morning, Deblon could have begun the meeting by explaining that they were in desperate straits— that they were a one-mile-long island in the middle of the mountains cut off from the world, that they would have to live off what they had for who knows how long, that their well water was most likely contaminated, and that, as town resident Angelique Lee put it, "Everything seemed one broken part away from collapsing."

Instead, Deblon told a joke. Using Peter Borden and his wife, Verna, as the butt of the joke, he told of a parrot that Verna had purchased at a local pet store for $50. When asked why the bird was so inexpensive, the pet store owner explained that the parrot had previously lived in a house of ill repute. Verna bought the parrot anyway and brought it home, where it started saying, "New madam, new madam," and "New madam, new house." After Verna invited a friend to see the bird, the parrot said, "New madame, new house, new girl." Verna was worried what Peter might think when he heard the bird. Instead, when Peter returned home that evening, the parrot greeted him with, "Hi Peter."

The congregated townspeople laughed. Not a nervous laugh, but a good, hearty, we-needed-that laugh.

"We were all so on the edge," said Lee. "You could laugh or you could cry. George let us laugh."

It was the first of many jokes Deblon would tell through the course of the emergency. When asked why he chose to address the situation with humor, he said there wasn't much anyone could do to change the disaster, and that he hoped to lighten the mood, at least for a minute, and let people relax.

"Humor is good medicine for everything," he said.

The laughter acted as a collective exhale, and shock was replaced by action. The first concern was to ascertain that everyone in town was accounted for and safe, and if there were any immediate medical needs. One by one, townspeople stood up—without being asked—and announced whom they had already contacted and whom they would check on after the meeting. At one point, someone asked if anyone had checked Evelyn Payette's destroyed trailer for her pets. She has a cute little dog named Bandit and two cats. Everyone shook their head, and two guys offered to check after the meeting.

Then others stood up and stated what they could do to help and what they had to offer. The Martins, owners of cv Oil in town, announced that they would fill propane tanks for grills if people would drop them off at the town hall by noon. Cell phone service was still out (the Federal Communications Commission reported that sixty-five hundred cell sites and towers were out after Hurricane Irene, including 44 percent of Vermont's sites). But the townspeople soon realized that it was only AT&T's cell service that wasn't working. Verizon wireless customers still had a signal if they stood on the village green. Those with Verizon as a cell carrier offered to lend their phones to anyone who needed to make a call.

Haskins began writing in a notebook a list of who had what to offer. Deblon assured the group that local contractors would begin rebuilding Route 100 that morning. The town would also have a medical clinic staffed by people like Connie Martin, Kathianne Mianulli, also a nurse, and Chris Masillo, a physician's assistant, though medical supplies at the moment were limited.

After the meeting, Angelique Lee, who lives in a charming house on the town green with her husband, Sean, and two teenage daughters, helped Haskins set up a bulletin board that would serve as an information center. On sheets of lined notebook paper, she wrote in large letters, "I can offer . . . Equipment and Supplies," and "I can offer . . . Medical Supplies," with space underneath for people to write their names and how best to reach them. She tacked them to the bulletin board, along with paper cups full of pens, then propped the board against the stairs leading up to the town hall.

On the green after the meeting, townspeople milled about, discussing who had a generator to run refrigerators and charge cell phones, who had potable water, who needed medicine, and who needed help. Chris Masillo and Whalen Layne headed to Payette's mobile home to look for her animals. They found her dog Bandit, put him in a bucket, and carried him to safety. The cats were nowhere in sight. They hoped the felines had escaped out a broken window. Others headed to the Stumpfs' house to help the couple salvage what they could from the overturned house in Guernsey Brook. Brian Mitchell, one of the wedding guests, stopped at the Original General Store that morning on his way back from exploring the damage north of town. He asked Lee Ann Isaacson, operations manager of the store, if her family was all right. Isaacson explained that the chasm on Route 100 north of town had severed her path home. Mitchell asked how he could help, and she put him to work taking food orders and bagging groceries.

After spending the night at the Swiss Farm Inn with her sons and mother, Marion Abrams headed back to her home on the West Branch to join her husband, Wilbur. As she walked down her driveway, she stopped in her tracks and muttered, "Holy shit." What had been their yard was now rocks and holes, their sons' toys (the ones that hadn't been swept away) buried in gravel and mud. The garage was tipped sideways, one door peeled up, their 1940 Chevy sticking out the front; and the chicken coop was flattened, with the chickens nowhere in sight. The deck, which leads to their front door, was hanging sideways, its supports undermined by water and the debris that must have slammed into them the day before.

As Marion and Wilbur stood there trying to figure out what part of the massive mess to tackle first, their neighbors Denny and Stacey Veilleux walked down the driveway. Marion knew them only by their first names. Denny looked at the house and turned on his heels to get equipment needed to help Wilbur shore up the deck so they could get back into their house. He also brought a generator.

On the southern end of Pittsfield, Jason Evans began pulling together food for what would turn into a huge party. The owner of the Clear River Tavern, which sits along the Tweed River near where the Route 100 bridge had washed out, Evans had not had much hope that the tavern would survive the flood. But at the town meeting that morning, he ran into Brian Merrill, who rents an apartment over the tavern. Merrill told Evans that the building had made it through. Evans drove to the tavern after the town meeting and was surprised to find no water inside anywhere. But without power, the week's worth of food stored inside the walk-in refrigerator wasn't going to last. Why not cook it?

He loaded up coolers and a portable grill and drove back to the Pittsfield green. He would host a barbecue for anyone who wanted to show up. Again, word spread quickly throughout town.

§ § §

IN SOUTH ROYALTON, Geo Honigford was up well before the sun on Monday morning. He hadn't gone to bed until after 10:30 the previous night. The White River was still rising, and how could he sleep with what looked like the Mississippi lapping at the hillside beneath his house? The flood peaked somewhere close to midnight.

By morning, the water had receded enough that Honigford could walk around his organic farm and survey what remained. In the gray light of early dawn, Honigford noted that half his field was still flooded, but his two greenhouses hadn't moved. He was pleasantly surprised.

"When I went to bed Monday night, I thought they wouldn't be standing in the morning," he said.

The greenhouses' plastic, though, was torn to shreds. Honigford and Mark Edsell had slashed the ends during the flood so the river could go in one end and out the other. Water, trees, and debris had washed through the greenhouses for hours, leaving the remaining plastic in tatters. Inside, tomatoes, sweet potatoes, and what was left of five thousand pounds of onions lay under a layer of brown silt. In his fields, popcorn (forty-five hundred pounds of it), sweet corn, cantaloupe, honeydew, peppers — anything you can grow in Vermont in August — as well as his hay crop lay under more mud and silt.

Honigford turned around and walked back to the house. By the time he got there, Edsell had arrived. The two men walked around the farm again, trying to evaluate what they could save and where to start. Edsell was not optimistic.

"[The produce] was covered in eight inches of silt," he said. "In good conscience, we weren't going to go to a farmers' market and sell it."

But he also knew that Honigford was not prepared to hear that. So, in the large greenhouse, the two men began pulling onions from the mud. As they worked, about twenty people arrived at the farm — friends, neighbors, other farmers, and students from Vermont Law School in South Royalton. They all chipped in, digging onions from the muck. Once unearthed, the onions were placed in bushel baskets, and Edsell towed the baskets to the upper greenhouse on a trailer behind the tractor. They managed to save about four thousand pounds of onions — the rest had disappeared, no doubt washed downriver. Once dried, the onions could be prepared for market. Or so Honigford thought.

It quickly became clear to Edsell that Honigford was having a hard time facing the destruction on his farm. The farmer was also thinking about his neighbors. He had seen the river flowing through the five houses south of his fields the previous afternoon. At the very least, their basements were flooded. He had a pump that he used for irrigation. If he could find it under the silt in his field, he could help pump out their basements. With Edsell assuring him that he would take care of the farm, Honigford walked down toward the river with his friend Greg Russ to look for the pump.

Downriver from Hurricane Flats, David and Peggy Ainsworth looked out the window at their cornfield by the river. A quarter of the corn was flattened. The rest of it—deep-green, majestic stalks with two ears on most stalks—was covered in brownish gray silt.

It was late August, and they now had nothing to feed their dairy herd through the coming winter.

 identifier ses ses ses

SOMETIME AROUND 10:30 or 11:00 a.m. Monday, Zack Thompson, who works for Casella Construction, spotted a boot. It was a dark green rubber boot and hard to distinguish from the trees, branches, and leaves. But it was definitely a boot.

The search parties looking for the Garofanos had worked their way about a half-mile downstream from the intake valve on Mendon Brook. Climbing over house-size mounds of debris, the searchers peered as deeply into the tangled piles as they could. Then Doug Casella gingerly pulled the piles apart with his excavator. It was painstaking and heart-breaking work.

As soon as Thompson spotted the boot, the searchers began pulling on the surrounding branches and logs with their hands. But nothing in the tangled pile budged. Casella moved in with the excavator and began delicately picking apart the pile, trying to free up pieces of debris without touching Garofano's body. It was, he said, the hardest thing he had done in his thirty-six-year career.

"It's one thing to dig somebody out who you don't know, to work around heads and bodies with the machine," he said, this time without smiling. "It's another thing to work around someone who you know and recognize."

Deputy fire chief Robillard and the state police working the scene told Casella that he and his crew could leave, that the trained rescue personnel could handle removing the body from the debris; Robillard knew it would be awful work. But no one left. Casella stayed at the controls of the excavator, and his crew stood nearby. When he needed someone to move a bit of debris by hand so he could better angle the excavator's bucket, everyone standing there went straight into the pile without hesitating. After two hours of delicate, gut-wrenching work, they extracted the water department supervisor's body from the pile.

It was a sad resolution to a tragic twenty-four hours. But at least they had found him.

The searchers then set out to find Young Mike. They assumed he lay somewhere nearby. But as Monday wore on, they saw no sign of the twenty-four-year-old.

7

DIGGING OUT

It was a mission impossible. . . . Every single road we opened just
felt like a miracle.

   § Sue Minter, deputy secretary of the Vermont Agency
     of Transportation, then Irene recovery officer

BY VIRTUE OF TOPOGRAPHY, ROADS IN Vermont tend to follow river
valleys, particularly in the mountains. The roads often follow ancient
routes first cut by wildlife, then Native Americans and the early Colonial
and British military. When those groups needed to traverse the mountains, they sought the easiest grade into the steep terrain, and a valley is
generally easier walking than a mountainside.

The first official roads created in Vermont were military roads. These
roads included the Great Albany Road, constructed in 1746 to connect
Fort Dummer near Brattleboro to Fort Massachusetts in North Adams,
Massachusetts (an extension of this road linked Wilmington to Bennington); the seventy-seven-mile-long Crown Point Road, laid out by
General Jeffrey Amherst in 1759 to connect Chimney Point on Lake
Champlain with Fort No. 4 on the Connecticut River (in what would
become Claremont, New Hampshire); and the Bayley-Hazen Road in
northern Vermont, which was begun in 1776. These roads traveled along
hilltops wherever they could—to avoid low-lying marshes. But they also
followed river valleys, such as the Otter Creek and the Black River in
places. Parts of Vermont state highways 9, 103, and 131 follow similar
routes today.

The development of other roads in the state is less clear. But early
settlers no doubt cut foot, bridle, and carriage paths to reach the closest

town, or to connect towns. And again, in the mountains, many of these trails were cut along the path of least resistance — river valleys.

In central Vermont, any road that traveled east of Rutland had to cross a formidable section of the Greens near the state's second highest mountain, 4,235-foot Killington Peak. Just to the west of Killington Peak, East and Blue ridges rise abruptly like an impenetrable wall, guarding the route east from Rutland. But between these two ridges is a narrow gorge cut by Mendon Brook. Most days, Mendon Brook babbles down through the gorge around large boulders on its way from its watershed on the western flanks of Killington and neighboring 3,967-foot Pico Peak. Usually, the brook is only a few feet wide.

This gorge was the obvious route from Rutland and Mendon over the mountains to Woodstock and towns on the eastern side of the state. But by most accounts, a road into Mendon Gorge and then over 2,150-foot Sherburne Gap wasn't created until after the Civil War. Early maps show a "Road Over the Mountains" traveling north of Rutland, through Chittenden, and over the mountains through Pittsfield to Stockbridge, where it joined a path that paralleled the White River to Bethel and on downstream. A map dated 1869 finally shows a road, through Mendon Gorge and over the mountains to the east, possibly Sherburne Gap — as well as a railroad to Woodstock (that by all accounts was never constructed). The road on the east side of the gap then followed the Ottauquechee River through Woodstock to Quechee. This road from Rutland to Woodstock and farther east would eventually become U.S. 4.

Farther north, the easiest route from eastern Vermont to the western side of the state followed the Winooski River. Over geologic time, the mighty Winooski carved a relatively wide and deep swath through the Green Mountain Range between 4,393-foot Mt. Mansfield, the state's highest peak, and 4,083-foot Camel's Hump. Today, U.S. 2 follows the Winooski from Marshfield, Vermont, all the way to Burlington; Interstate 89 also follows the river from Montpelier to Burlington.

Vermont's U.S. 2 and 4 gained status as "highways" in 1926 when the federal government established the U.S. highway system. No new actual "highways" were constructed. It was simply a new countrywide numbering system to help American automobile drivers get from Point A to Point B via the most direct route — with standardized road signage.

(Until then, road dangers were conveyed in whatever language the sign maker chose. The favored sign at railroad crossings was a skull-and-crossbones. And one forty-foot sign in Tennessee warned motorists, "Drive Slow — Dangerous as the Devil.")

Other federal highways in Vermont were U.S. 5, the north-south route paralleling the Connecticut River on Vermont's eastern border, and U.S. 7, Vermont's north-to-south western corridor that follows several rivers, including the Battenkill and Otter Creek (Vermont's longest north-flowing river).

But this highway designation did not mean the roads were impervious to danger. In Vermont, many of the roads were still dirt in the late 1920s. In the Flood of 1927, U.S. 2 was engulfed in several places, and U.S. 4 was completely washed away in Mendon Gorge. U.S. 4 in Mendon suffered similar damage again in the Hurricane of 1938. Each time the road was rebuilt, and between 1957 and 1959, U.S. 4 from Rutland to Sherburne Gap was straightened and widened to three lanes. But it remained in Mendon Gorge. There is no other path for the road to take over the mountains there. The same can be said for many roads in Vermont. Short of tunneling through the mountains, or switch-backing up and over them, Vermont roads simply have to follow river valleys. Fluvial erosion caused by flash flooding is part of the geologic cycle — a mechanism for turning mountains into plains. And building what are considered permanent structures like roads and buildings near rivers and streams where flooding is inevitable can cause problems.

ℑ   ℑ   ℑ

AFTER HE DELICATELY pulled apart the huge pile of debris that engulfed Mike Garofano's body, Doug Casella took a break. He had heard that roads around Rutland were washed out and that his company's equipment and expertise might be needed. He wanted to see the damage for himself.

Leaving the Rutland Reservoir, he turned left on Post Road in Mendon and drove up the hill toward U.S. 4. He turned left onto the highway and stopped at the road barricade near Sugar & Spice, where the state policeman guarding the road closure let him through. Casella rounded the sweeping corner, then stopped.

"Holy shit," he muttered, when he saw what Mendon Brook had done to U.S. 4. "That's a big hole."

Having grown up along U.S. 4 and fished in Mendon Brook with his brother John, Casella was having a hard time believing that the little brook they used to hop across when they were kids could cause this much damage.

Kent Belden and his crew were already on the scene with a couple of excavators and a bulldozer. Belden had also grown up nearby—at Pico Mountain, six miles farther up the road. He had learned to drive heavy equipment on the mountain, helping his dad cut new ski trails (when Bruce and Verlene Belden bought Pico in October 1964, the ski area was still small, with only a T-bar on the lower mountain and no ski lift to the summit). Back then the ski business was 50 percent skiing, 50 percent construction, said Belden. He learned to ski at Pico too. Like many people in Rutland, both Belden and Casella had friends trapped in the mountains by Irene.

Before Belden could begin filling the five holes along U.S. 4 here in Mendon, he and his crew had to move the brook back to its original channel—or at least away from where the road had to go. They also had to remove guardrails, broken telephone poles, washed out metal and plastic culverts, a tumble of displaced sewer line fragments, trees, and whatever else the brook had torn up and left as detritus in the gorge. Belden mostly remembers the trees—thousands of trees tangled into huge messes that had to be removed. He had no idea when he and his crew would be able to finish building a temporary road—a few days, perhaps. They were working as fast as they could.

Watching Belden work, Casella knew immediately that his company could help. Yes, U.S. 4 was "a big hole." But Casella was used to moving dirt—a lot of dirt.

"That's what we do," he said.

For a man who is as comfortable driving his wife's sedan as he is a sixty-ton off-road Euclid—a truck so huge that a single-family home can fit in the truck bed, and so tall that the driver has to climb a ladder to reach the cockpit—he knew that rebuilding U.S. 4 would not take as long as many were thinking. On a recent project, Casella Construction had moved a million and a half yards of material. Filling the five gaps on U.S. 4 here in Mendon would take a fraction of that much material, he estimated. Probably a hundred thousand yards. But where could he quickly get that much?

🌀 🌀 🌀

ON THE OTHER SIDE of Sherburne Gap, Craig Mosher sat in his excavator in the Roaring Brook trying to rechannel it—or rather, put it back in its previous channel—so he could begin rebuilding U.S. 4 in Killington. As he worked, another of his employees joined him at the scene. Gene Westney from Bridgewater made it to Mosher's garage Monday afternoon, jumped in Mosher's rubber-tired loader, and rumbled along the four miles of U.S. 4 to the washout where Mosher and Bourassa were working. Once on site, he began scooping up gravel and dirt that had buried Goodro Lumber and carrying it toward the huge gap on U.S. 4.

At some point, Mosher's cell phone rang. It was Bruce Nichols from VTrans.

"Craig, I know you and know what you're doing," he told Mosher. "I'll catch up with you at some point."

"That's fine, Bruce," replied Mosher.

Before he hung up, Nichols asked Mosher when he thought he could get the road reopened.

"We'll have traffic through here tomorrow night," said Mosher.

Nichols was relieved.

Then, out of nowhere, Josh Pockett—another of Mosher's employees—arrived at the scene on an ATV. The heavy machinery operator lives in Pittsford, north of Rutland. He knew Mosher could use his skills in the mountains. But he also knew that the road into the mountains was blocked. So he loaded his ATV into his truck, drove to where U.S. 4 was closed in Mendon, parked at Sugar & Spice, and convinced the police to allow him to drive his ATV up through Mendon Gorge. Once through that mess, he drove the ATV another ten miles to where Mosher was working.

"What do you want me to do?" Pockett asked Mosher.

"Go get a dump truck."

By sundown on Monday, Mosher had the Roaring Brook back in its original channel flowing under U.S. 4, not alongside and over it. They would focus on rebuilding the roadbed on Tuesday.

Back at Mosher's, Westney headed home to Bridgewater. But Bourassa and Pockett would have to spend the night. Mosher lives over his office and had little food in the house. But he had plenty of beef (in addition to pasturing the Scottish Highlanders Big and Rob, Mosher also occasionally raises beef cattle).

"You don't need much else!" he said, laughing.

By candlelight and flashlight, the three men dined on steaks, then fell asleep.

§   §   §

DOWN IN WILMINGTON, Lisa Sullivan and Laura Sibilia had prevailed in their mission to open downtown to business owners. Monday afternoon, proprietors received permission from town officials to check out their properties in downtown Wilmington. Of the forty-five businesses in the downtown area, floodwaters from the Deerfield River had damaged forty. To keep potential looters or sightseers from wandering into the destroyed area, town officials set up a pass system. Those who could prove they had a reason to be in downtown Wilmington could get a pass from the police department in its temporary headquarters at the high school. Sullivan also learned that the town would give passes to volunteers to help business owners clean up.

In their brief visit to her store that afternoon, Sullivan and her husband, Phil Taylor, knew that almost their entire inventory of books, cards, music, and gifts was either washed away or sodden and muddy, and that the shelving was a-goner. Taylor, a builder, also knew it would be crucial to get all the wet material—including wet wallboard and insulation—out of the building as soon as possible to prevent mold and mildew from spreading to what little remained unscathed. With help, they could clean out the store quickly.

That evening, Sullivan posted a note on Bartleby's Facebook page. "We think you might be able to come and help us tomorrow, if you would like to," she wrote. "Go to the high school and try to get a pass."

§   §   §

IN BOSTON, Tracy Payne was beginning a long descent into hell. With roads washed out and bridges undermined across southern Vermont, she had no way to reach Jamaica. Although initially open, bridges on Route 30 south of Jamaica had been closed until their stability could be verified, and roads approaching town from the north were questionable. People knew what roads were passable only if they actually traveled them. With the route uncertain, Payne stayed in Boston with her partner, Kelly Esposito. But time was ticking. With the plan to move to Vermont on September 1, Esposito had given her Boston landlord notice that she would be out on August 31. It was August 29.

"It was grueling because I wanted to get back up there, but I was locked out," said Payne. "I couldn't get in."

She stared at her mother's violin, the only piece of her past that she still owned.

In Jamaica, town officials continued assessing the damage to the outlying areas. Stewart Barker and Brian Chapin drove ATVs on a reconnaissance mission up West Jamaica and Pikes Falls roads. Both back roads ascend into steep mountain valleys west of town, with each following a brook. Several times they stopped their machines and stared down into deep canyons cut by rushing water. With no way across these abysses, they figured out where they would have to cut paths in the woods to navigate around them. They knocked on the doors of every home, asked if everyone was accounted for and who needed what, then marked the front door of each house with painter's tape to indicate that the home had been checked.

Where they had cell phone coverage, they called back to the Three Mountain Inn and updated emergency management director Paul Fraser and Ed and Jennifer Dorta-Duque, who were running the command center, on whom they had found, who needed to be rescued, who had animals, who needed special care, and other details. At one point during the day, a property owner near a long washed out section at the far end of West Jamaica Road called the emergency command center to say that he could not reach his home. Barker and Chapin took a circuitous detour through Wardsboro to reach the property. Legend has it that en route to the property they found an excavator with the keys in the ignition and used it to fix a section of road. In truth, the stranded homeowner told Barker and Chapin when they arrived that they were welcome to use his heavy equipment to repair the road. Chapin jumped on the excavator and Barker fired up the bulldozer. The two men spent three hours fixing a culvert and about a quarter-mile-long section of West Jamaica Road.

Mission complete, they returned to the Three Mountain Inn in Jamaica and planned a rescue mission for Tuesday. They would need more than two ATVs to bring people who wished to leave their homes down to town. So Ed Dorta-Duque called a local who he thought could round up a few more off-road vehicles.

§ § §

PROPRIETORS OF the Pittsfield Pitt-Stop and the Swiss Farm Inn, Joyce and Roger Stevens remember thinking that all the hoopla about Hurricane Irene heading to Vermont was a big joke. The couple had lived in Pittsfield since June of 1998, moving there nine days after their youngest daughter was born, and they had weathered a few storms. But nothing like what they'd experienced at their previous home: the Caribbean island of St. Croix, where they managed the Cormorant Beach Club. One of the U.S. Virgin Islands, St. Croix sits in "hurricane alley" and is regularly pummeled by tropical storms that form off the Cape Verde Islands near Africa. In the late 1990s, hurricanes Marilyn, Lenny, and Georges all caused significant damage on the island. After one hurricane — Joyce doesn't remember which — they lost power for seven months.

So when Irene began causing havoc in Pittsfield on Sunday, the Stevenses knew what to do. During the storm, the Pittsfield Pitt-Stop, a store and gas station on the north end of the village green and across Route 100 from the Original General Store, had served as an ad hoc communication command post. Now the store was the go-to place for supplies for people trapped in town. Joyce had already moved the essential food — milk, eggs, and so forth — into one walk-in refrigerator powered by a generator.

With no way in or out of town, and no idea how long the isolation would last, Joyce also knew she had to ration gas. But with no power, the computer that runs the gas pumps wasn't working. And the generator produced only enough amps to power the walk-in refrigerator.

So on Monday, Sean Lee, who lives next door to the Pitt-Stop, went to work. A computer programmer who consults for a number of businesses including the state's ski areas, Lee "MacGyver-ed" the pumps, joked his wife, Angelique; he figured out how to override the pumps' computer and make them work manually. The Pitt-Stop could now sell gas again.

"When everyone came down to fill their generators, I said that's fine, you can fill your five-gallon gas cans and that's it," said Joyce. "People came down with cars, I said absolutely not."

Without power, the store's credit card machine and the ATM also weren't working. So Joyce allowed people to start tabs at the store—even people who were just visiting Pittsfield or became marooned when they were driving through town and the roads washed out. People were very honest, she said. Even when they took bags of ice from the outdoor ice cooler, they came in the next day to pay. Or they put the purchase on their tabs. At the fifteen-room Swiss Farm Inn, though, she wouldn't let stranded visitors pay for shelter.

"It's a different situation than if you're coming to stay here for the weekend," she told them.

Around lunchtime Monday, people began gathering on the village green near the Pitt-Stop. Jason Evans had fired up his portable grill, and he and his wife were setting up for the barbecue. By 1:00 p.m. Evans estimated that 250 people had arrived—just about everyone in town except for the guys rebuilding the roads—and the line for food stretched around the town hall. The satisfying smell of barbecued steak and grilled burgers filled the dry late-summer air. The Stevenses rolled over a freezer of ice cream from the Pitt-Stop. Without enough electricity to keep the freezer going, the ice cream was rapidly melting. People helped themselves to pints of Ben & Jerry's and drank the softened ice cream. Kids giggled in delight as they ate the free ice cream and ran around the green without parents worrying about traffic barreling through town on Route 100. A few people prepared plates of food and took them to the road crew. Except for the hum of generators and heavy equipment in the background, it could have been the Fourth of July.

After lunch, clean-up around town continued. A few of the wedding guests helped Lee Ann Isaacson's daughter remove furniture, shovel mud, and divert water from her house. With AT&T still out, the guests with Verizon cell-phone service lent their phones to others so they could call family and friends. Brian Mitchell lent his phone to an elderly couple who had been unable to let family know that they had survived the flood. "The woman cried," he wrote in his memoir, which he submitted to the town archive. "I did too."

With a curfew set by Doug Mianulli (from "sun up to sun down," he had said at the meeting that morning, until corrected), the town was subdued—from exhaustion and the realization that they might be stranded for a very long time.

IN SOUTH ROYALTON, Geo Honigford and Greg Russ found the irrigation pump buried under silt and muck near the river and dug it up. They loaded it into Honigford's truck and headed a half-mile south to the five homes that sit in a small cloister by the river south of his fields. The road south was covered by silt in a low spot near Honigford's field, so they drove on a dirt road paralleling South Windsor Road but higher up the hillside. When they pulled to a stop at the first house, owned by Bill and Nancy Murphy, they looked around in awe. Three campers lay in an L-shape next to a huge hole in what had been the Murphys' lawn. The previous day, the campers had been parked in a small campground in a wooded glen between the Murphys' house and the river. As the water rose on Sunday, the campground's owner had moved the campers up the road and parked them alongside the Murphys' lawn. He did not move them high enough, though. The floodwaters caught the campers and carried them toward the Murphys' house, where they became caught in the yard. For hours, water eddied around them and gouged the hole. The eddies also tore up the water line. By morning, the holes were still full of muddy floodwater.

Nearby, a picnic table was caught in a tree, a green shed in another. The shed, Honigford would discover, belonged to the town school, a mile and a half upstream. In the field in front of the trees, Honigford saw a few onions poking through the muck and realized they were his.

He then looked back at the Murphys' house and noticed that the high-water line—marked by a layer of mud—reached about a foot and a half up the side of the house. Murphy, a retired teacher who had evacuated with Nancy on Sunday when he saw how fast the river was rising, was in a daze. The house that they had lived in since 1980 was a muddy mess, the pine-board and tile floors that Murphy had laid himself buried under layers of muck, and everything in the basement was submerged under eight feet of water. When Honigford arrived, Murphy was outside with a friend trying to siphon water from the basement with sections of garden hose. It was like trying to bail a boat with a teacup.

"He had this look like a bomb just went off," remembered Honigford.

Honigford pulled his pump from his truck and began to hook it up. But when he tried to start it, the engine wouldn't turn over. The farmer jumped back in his truck. He had a part at his house that would probably fix it. But he wasn't optimistic. Even if he managed to start the pump, it would take a long time to drain all the water from the Murphys' basement. And the neighborhood had four other flooded houses that needed pumping.

En route back to his farm, Honigford passed a member of the South Royalton fire department. He waved the guy down.

"Hey Chris, you guys must have big pumps at the fire department, don't you?" asked Honigford.

Yes, they did.

"Could you pump out a basement?" he asked.

The fireman agreed, and twenty minutes later he returned with a pump and began helping Murphy and the other neighbors in the development. Meanwhile, a town official called Honigford and asked if he could help repair a washout on a town road with his tractor. Honigford drove to the washout but realized that he could do little to help. It was a massive hole in the road, and a neighboring farmer was already working on it. He turned around and headed back to help his neighbors. On his way home, Honigford drove through the village of South Royalton. In the green, chef Bill Therrien from the popular Five Olde Tavern in town had set up grills and was cooking lunch for the townspeople from his food stores, which—like Jason Evans's in Pittsfield—would spoil quickly without power. Honigford stopped, stepped out of his truck, and walked over to the gathering. After chatting with a few friends, he made an announcement.

"Enjoy your lunch," he remembered saying, "but there are people down the road who are struggling and would welcome your help."

A short while later, about seventy-five people made their way down South Windsor Street to the small five-house development. Some of them the Murphys knew, but most of them they had never met.

From his experience as a builder in the winter months, Honigford knew how to save a building that had suffered water damage. Everything wet needed to be removed—including floors, walls, and insulation. But he was reluctant to tell property owners what to do—and no one really wanted to hear that their homes had to be partially destroyed in order to be saved. Instead, the volunteers pulled wet belongings out of the houses and basements, shoveled silt, and began scrubbing floors and walls. As belongings came out of the houses, they were put into differ-ent piles: one pile for trash, one for salvageable items, another for ques-tionable items.

By late afternoon, Nancy Murphy had had enough. She thanked ev-eryone for showing up and asked if they could please leave for now.

"I just want to sit down and pretend this didn't happen," she told the group.

"She was exhausted," remembered Mary Russ, a friend of Honigford's who had been helping since the morning. "Everyone was exhausted. The Murphys looked completely stunned."

After everyone hugged, the volunteers left, and Honigford helped Bill Murphy rig up a makeshift fan to air out his basement. Then he headed up the road to his farm. There, he, Edsell, Honigford's wife, Sha-ron, and a couple of friends gathered at the kitchen table. They talked about the day—what they had accomplished and what still needed to be done. And they realized that the clean-up effort had been leaderless. Honigford, Edsell, and the other volunteers had deferred to the property owners for direction, and then waited for the owners to tell them what needed to be done.

"We realized it was terribly inefficient," said Honigford. "The land-owners were in shock, incapable of making decisions and incapable of making good decisions. They were wandering around in a daze."

Edsell, who has spent years working for various grassroots organiz-ing campaigns such as the state public interest research groups (PIRGs), MoveOn.org, and Corporate Accountability International, knew that the recovery effort needed more structure. It needed a rough chain of com-mand, priorities determined, supplies procured and distributed, volun-teers recruited and coordinated, and donations solicited. In the clean-up effort on Monday, volunteers had wasted time scrubbing floors and walls that instead should have been torn out. Clean-up at each house needed a leader who could direct the work and ensure that everyone's efforts were expended wisely.

Edsell was no longer a farm manager. He was back in his role as an organizer.

8

VERMONT INGENUITY
AND VOLUNTEERISM

Irene gave every guy who had a tractor the opportunity to tell
his wife why he bought the tractor. We joke about it, but that's the
thing that pulled us through. That and the fact that every one of our
towns had two to three contractors with a lot of heavy equipment
who were on the road even while the rain was falling.

    〜 Mel Adams, flood recovery special projects manager for
      the town of Killington

BY TUESDAY, GOVERNMENT OFFICIALS HAD a better sense of the state
of the state. And the numbers were staggering. At least a portion of every
highway in Vermont, except for I-89 and I-91, was closed—with a total
of 146 separate state road segments washed out or collapsed, and 531
total miles (a quarter of the network) closed. Additionally, VTrans closed
thirty-four bridges, and another two hundred were damaged. Those
numbers didn't include damage to town roads, where an additional
2,260 road segments were damaged and 175 segments closed, including
ninety bridges. Because of the immense amount of road damage, people remained trapped in thirteen towns: Marlboro, Wardsboro, Stratton,
Cavendish, Plymouth, Killington, Mendon, Pittsfield, Strafford, Stockbridge, Rochester, Hancock, and Granville. Nine of these towns sit along
Route 100, nestled in the middle of the Green Mountain Range.

    Each town faced myriad problems. With no power to pump water
from wells, municipal water and sewer lines severed, and surface water
sources compromised by floodwater polluted with propane, gasoline,
heating oil, and sewage, people in the isolated towns had no drinking
water. Food supplies were running low because they had no power to

run refrigerators and freezers, so perishables were rapidly spoiling. And anyone experiencing a medical emergency had to hope there was a doctor either living or stranded in town. The situation in the mountains seemed desperate.

"I think it's probably a very scary thing to not know when you can get out of town and to have a water system that's not working and a general store that has run out of bottled water," Mark Bosma, spokesman for the Vermont Division of Emergency Management, told a *New York Times* reporter. "People are extremely nervous about being isolated."

VTrans made it their number one priority to reconnect these isolated communities and decided to redeploy its forces into two primary incident command centers — one in Rutland, the other in Dummerston. (A third incident command center set up in Berlin directed road, bridge, and railroad repairs in northern Vermont, which was far less affected by Irene.) Sleep was no longer part of the program.

"It was a pretty big decision to totally redeploy our forces," said Sue Minter, then deputy secretary of VTrans. "But I think it was the most important decision."

To those on the outside, the sense of urgency grew throughout Monday and swelled on Tuesday. cvps made a corporate decision to do whatever it took to restore power to customers: they would reach customers by any means possible. Greg White, director of engineering and system operations at cvps, hiked five miles into Rochester (and back out again) to evaluate damage to the destroyed substation. Ben Bemis, Royalton operations supervisor, rode his off-road motorcycle to assess damage in Rochester. And three employees — Duane Dickinson, Tim Madore, and Charlie Daigneault — mountain biked into Wardsboro and West Jamaica. Where linemen couldn't get trucks in to replace washed-out and broken power poles, they tacked power lines (on insulators) to trees.*

"People have enough problems not being able to get in and out of their hometowns," said cvps spokesperson Steve Costello. "We've at least got to be able to get them power back."

*For its response to Irene, CVPS received the Edison Electric Institute's 2011 Energy Recovery Award, the electric industry's highest honor for storm recovery. EEI president Thomas Kuhn credited the utility for its preparation, planning, and plan execution, as well as CVPS employees' "uncommon ingenuity and dedication to customers," in allowing the company to restore power quickly, in many cases before the towns and homes were accessible by road.

Across the state, volunteer groups sprang up on Facebook. Frustrated because she could not find a place to volunteer on Monday, Katye Munger created her own relief effort in Rutland. She contacted Jim Sabataso, also a Rutland native, and told him that she wanted to start gathering supplies for people in the isolated towns — people like her friend in Pittsfield who posted on Facebook that she needed diapers for her baby. Sabataso received permission from his parents to begin collecting supplies in an empty storefront next to their restaurant, The Palms, in downtown Rutland. Meanwhile, Munger joined forces with Aaron Kraus, who also had grown up in Rutland and had created a clean-up event called Restoring Rutland. His initial idea was to bring together his friends to help clean the flooded parts of Rutland the weekend after Irene. Kraus would lead the clean-up event, and Munger spearheaded donations.

At 1:23 on Tuesday afternoon, Kraus suggested to his Facebook friends that they "like" Restoring Rutland. Ten minutes later, he added: "We are set up at 34 Strongs Ave in Rutland to collect supplies. We need volunteers!! Also we will be collecting bottled water, dry goods, food, toiletries, supplies such as boots, shovels, buckets, sponges as well as pet food. These donations will be taken to Mendon and Killington areas. Please come down, bring what you can, and stay to help out!!!"

People began dropping off supplies in droves that afternoon. Casella Waste Management, which was going to carry large roll-off dumpsters to Killington to handle the isolated town's growing trash problem, offered to fill the empty dumpsters with boxes of supplies to be dropped off in Killington the next day. By 7:55 p.m. Tuesday evening — a little over six hours after Kraus had started the Facebook page — more than a thousand people had "liked" Restoring Rutland.

Elsewhere in Rutland, Lyz Tomsuden, a graphic designer, created the outline of Vermont in black silhouetted against a green background with the Army-inspired message "I Am Vermont Strong" written across the image. She and her partner, Eric Mallette, set up a webpage, then a Facebook page, offering to sell "I Am Vermont Strong" T-shirts to raise money for the Vermont Foodbank. Facebook fans began peppering them with questions about where they could buy the shirts. They sold forty shirts in the first three hours on Tuesday.

Farther north, Sarah Waterman from Winooski and Matt Sisto of Burlington set up a WordPress blog called VTResponse.com in response to all the #VTresponse tags on Twitter. In 2005, Waterman had volunteered in Biloxi, Mississippi, after Hurricane Katrina, so she had an idea what was involved with disaster recovery. She wanted to set up the website in part because of the memory of watching so many people ask for help in the Gulf region and not get it, she later told the *Atlantic*. VTResponse .com aimed to match donations and donated services with those individuals and communities that needed them, and to coordinate volunteer efforts. By Tuesday, VTResponse.com had received thirty thousand page views.

In offering help, people gravitated toward their strengths. Matt Dunne, a former Vermont state legislator who was the head of community affairs for Google, had experience working with a crisis map team in flooding situations in Council Bluffs, Iowa, and elsewhere. When he realized the extent to which Irene had damaged roads in the state (he lives in Hartland, Vermont), he called Sue Minter, whom he knew from working in the legislature, and offered to create an online map for VTrans that would show the public which roads were open and which were still closed. For anyone trying to get around Vermont in the days and weeks after Irene, this map became an important resource.

In Bennington, Natasha Garder said she felt moved to do what she does best after the storm. Garder and her fiance, Matthew Littrell, owners of the Crazy Russian Girls Wholesale Bakery, provided food to the emergency shelter in town, and the bakery became a drop-off location for donated clothing and other supplies.

In the isolated towns, anyone with an excavator, bulldozer, backhoe, and tractor was helping to patch up and rebuild the washed-out roads — filling in breaches or creating detours. Where the chasms could not quickly be filled, resourceful Vermonters found other ways around. In Mendon, word got around that a half-mile-long trail through the woods (an ancient road) connected a driveway at the end of Journey's End Road, on the uphill side of the U.S. 4 Mendon Gorge washout, and another driveway at the end of Helvi Hill Road on the Rutland side. Jane and Merrill Outslay, who own the popular A Crust Above pizza restaurant in Rutland, were the first to remember that the path existed. After closing A Crust Above on Sunday during the storm, they heard that U.S. 4 was washed out, leaving them no way to reach their home on Journey's End by car. Instead, they drove to the top of Helvi Hill Road, parked beside the road, and walked up the wooded path — then blocked by a few downed trees — in the rain. The path came out in their neighbor's driveway. The next day, they walked down the path to Helvi Hill, got into their car, and headed back to work. Although the path was not wide enough for a car, it was an easy walk or bike ride, especially after Merrill, sixty-nine, used a hand saw to remove the fallen trees and limbs. The trail was muddy in places and crossed private property. But it provided a much-needed escape route for people stranded in Mendon and Killington. Later in the week, Killington resident Lindsay Cone, an NCAA ski champion at the University of Denver, made national TV news by pulling her rolling suitcase down the path. She did not want to miss her plane back to Denver for the start of her senior year.

In Royalton, residents living on the back roads west of town used what was dubbed the Hillbilly Highway, an impromptu exit off Interstate 89, to reach town. Adam Lyman and his father created the Hillbilly Highway — alternatively called Exit 2½ — during the storm when they realized that flooding from the White River had cut off their route home (they had been moving trailers to higher ground from Lucky's Trailer Sales on Route 107 near I-89's Exit 3 in Royalton). They asked a policeman, one of Lyman's four-wheeling buddies, if they could cut through the chain link fence that parallels the interstate off the southbound lane about a half-mile south of Exit 3. Jim Bigelow was sitting at his kitchen table during the storm when he suddenly saw headlights coming through the trees and shrubs that provide a privacy barrier between his land and the interstate. He immediately recognized Lyman and waved him through. The next morning, another local called the Bigelows and asked if he could drive on the impromptu exit to reach town. So began a regular stream of traffic that bounced across the grassy shoulder, through a narrow band of trees, onto the Bigelow's driveway, then onto Royalton Hill Road. Later in the week, orange barrels and a sign that said, "Locals Only" marked the Hillbilly Highway. And Jim's wife, Rachel, set up a farm stand near the break in the fence to sell sweet corn.

In addition to local efforts to provide aid to the isolated towns, the Vermont Army National Guard began airlifting supplies to the thirteen isolated towns late on Tuesday. First, they used smaller two-seater UH-72 Lakota and Bell OH-58 Kiowa helicopters to scout suitable landings in each town. Then they began flying in huge tandem-rotor Chinook helicopters that landed in open fields. Guardsmen rolled pallets of ready-to-eat meals (MREs), water bottles, blankets, medicine, diapers, baby formula, and tarps off the choppers' rear loading ramps and left them in the fields for townspeople to collect. The helicopters gathered a crowd wherever they landed, and people waved, often with both hands, as the choppers took off.

ʕ   ʕ   ʕ

EARLY TUESDAY MORNING, Kent Belden and his crews had one narrow dirt lane of U.S. 4 open through Mendon Gorge. On one of the worst washouts, his crews laid down a large wooden mat to keep the heavy utility trucks from sinking into the soft dirt. It was marginal, said Belden, but he and his crew had finished it in half the time he thought it would take.

At 9:30 a.m., seventy-five line workers from Hydro One, Ontario's largest electric utility, and Bemis Line Construction, a Vermont company, drove up the temporary road. The crews from Ontario had come to Vermont on Monday to support CVPS's and Green Mountain Power's efforts. They expected to find the type of damage they usually see from hurricanes — mainly lines damaged by blown-over trees. Instead, the Hydro One guys were shocked by the number of washed-out roads and the rock-strewn, rubble-filled landscape. They noticed little oddities, like grass caught in insulators high on still-standing poles, and grass clumps hanging from wires — indications of how high the water had risen during the flood.

"You see these little streams flowing by, you can't really picture what that rush of water must have been like," said Bill Smeaton, a Hydro One superintendent.

After the convoy of utility trucks made it through the gorge, Belden and his crews returned to stabilizing the road and installing the Alpine Pipeline's temporary sewer line.

On the other side of Sherburne Pass, Craig Mosher and his men had put the Roaring Brook back in its channel and started rebuilding U.S. 4 on Tuesday morning. If they could get one lane open, people in Killington would have an escape route. Although U.S. 4 was beat up through Bridgewater and Woodstock, it was at least passable, even if the Ottauquechee River had taken out big bites. The gulf in the road created by the Roaring Brook was the only place on the east side of Sherburne Pass where the road had been completely severed. Mosher thought that he and his "miracle men," as they were called by a few locals, could get a passable road open by evening.

꙳ ꙳ ꙳

LISA SULLIVAN had not always been a bookseller in Wilmington (or Brattleboro). She started her career as Red Hat's first official employee. Headquartered in Raleigh, North Carolina, Red Hat was an early pioneer in the open source software movement, and Sullivan is credited with building the company's brand from its start in the early 1990s. High-tech marketing is a fast-paced life, and after seven years Sullivan decided to leave Red Hat and start a family in a quieter environment. In 2002, she and Taylor moved to Wilmington, where Sullivan started a boutique marketing agency, Hats Off Communications. She soon realized that she wanted to balance her business with work outside her home. One of her favorite stores in Wilmington was Bartleby's Books, which had opened on North Main Street in 1989. So she applied for a job, and the book-store's owner, Ariel Redden, hired her. By 2004, Sullivan and Taylor were business partners with Redden. Not long after, Sullivan, Taylor, and Redden purchased the Book Cellar in Brattleboro. Founded in 1948, the Book Cellar had been closed for most of 2004, its owner almost bankrupt.

"It had quite the history, being the oldest bookstore in town," Sullivan told the *Rutland Herald* at the time. "That was part of the appeal for us."

And they figured that running two bookstores within twenty-five miles of each other would not be twice the work. The Book Cellar reopened on November 18, 2004. Four years later, Sullivan and Taylor bought out Redden and became the sole owners of Bartleby's and the Book Cellar. That same year, they purchased a building on West Main Street in Wilmington and planned to move Bartleby's there. Built around 1833, the building offered another seven hundred square feet of retail space on the first floor and had a second floor where they could hold book read-ings and community events.

Since moving to Wilmington, Sullivan and Taylor had also become ac-tive in the community. Taylor is on the Wilmington school board, and Sul-livan was involved with the Mount Snow Valley Chamber of Commerce. She is also on the board of the New England Independent Booksellers

Association and has been described as "a force of nature who seems to know how to do things before anyone else has even figured out where to start," according to a fellow independent bookseller who admires her.

"If there was an award given for the most worthy bookstore owner in America, it ought to go Lisa, because she is a remarkable human being, and I promise you her bookstore . . . will not be one of those that slips away because of Amazon," wrote author Jon Katz on his website after visiting Bartleby's. "She is impressive — agile, open to the future, willing to change, and she is piling all of her energy into creativity, new ideas and her love of books and the people who buy them rather than into laments about the Kindle."

With many connections in the area and many fans of their bookstore, Sullivan and Taylor walked down to Bartleby's on Tuesday morning and found more than twenty people, some of whom they had never met, at the store ready to help clean out the flooded store. Volunteers had showed up to help other Wilmington businesses as well. They walked through a couple of inches of muck in the shop and took any undamaged inventory to the store's second floor. Sullivan estimated that they could save about 10 percent of the bookstore's inventory. She and Taylor then told the group that everything else in the store had to be removed — all the sodden books, CDs, cards, shelving, tables, anything that was wet. There were no dumpsters yet, so they told the volunteers to pile the spoiled inventory and debris in the store's small parking lot on the west side of the building. Then they shoveled the mud out of the store.

"They literally got every last book that was ruined out of the store," said Sullivan, still marveling at the altruistic energy.

Sometime during the morning, store manager Ana McDaniel arrived. Normally a half-hour drive from her home in Brattleboro, the trip to Wilmington had taken her four hours.

Up the road on East Main Street, six volunteers, including Larry Nutting, arrived at the town clerk's office to help Susie Haughwout and assistant town clerk Pat Johnson move the town records that were still in the vault to Johnson's barn. As floodwaters rose on Sunday, Haughwout had decided to take only the books and records that sat below eye-level in the vault; the floodwaters, she hoped, would not rise much higher than they had in 1938. Although undamaged, the remaining books and records in the vault could not stay in that damp environment. A local man arrived with a flatbed truck, borrowed from the Deerfield Valley Transit Association MOOver, and they began loading the vault's contents onto it. The truck bed was covered with a thin layer of dirt and dust, but it would have to do. They drove to Johnson's house and placed the books and records inside the barn.

"We were telling everyone that they were moved to a secure location," said Haughwout, shrugging her shoulders. "There wasn't anything else we could do."

Haughwout knew that they had to get the town office running again as soon as possible. The damaged businesses would need their real estate records in order to file for grants and loans.

With clean-up underway at Bartleby's, Sullivan put on her Chamber of Commerce hat and set out to see what other business owners in town needed. She found people "sort of paralyzed," she said. They weren't sure what to do. Some had talked to their insurance companies, which instructed them to close and lock their shops and not take anything out. Sullivan and Taylor knew differently — partly because they had faced a destroyed business less than six months earlier. Sullivan had talked to her insurance agent that morning and informed him that they were going to get everything out of Bartleby's. The agent said that was fine, but to take pictures first. Gradually that day, other business owners in downtown Wilmington seemed to take note of the clean-up effort underway at Bartleby's.

"I think it helped some people realize that they needed to get everything out of their building," said Sullivan.

By late Tuesday afternoon, Taylor began pulling out wallboard and insulation and other wet building materials before mold and mildew could grow. Bartleby's had flood insurance to cover part of the cost of rebuilding. But most business owners in Wilmington were far less fortunate. For homes and businesses within a mapped floodplain, flood insurance payments can run between $1,000 and $3,500 per year. That's a big hit for small retail businesses that run on the margin.

§ § §

IN JAMAICA, Ed Dorta-Duque walked out of the Three Mountain Inn and discovered that the call he had made the previous afternoon for ATVs had worked. Sixteen machines were in the inn's driveway. They would use them to evacuate stranded residents on West Jamaica and Pikes Fall roads.

Other donations were pouring in as well. Mo's Market in East Jamaica, Al Ducci's in Manchester, the Red Fox Inn in Bondville, Smokin' Bowls in Winhall, and Stratton Mountain Resort were among the many who brought food to Jamaica's emergency shelter to feed volunteers and victims. And when Mocha Joe's Coffee Roasters in Brattleboro called the inn to see if they were ready for their weekly shipment of coffee, the Dorta-Duques asked if they could order much more than their usual few pounds. They explained that they were serving as the emergency shelter and command center and that coffee was a popular amenity. Mocha Joe's donated twenty-five pounds of coffee beans.

In town, Wesley Ameden — along with other local contractors, the town road crew, and myriad townspeople who pitched in and worked as flaggers directing traffic — had finished the temporary Water Street that connected Route 30/100 north of the washed out bridge to the Depot Street Bridge; it was passable Monday night by 10:00 p.m. With Route 30/100 still closed south of town, this detour opened up Jamaica to points north. With two excavators, a bulldozer, and a dump truck, Ameden continued to shore up the new road.

A CBS news crew drove into town on Tuesday and filmed the road crew at work. Interviewing emergency management director Paul Fraser, CBS reporter Wyatt Andrews asked, "Is it fair to say you are moving this creek from there to there?" As he asked this, Andrews pointed to where the creek was now flowing and where it had flowed during the storm.

"I like to say we're returning it to where it came from," replied Fraser.

"You didn't ask permission?" asked Andrews.

"Well, we'll apologize later," said Fraser. "This had to be done."

Later, Fraser and Ameden's stepmom, Karen, were talking about the interview and thought the quotation might make a good T-shirt. Shortly thereafter, D&K's Jamaica Grocery Store began selling "Fix It Now, Apologize Later" T-shirts for $20. Proceeds would go toward flood victims in Jamaica.

ʂ   ʂ   ʂ

VERMONTERS ARE a resourceful lot — both native Vermonters and those who have moved here from elsewhere. Whether it's climate, topography, lack of population density, or all of the above, the state typically does not attract the sort of person who calls AAA every time the car won't start. Help, even if called, does not often arrive immediately. Those who are the most comfortable living in small town Vermont usually know, at the very least, how to jumpstart a car or build a fire in a woodstove or fireplace—and can list a dozen different uses for duct tape (and not one of those uses is patching ductwork). Those who come to Vermont—and stay—typically enjoy the outdoors, whether skiing, snowmobiling, hunting, cycling, hiking, four-wheeling, golfing, fishing, you name it.

Ask those in Pittsfield how they ended up in town, and many will point to nearby Killington, where they came to ski then decided to stay. Several locals are—or have been—ski patrollers at Killington or neighboring Pico. Pittsfield also has an avid cycling community, and a few of these cyclists and adventurers have developed a single-track mountain bike trail network through the hills above town that's grown in popularity. Joe De Sena's Death Races have further marked the town as an adventurer's paradise.

So when Irene left Pittsfield literally landlocked, most people didn't panic. They rolled up their sleeves and quickly settled into a new routine. At the Borden house on the West Branch of the Tweed (just downriver from the Abramses), Peter left early for the town officials' meeting at 7:00 a.m., while Verna—a schoolteacher in Rutland who was unable to reach work—and their sons, Andrew, fourteen, and Peter, ten, started the day with chores. With no power or water, they couldn't do dishes or laundry, so household responsibilities were limited to picking up the house and filling the bathtub with brook water so they could flush the toilets during the day (many in town now know that it takes three-and-a-half gallons of water to flush the average toilet). Young Peter suggested they form a bucket brigade. And so began their morning.

"It reminded me of Little House on the Prairie where the wife tended to things at home while the husband was out doing things," said Verna with a laugh.

After the town officials' meeting every morning at 7:00 a.m., the whole town convened for another daily town meeting at 7:30. With so many people attending this meeting, they moved it from the town hall to the church, where townspeople filled the pews. The pastor again began the meeting with a prayer, and George Deblon followed with a joke. People were encouraged to list on the large bulletin board outside the town hall what supplies or help they could offer, as well as indicating if they needed help. cv Oil again offered to fill propane tanks for gas grills if the empty tanks were left at the town hall by 1:00 p.m. The Original General Store offered cooler space to anyone needing to refrigerate food or medication. A tanker truck full of potable water was parked outside the fire station for people to fill water jugs. And the Pittsfield Pitt-Stop reminded people that they could fill up five-gallon gas cans at noon and 5:00 p.m.

A parent announced that she would set up a temporary classroom on the town green for the seventy-two school-age children in Pittsfield. The town does not have its own school, so under normal circumstances, these kids usually head off to class in every direction — north to Rochester, south to Killington, east to Woodstock and Sharon, and west to Rutland. Most schools were scheduled to open on Wednesday, August 31 (though very few actually did, thanks to Irene). If the local children could attend school on the village green starting Wednesday, it might give them a sense of normalcy, and at the very least give them someplace to be during the day while their parents helped dig out the town.

Also during the meeting, Joe De Sena announced that a helicopter had been chartered by a few of the wedding guests and would arrive later in the day. He wanted to know what the chopper should bring in. His announcement was reportedly met with a chilly response. Brian Mitchell, who was attending the town meeting, remembered one of the constables saying, "If they're flying into *our town*, they better be bringing supplies." After the meeting, De Sena took lists of needed supplies from the town office and provided it to the helicopter charter company.

After the meeting work continued on road rebuilding and helping people salvage what they could from their lost homes. Constable Mianulli helped Heather Grev and Jack Livesey get into the little white house they had rented — now tipped at a precarious angle in the mud. Grev had made a list of important documents and other items she hoped to find. On the list were their passports and birth certificates, as well as two airline tickets to Denver and tickets to see the Bronco-Raiders football game on September 12. Grev's grandfather had recently passed away and left her money that she used to cover her bills, then to pay for the trip. "Your grandfather wanted you to do something really fun," her father told her earlier in the summer. Miraculously, she found all the tickets, as well as their passports and birth certificates.

"It was crazy," she said. "I thought we were crazy for wanting to go. But what else are you going to do?"

She also found clean laundry still folded and stacked on her bed. But most of their possessions were beyond salvage.

Two houses down, Traci Templeton painted a large green sign and wrote in big black letters, "Irene You Bitch." She leaned the sign up against the ruined home where she and her daughter had lived for nine years. Then she went back to work making lunches and dinners for the road crew.

Local contractors continued to make Route 100 passable. The raging Tweed River had undermined the southern abutment of the bridge south of town after trees and other debris had clogged the bridge and caused the river to overflow the road. With the northern end still firmly on its abutment, the bridge tipped like a ramp into the mud. Contractors filled the gap with dirt and gravel and made the sloping bridge passable. The dirt section was only one lane wide, but that was all they needed. For now.

About a quarter-mile south of the destroyed bridge, near Brian Halligan's demolished home, vehicles could skirt a collapsed section of Route 100 by driving onto the road's dirt shoulder. From there seven miles south to Killington, Route 100 was passable in at least one lane. Emergency management coordinator Peter Borden told a *Rutland Herald* reporter that Pittsfield was "trying to kick its way to Killington."

"We're digging our way out," he said.

VTrans's District 3 general manager Bruce Nichols made it to Pittsfield on Tuesday by driving an ATV from the Rutland side of the U.S. 4 washout. No one from VTrans had been in contact with Pittsfield town officials since Sunday, so he had no idea what to expect.

"When I got there and I saw the devastation, my jaw dropped," he said.

But he was immediately impressed by how much work the contractors had already done to make Route 100 passable.

"We saw what needed to be done, and there was no other option," said David Colton, who is also Pittsfield's fire chief.

Nichols was even more impressed that they had done the work without knowing if they would get paid. In fact, no one in town was talking about reimbursement.

"We're not worrying about money right now," said Patty Haskins at the time. "It will come out in the wash later."

Although the power was still out, Haskins managed to file the town's disaster declaration form with the state on Tuesday—a necessary step for the town to receive aid. State officials had asked her to fax it, but under the circumstances she would have had better luck sending it down the Tweed in a bottle. Instead, the enterprising Angelique Lee came up with an idea. Brian Mitchell was charging his iPhone and iPad at the Lee's house (they had a generator). With cell reception on the town green, Mitchell was able to check and send email. Could he email the town's disaster form to the state? asked Lee.

Sure, said Mitchell. It would be easier, however, to email the documents from Lee's laptop. After a lengthy phone call with his cell-phone service provider, Mitchell set up his iPhone as a wifi hotspot and tethered it to Lee's laptop. Lee took a photo of the form, cropped it on her laptop, and emailed it to the state. Thereafter, the Lees put out a sign offering free wifi from their house on the green.

Pittsfield made national news on Tuesday night after CNN ran a story about the wedding guests stranded in Pittsfield. Some of the guests had already left on a helicopter chartered by Scott Redler, a Wall Street trader, to ferry out himself, his mother and father, his wife, and their three-year-old daughter. Redler's mother was reportedly running out of breast cancer medication. Although rumors abounded that the helicopter had arrived with no supplies, Mitchell reported that the chopper brought in fifty pounds of brown rice, fifty pounds of black beans, two cases of diapers, two large containers of vitamins, cases of bottled water, and a few medications that locals had requested. Joe De Sena said the helicopter made eight trips total and brought in supplies with each trip. He gave the supplies to the town.

That wasn't the only helicopter to whirl into town on Tuesday. Town officials received word that an Army National Guard helicopter was coming to Pittsfield sometime that evening. But they had no way to communicate with the Guard. Colchester Technical Rescue pulled into town around 6:00 p.m. They were the first outsiders to reach Pittsfield since before the storm, and some said it was like seeing the first Allied vehicles arriving in occupied Europe during World War II. Town officials asked the Colchester team if they could reach the helicopter through their dispatcher, to no avail.

Then, out of nowhere, townspeople heard a distinct chopping sound coming over the ridgeline northeast of town. A small National Guard helicopter hovered above a landing zone created for medical airlift choppers behind the Pittsfield Fire Station. It was a reconnaissance helicopter sent out to find a place for a thirty-thousand-pound Chinook to land the next day. Along with the Colchester Technical Rescue team, these National Guardsmen were the first outsiders that most Pittsfielders had seen in almost seventy-two hours.

"It was acknowledgment that somebody from outside knew we were here," said Angelique Lee. "It wasn't just stranded wedding guests on CNN."

§ § §

GEO HONIGFORD hadn't always been an organic farmer. He grew up in a small Ohio town, went to college, and became a high school social studies teacher. He wanted to see the world, so he enrolled in the Peace Corps and for two and a half years helped build rice patties in the West African nation of Sierra Leone. During that time, he met Sharon O'Connor, who would become his wife.

Asked if he always wanted to farm, he said no, not until his Peace Corps experience.

"After I grew my first crop of rice, then I knew I wanted to farm," he said.

When they returned to the United States, Honigford didn't immediately jump into farming. He and O'Connor settled in Ohio for a year, then moved to New England. He held a variety of jobs, including park ranger, building contractor, and teacher. One year he taught in a juvenile correction facility. In the early 1990s they moved to Raymond, New Hampshire, where Honigford found a job teaching social studies. But he hadn't given up the idea of farming. A Peace Corps connection put Honigford and O'Connor in touch with a farm in Norwich, Vermont, where they started working in their free time.

"As soon as I discovered Vermont, I was like, cripe, why would I live anywhere else?" he said.

In 1995, Honigford convinced O'Connor that they should buy an old farm a mile south of South Royalton. The 1780 farmhouse that sits on South Windsor Road on a bluff above the White River was a wreck, but Honigford convinced his wife that he would fix it up. She reluctantly agreed, and that summer, in addition to fixing the house, they began slowly rehabilitating the thirty-seven acres of monocropped field. They called it Hurricane Flats — a name they found in the annals of town history. The topography of the valley invites a persistent, strong wind that whips down the valley each spring.

Honigford and O'Connor, who works as a statistician for the Dartmouth Medical School in nearby Hanover, New Hampshire, have since grown the farm to the point where people look for their produce at the Norwich and Lebanon, N.H., farmers' markets from spring until October, or stop by the farm's own farmstand. Hurricane Flats is particularly known for its melons and sweet potatoes. But even with an established reputation, farming is not a lucrative business. So Honigford often supplemented the family income by rebuilding and restoring houses during the slower winter months, then selling them.

Like everyone whose business is tied to the weather and the land, they have had good years and bad since they bought the farm. And 2011 was offering a little bit of everything.

"No matter how straightforward, predictable, and manageable something can seem, life has its ways of derailing those plans," wrote farm manager Mark Edsell on Hurricane Flats' new blog on July 27, 2011.

"Growing vegetables in Vermont can sometimes be a frequent reminder of that fact," he continued. "And this season so far has definitely thrown its share of curveballs. A spring of record breaking rainfall has given way to a summer peppered with all manner of extreme weather: record temperatures, sweltering humidity, torrential downpours, and even a few extended dry spells that left us with some very thirsty plants. Thankfully, one great advantage to growing a wide variety of vegetables is that no matter what Mother Nature offers, there is always something that flourishes. The heavy rains and overcast skies in the earliest parts of the season have yielded bumper crops of broccoli, lettuces, and potatoes. Last week's sultry heat wave helped to push along the sweet potatoes, melons, and corn. In fact the popcorn is now taller than we have ever seen it!"

Edsell ended the blog by presciently writing: "With plenty of time left in the growing season, we're certain we'll get a few more surprises along the way."

Little did he and Honigford know that in one month, Hurricane Flats' sweet potatoes, melons, corn, and popcorn would become buried in silt or swept downstream.

But on the Tuesday after the storm, Honigford was not thinking about the farm revenue that had washed away. He wasn't ready to face it. Nor was he ready to deal with the fact that big chunks of his field along four hundred feet of the White River were gone. It was easier to offer help to his neighbors. Their lives had been disrupted by Irene far more than his. At least he and his family still had a house to live in. Since Honigford knew people who lived in the five-house development — and more important, they knew him — he would be the leader of the clean-up effort there.

When Honigford and Edsell arrived at the small housing development south of Hurricane Flats that morning, Edsell set up a checkpoint where volunteers would stop first. Before he sent them to Honigford for a clean-up assignment, Edsell asked them to contact everyone they knew. "Go through your cell phone and tell everyone you know to get down here," he suggested. Edsell also asked people to put up flyers around town to recruit even more volunteers.

Honigford and Edsell numbered the houses one through five, and Honigford instructed volunteers what to do at each house, such as removing everything from the basements and mucking them out. He and Edsell even wore orange traffic vests so they looked official — and so people could find them.

"Geo took control, and I'm very thankful for that," said Bill Murphy, who calls Honigford the "hardest working farmer you can imagine." Murphy just wanted to be in the basement of his home, working to save what he could, not figuring out how others could help him and delegating the responsibility. Murphy was also grateful that someone else would tear out the pine-board and tile floors that he had painstakingly laid more than thirty years before.

That night, as Honigford, Edsell, and others sat around the kitchen table again, they knew they needed to recruit more volunteers. Edsell advised them all to send out more emails — "to every single person you know, not just the people you think will respond yes," he told them. "Everybody gets asked. It's Organizing 101."

ⓢ ⓢ ⓢ

BY TUESDAY EVENING in Killington, Craig Mosher and his "miracle men" had created a narrow, one-lane dirt road across the Roaring Branch. It was by no means a highway, but the path was stable and smooth enough for passenger cars to drive without bottoming out. Word spread throughout Killington that anyone wishing to leave town should head east on U.S. 4 between 6:00 and 7:00 that evening. All cars would be assisted by police, and drivers were cautioned that "obstacles still remain in road" and that they would drive at their own risk. They would be allowed to leave but not return. And the escape route would be open again on Wednesday from 8:00 to 10:00 a.m.

About eighty cars drove out on Tuesday night.

ⓢ ⓢ ⓢ

LATE TUESDAY NIGHT, Governor Shumlin returned to Montpelier and asked his staff to come into his office. After two days of touring the state, flying over mountain ridge after mountain ridge, touching down in one devastated community after another — "every one looking worse than the one you'd just seen" — he knew that the damage was much more than the state could handle on its own.

"We cannot get Vermont back on its feet without outside help," he told his staff. "We've got to do everything we can to bring in as much help as we can from outside the state."

He then picked up the phone and dialed President Obama. Vermont needed help, he said. Would the president make a major disaster declaration so that the state — and individuals in the state — would qualify for federal assistance?

Then he called his fellow governors around the Northeast and asked if they could spare their National Guard units.

ⓢ ⓢ ⓢ

IN BED TUESDAY NIGHT, Geo Honigford again couldn't sleep. They needed to finish cleaning out his neighbors' houses by Wednesday afternoon, or the houses themselves would be lost to mold and mildew contamination. He thought of all the people he knew around New England from past teaching jobs, or whom he had met at the farmers' markets or other events. If they could only lend a hand . . .

At 4:00 a.m. he got out of bed, turned on his computer, and wrote a message to everyone on his email list.

"I'm not much for asking for help, but we are in critical need," he began. "The need is my neighbors, we have been fighting two days to attempt to save their five houses. Like all of us, they have no flood insurance."

Honigford wrote that his neighbors' homes are the bedrock of their lives and the center of their financial security. But when mold takes hold, it will be too late to save the houses.

"We have until the end of today (it's 4:00 now) to get the mud and trash out. Many of you have helped already, but we need a big push today to finish this job, and we need bodies. Our terms: we can supply food and drink and muddy working conditions with no chance for advancement."

He asked volunteers to bring flat shovels, five gallon buckets, generators, drop lights, and power cords.

He concluded his message: "Here's how I see it, you can go to work and continue with your lives, or you can give us even a few hours for a day and make a huge difference in someone's life."

Then he hit send.

9

GETTING AROUND

There's probably not one person in town who didn't do
something for someone.

‍ Jane Pixley, Cavendish town clerk and treasurer

BY WEDNESDAY MORNING, PEOPLE LIVING IN twelve of the thirteen
isolated towns had an escape route. Not for high-speed traffic: many of
the repaired roads were dirt and only one lane wide, with steep drop-offs
on at least one side. Locals were advised that the roads were for emergency crews only, but they were a link to the outside world and a way for
utility crews and emergency responders to reach the towns. And many
locals drove the roads anyway—and no one stopped them. Only Wardsboro remained cut off.

In Killington, as Craig Mosher reinforced the Roaring Brook's channel
to keep the brook away from U.S. 4, another three hundred cars—mostly
stranded tourists—drove east on U.S. 4 on Wednesday morning. That
afternoon, the town of Killington posted a road schedule on its website and Facebook page: westbound, U.S. 4 would be open daily from
6:30 to 7:30 a.m.; eastbound, from 8:00 to 9:00 a.m. The road would be
closed at all other times. They also posted a Marble Valley Transit Authority bus schedule for those trying to reach Rutland. But the trip to and
from Rutland would involve walking—or riding in a golf cart—along
what would become known as the Woodchip Parkway in Mendon. But
as of Wednesday, no woodchips had yet been dumped on the path. That
would come in later days.

Bill Smeaton of Ontario's Hydro One was impressed by the spirit of
many Vermonters, particularly in the isolated towns. Hydro One regularly responds to hurricane destruction, often in Florida. But in those

responses, Smeaton and the Hydro One crews typically found that residents had left areas that had been without power for days. In Vermont after Irene, people in the "island" towns were stuck. They had no choice but to cope.

The seemingly desperate circumstances did not dampen generosity or the can-do attitude. While the *Wall Street Journal* reported "tempers frayed over recovery's pace" in New Jersey and Connecticut, where "frustrated residents" were "angered by days without power, continued flooding and what they perceived to be a slow government response to Hurricane Irene's destruction," people in Vermont cheered when utility trucks rolled into town, thanked National Guardsmen for responding to the disaster, hugged the governor, and baked cookies for the local contractors rebuilding the roads. In one town—Smeaton can't remember exactly which—a woman at a corner store plugged a coffee pot into an outdoor plug powered by a generator and left Styrofoam cups next to it for the utility workers and road crews to help themselves.

By Wednesday morning, cvps and the six hundred or so other companies that had come to Vermont to assist the utility had restored power to more than 59,500 of the 73,000-plus cvps customers who lost power as a result of Irene, leaving 14,300 still in the dark. But the crews moving into the isolated towns brought more than new poles, wire, and substations when they rolled into these villages. cvps spokesman Steve Costello accompanied crews that finally made it into Rochester on Wednesday. At the time, the town had no cell phone service—except from the top of a couple of hills outside town, reached only by hiking—and Costello heard that townspeople were desperate to see what was happening in the outside world. He received bundles of papers from the *Rutland Herald*, and he bought every *Burlington Free Press* he could find at stores between Rutland and East Middlebury, where the cvps trucks turned east to drive over the mountains to Rochester. When he arrived in Rochester—after driving a series of back roads over Middlebury Gap, then down through Hancock—he began handing them out to townspeople, who flocked to the street to greet the utility trucks.

"You would have thought I was giving out gold bars," Costello said. "You'd hand [a paper] to someone and five people would be reading it."

ⓢ ⓢ ⓢ

DUMPSTERS BEGAN ARRIVING on Wednesday in downtown Wilmington. Huge dumpsters the size of trucks. They arrived because Lisa Sullivan worked hard to get them. Volunteers poured into town, too, many
from Mount Snow just up the road in Dover. The resort had also been
damaged, with its vast parking lots covered in gravel and mud. But every
day, resort general manager Kelly Pawlak arrived in her muck boots and
led crews to downtown Wilmington to help business owners dig out.
The resort also opened up its Snow Lake Lodge — rent-free — to flood
refugees who had been staying in Wilmington's high school.

On East Main Street, volunteers stripped the town office of debris, ruined furniture, and sodden wallboard, emptying it all into a dumpster.
On West Main Street, another crew of volunteers helped Sullivan and
Taylor load wet books, destroyed shelving, silt-filled displays, soggy drywall and insulation, and whatever ruined merchandise had been hauled
out of the building the previous day into the giant dumpster sitting in
front of Bartleby's.

Sullivan and Taylor estimated that they had incurred $300,000 in lost
inventory and building damages. Their flood insurance policy would
cover only $150,000, and FEMA does not give disaster grants to busi-
nesses — a revelation to many business owners who initially had thought
that FEMA money would help them get back on their feet. Funds would
have to come in the form of grants from local fundraising groups and
small business loans. In a small town and in a business that is being
undermined by Amazon and electronic book sales, taking out a loan can
be a risky proposition.

Still, Sullivan didn't have the same sense of despair that she had felt
in April after the fire that destroyed her other bookstore.

"After the Book Cellar fire, I felt a personal sense of 'Oh, it's too
much,'" she said. "It felt like it was about me as opposed to . . . I can't
quite describe it. But in the Wilmington flood, I felt like the easiest thing
is getting that bookstore open again. It's so straightforward. We need
to rebuild the building, we need to buy the books, we know the steps
to take."

What Sullivan didn't know how to do was get the town back. She
worried about other downtown business owners who did not have flood

insurance and how they would afford to reopen—even how they would afford to live in the coming months. Many of Wilmington's business owners are in their sixties and seventies, and they had invested their life savings into their stores. How could they afford to repay huge loans needed to reconstruct their buildings and restock inventory? Could she do anything to prevent Wilmington from becoming a boarded-up ghost town?

With Taylor rebuilding Bartleby's, Sullivan began doing what she could for the town. She walked door to door downtown asking business owners what their major issues were. From their responses, she began making more phone calls. She called the Vermont Department of Labor and asked if they could send someone to Wilmington to help business owners file for unemployment. And she asked business advisors from the Vermont Small Business Development Center to come to town and consult with owners on how they could rise up from the muck.

"Every button that had to be pushed, she pushed," said Laura Sibilia, who worked with Sullivan at the Mount Snow Valley Chamber of Commerce.

Sibilia credits Sullivan's loss of the Book Cellar with actually helping Wilmington in the days immediately after Irene.

"Lisa and her manager knew what they would have to do for Bartleby's—she knew—so the absence of fear of the unknown I think really allowed and empowered her to go help other people function and learn," said Sibilia. "She knew what it felt like for them not knowing what to do or where to start. We were all lucky because of that."

Mostly though, Sullivan knew she had to reopen Bartleby's. And several other business owners in town knew they had to reopen too. On the knife-edge financially, many did not have a choice. Everything they had worked for their entire lives was in their stores and restaurants. If they did not bring back their businesses, they would have nothing.

At 10:28 p.m. Wednesday night, Sullivan posted a note on Bartleby's website:

It is with a heavy heart that I write this post about the flooding in Wilmington. Bartleby's is currently closed (as is the whole of downtown Wilmington) due to devastating flooding. We have lost the majority of our inventory as well as all of our shelving and we'll require extensive renovations, but the building is sound and we are one of the more fortunate sites in the village. Some buildings washed away down river and others have been condemned. The incredible strength and support that we have experienced over the last few days have been the lifeline we've needed. Friends and neighbors have come together to help our community. The downtown businesses are getting cleaned up more quickly with so much volunteer help. Bartleby's will reopen and we will do whatever we can to help other businesses and individuals affected. We are blessed to live and work in this community. Wilmington will be put back together!

We will post updates as we have them. Thank you for your support.

Lisa

֍ ֍ ֍

IN THE YEAR since Tracy Payne had purchased her house on Water Street in Jamaica, she had poured her soul into it—and most of her money. She gutted the 1840s farmhouse down to the clapboards and then rebuilt it the way she wanted it—an open floor plan on the first floor, a master suite on the second, and two bedrooms on the third floor, one for her mom when she visited. Contractors had done some of the work, but she was particularly proud of the work she had done herself, such as the tiling in the bathroom. She even hung drywall, a challenge for someone as petite as Payne, who is not much above five feet tall. For the kitchen, she bought the appliances of her dreams, like a stainless steel refrigerator with French doors. The only appliance that she had yet to replace was the furnace—and she'd planned to replace it in early September 2011. Inside her home were her three guitars, which she had owned for thirty years, family heirlooms, and small possessions that she loved, like a heated mattress pad and a toothbrush holder she had purchased on a trip to Mexico.

"I had weeded all the junk out of my life by the time I got to Jamaica," she said. "I only had the things that made me comfortable, made me happy. I was content. I didn't need or want for anything else. I had no mortgage, and all the renovations were paid for. My mother helped me with everything."

In fact, the money she used to buy and renovate the house on Water Street had meaning attached. It came from her brother's life insurance policy after he passed away suddenly in 2008. Payne's parents were the policy's beneficiaries, and Payne's mother wanted to put the money toward something good. She gave it to her daughter to buy and renovate the house in Jamaica.

"She wanted me to have stability and not have to rely on anyone else," said Payne.

Her mother had yet to visit her daughter's new house. But Kelly Esposito was preparing to move in—to start a new life with Payne.

After buying the house in September 2010, Payne had purchased homeowner's insurance but not flood insurance. On Water Street near the Ball Mountain Brook, the house was technically not in the mapped floodplain (flood studies do not take into account fluvial erosion: rivers and streams eroding their banks and moving across the landscape, taking their floodplains with them). Given the house's proximity to the brook, she considered purchasing flood insurance but quickly put it out of her mind. She didn't know what it would have cost, but she didn't want to spend any extra money if it wasn't absolutely necessary.

"My house was built in 1840," she said. "It had been there for so long, survived the 1927 flood, 1938 flood, 1973, 1976. It survived all of that."

But it did not survive 2011. And after the raging Ball Mountain Brook swept away Payne's home, along with Brett Morrison's, Karin Hardy's, and Dave Kaneshiro's, it also swept away roads and bridges leading to Jamaica, making it impossible for Payne to return immediately to the town to see the devastation for herself.

Payne and Esposito were finally able to make it to Jamaica from Boston on Wednesday. They drove straight to the Three Mountain Inn, and the Dorta-Duques put them in the inn's best room, the private Sage Hill Cottage. Then, the Dorta-Duques, as well as Judy Flowers, a Jamaica resident trained in psychology, accompanied Payne and Esposito on four-wheelers the short distance from the inn to the Depot Street Bridge. After crossing the bridge, they stopped, and Payne slid off the four-wheeler. No one said a word.

This wasn't like disasters often broadcast on the news—like inundation flooding along the Mississippi or tornadoes in Missouri. In those disasters, the victims can still stand on their land and sift through what remains. Here, along the Ball Mountain Brook, nothing was left of Payne's property but her barn. The shed by the river was gone. So was the big tree in her front yard. And there was no trace of her house, not even the foundation. The land she once owned had been scoured away and become the riverbed surrounded by a field of rubble. Wesley Ameden and others had put the brook back in its former channel. But now, running right where Payne's house had once stood, was the new Water/Back Street. The temporary road was adjacent to the brook and passed torn-open foundations and various pipes sticking out of the embankment, the homes to which they had once been attached ripped away.

"It was like Armageddon," remembered Payne. "I was in shock."

At the moment, though, Payne held it together. The reality of it—the fact that Irene had essentially erased her life—would sink in over time. Then the tears would come, the crying that originates in pain so deep it touches the soul. She would feel hollow, as if no life remained, nor would it return. That would all come later.

First, she had to deal with the logistics of losing everything. She called her insurance company, and they informed her that they could do nothing to cover her loss because she did not have flood insurance.

"What about my belongings?" she asked.

No, they were sorry, but even household possessions are not covered under homeowners' insurance if they are destroyed by floodwaters. Payne hung up. After all the money she had paid to purchase homeowners' insurance, she realized she was not going to get a penny back.

"All this money that just went through my hands, all this cash I had just handed out to contractors, everything gone, just poof . . . you can't even imagine. . . ."

ʃ   ʃ   ʃ

ON A MAP, Pittsfield and the town of Chittenden are neighbors. Except separating the two towns is the Green Mountain Range, reaching over 2,500 feet in elevation. As the crow flies, Pittsfield is only seven miles east of Chittenden, but only snowmobile and hiking trails connect the two towns through the mountains. The paved route from Chittenden to Pittsfield is twenty-one miles long, via U.S. 4 to Killington then north on Route 100.

Jan Sotirakis, who grew up in Pittsfield and now lives in Chittenden, and her nephew, who grew up in Stockbridge, had been following their friends' Facebook posts and knew how badly these towns had been damaged. She also knew that they needed supplies. A lifetime member of the Chittenden Volunteer Fire Department, Sotirakis began soliciting donations of food and water from locals, who dropped off supplies at the firehouse. Many donated cash, so Sotirakis would turn around and buy whatever supplies she saw requested on Facebook: cat and dog food, baby formula, facial cream for a teenager concerned about her complexion, cranberry pills for someone with a urinary tract infection, buckets and bleach, goat food, the list was endless. In the first few days after the storm, Sotirakis sent volunteers out to buy $10,000 worth of food and supplies.

But how to get them to Pittsfield? Some people suggested hiking supplies to Pittsfield over the Green Mountains, or carrying them on ATVs via a four-wheel-drive road that starts near the Chittenden Reservoir and feeds into Old Turnpike Road in Mendon, then intersects U.S. 4 above the big washout in Mendon Gorge. But there was an easier path. On Wednesday, Sotirakis received permission to drive a convoy of pickups up the temporary road on U.S. 4 into the mountains.

Few in Pittsfield knew that help was on the way. It was day three of their "captivity," and they were moving forward as best they could in a quiet, stubborn way. A homeowner south of town put out a roadside table with vegetables from her garden. Next to the table stood a sign saying, "All I have 2 offer is fresh corn, squash, cukes, and more." On the village green, a handful of kids attended school on a picnic table under a tree in front of the town office. At the north end of the green, Gary and Janice Stumpf were standing next to their cars. Inside their vehicles were a few possessions they had managed to salvage from their upturned house. Dressed in a Hawaiian shirt and shorts, Gary said they had just burned the house; a small pile of ashes still smoldered next to the Guernsey Brook. It was the only way to clear the box culvert under Route 100 where the brook had created a chasm in the road. With the culvert cleared, they had started rebuilding the road there. Despite the fact that they were homeless and Gary—a laid-off paper broker—only had the clothes he was wearing, he was more worried about his neighbor than himself. The Guernsey's floodwaters had possibly undermined their home's foundation, and he feared that they would soon be homeless too.

At lunchtime the road crew stopped working on the chasm by the Stumpfs' property long enough to eat chicken sandwiches, meatballs, onion rings, apples, and cookies prepared by Jason Evans, Traci Templeton, and the Stevenses at the Swiss Farm Inn. In the village, a few wedding guests stopped at the town office to say good-bye. They'd heard that they could get out via U.S. 4 east in Killington and did not want to take valuable supplies with them. They handed Patty Haskins plastic bags with a few apples and some nuts. Upstream on the West Branch, Joe De Sena lent the Abramses his bulldozer so they could build a protective berm between the brook and their house. Their yard was still a mess, but they needed to protect their house from further flooding. Though the weather had been gorgeous for three straight days, more rain was predicted for Thursday through the Labor Day weekend. Rain was one item that Pittsfield did *not* need.

Then around 1:30 p.m., a *th-wapping* sound was heard over the ridge northwest of town and a giant Chinook helicopter swooped low over the village. It settled in a field behind Colton's garage south of town, and with the helicopter's tandem rotors still whirring, National Guardsmen began unloading pallets of MRES, bottled water, blankets, tarps, and baby supplies off the chopper's rear loading ramp. Townspeople flocked to the field on foot, bikes, and in cars down dusty Route 100 and watched as the Guardsmen pulled pallet after pallet from the belly of the chopper and left them on the grass. After the chopper took off, with a Guardsman sitting in the still open rear hatch waving to the crowd, the people who gathered to watch the airdrop were almost jubilant. Down in the field, they quickly formed a bucket brigade, loaded the supplies into a trailer and two pickups, and took them to the fire station.

Around 3:00 p.m. the first convoy—three pickup trucks, with one hauling a trailer—from the Chittenden Fire Department pulled into Pittsfield. They had started in Chittenden at noon and, as emergency vehicles providing an essential service, had been given permission to drive up through the construction on U.S. 4. Each truck had a small American flag attached to its radio antenna, signifying that it was part of this convoy. Loaded into the trucks were diapers, baby formula, pet food, toiletries, and a huge assortment of nonperishable foods, from tuna cans to cereal boxes.

When the convoy arrived in Pittsfield, people stood on the green and stared, then began clapping and cheering. The trucks stopped at the Pittsfield Fire Station, where several townspeople helped unload them.

Inside, more volunteers arranged the supplies by category—like a grocery store.

"Residents of our neighboring town of Chittenden have brought us to tears with their generosity," wrote Angelique Lee in a "Postcard from Pittsfield" for VTDigger.com.

That evening, Restoring Rutland posted on their Facebook page that "it took some doing, but we got through to Pittsfield today."

One of Restoring Rutland's many fans commented, "There are amazing people in Vermont."

§ § §

AS WORK CONTINUED on the five flooded homes on South Windsor Road in South Royalton, Geo Honigford was impressed by the number of volunteers who showed up on Wednesday. Some had seen his email plea; others came from the Vermont Law School, which had given students permission to skip class if they were participating in clean-up efforts. Dumpsters were delivered to the five-house development, and some of Bill Murphy's friends showed up with heavy equipment to fill in the holes left when the river had eddied around the trailers in the Murphys' yard. They called themselves "Mini FEMA."

"I paid them the best I could," said Murphy. "But they didn't ask for anything."

At lunchtime, a chef from the Canoe Club in nearby Hanover, New Hampshire, arrived and cooked for all the volunteers. He was a friend of the Murphys' son and would not accept payment.

Murphy credits another neighbor, Walter Hastings, for donating chlorine and chlorine sprayers to keep the mold and mildew at bay. Someone else delivered buckets, rubber boots, and gloves, but Murphy had no idea who'd donated them. They were part of the supply chain created by Edsell. Other people took mud-covered household items from the five houses, such as pots, pans, and photographs. They cleaned and returned them.

"The outpouring of help was incredible," said Murphy.

By Wednesday afternoon, the five homes on South Windsor Street were cleaned out—basements drained and mucked, sodden possessions removed, ruined wallboard and flooring torn out, garages swept. The emergency phase was over. It was now up to the homeowners to rebuild as best they could.

At that point, Edsell elbowed his way into a similar recovery effort dubbed Operation Revive Royalton, started by state representative Sarah Buxton, who was working with a dozen or so other homeowners in town who had suffered flood damage. Operation Revive Royalton already had a command center set up at the local high school. Together, Edsell and Buxton created a website (thanks to some of Buxton's campaign colleagues), recruited a half-dozen other people with skills similar to Honigford's to work as site captains at each house, and brought volunteers to town in droves.

Honigford, however, was still not ready to face the mess on his farm. It was easier helping others. So he too offered his services and expertise to Operation Revive Royalton. As Edsell said of his friend and former boss, "Geo needed to save everything he could because he couldn't save his farm."

§ § §

IN RUTLAND, Doug Casella and his guys continued to help search for Young Mike Garofano and to rebuild the pipe to the Rutland City Reservoir. The brook had destroyed the intake pipe that recharges Rutland City's Davis Reservoir, and the ninety-million-gallon reservoir contained only enough drinking water for thirty days—down to twenty-six now, inasmuch as water had not flowed into the reservoir since Saturday, when Mike Garofano had closed the valve in anticipation of the storm.

As Casella worked at the reservoir, he mulled over the most efficient way to fix U.S. 4. The main problem was material. Contractors would need at least 100,000 yards of rock and gravel to fill the five huge holes on U.S. 4 in Mendon—one of the most damaged stretches of road in the state. Trucking that much material in conventional dump trucks, which hold only around ten to twenty cubic yards, would require anywhere from five to ten thousand loads. Large off-road trucks can hold forty to sixty tons, or from twenty-five to thirty-seven cubic yards of gravel (assuming a cubic yard of gravel weighs around 1.6 tons). So using the larger off-road trucks would require less than half the number of loads. And if the material had to be hauled using the smaller highway dump trucks from pits a long distance from U.S. 4, that would add significantly to the project's time schedule. Rather than weeks, it would take months.

And there was pressure to get the road open as soon as possible. With about nine thousand cars each day driving from Rutland to Killington—the greatest volume of traffic that U.S. 4 sees in Vermont (east from Killington, only around five thousand cars per day drive the U.S. highway)—U.S. 4 is one of the most heavily traveled roads in the state. People who live in the mountain towns of Mendon, Killington, Pittsfield, Bridgewater, Rochester, Stockbridge, and Plymouth regularly travel the road into Rutland to reach work and run myriad errands, from grocery shopping to doctor's appointments. Tourists coming to Vermont for foliage season also travel U.S. 4, and the state's hotels, restaurants, and shops count on a lucrative foliage season to stay in the black. Casella knew this well. Foliage season was crucial to the Killington Pico Motor Inn's bottom line—the motel once owned by his parents. Foliage season tourism brings in around $332 million to the state annually, or about 11 percent of the state's overall economy. It was now August 31, and the trees would start changing to their brilliant yellow, orange, and red hues in less than a month.

Sometime on Wednesday, John Casella, Doug's brother, telephoned Bruce Nichols and asked the VTrans District 3 general manager if he would meet with Doug at the reservoir. Doug, said John, has an idea of how to fix U.S. 4 quickly.

With most of the roads in his district looking as if they had been dive-bombed, Nichols needed some good ideas. So he hopped in his truck and drove to the Rutland Reservoir. Doug and John were waiting for him, as was Rutland mayor Chris Louras.

Doug Casella laid out his idea: if he could gather the gravel that had washed down Mendon Brook and settled in the brook's alluvial fan (the flatter floodplain below the reservoir's intake house, where the brook comes out of the mountains and into the broader valley), his crews and Belden's could rebuild the road quickly—in less than three weeks. Much of the gravel in the fan, after all, had once been U.S. 4's roadbed; the floodwaters had washed it away and deposited it downstream. Why not just put it back where it came from? He could bring in his company's biggest trucks—sixty-ton Euclids used in mining and heavy earth-moving operations, and forty-ton off-road trucks as well. With their huge off-road tires, these trucks could drive into the brook, where excavators and other loaders could load them with rock and gravel and send them back up Meadow Lake Drive and U.S. 4 to the five big holes in the road. Under normal circumstances, he would need a number of permits to excavate gravel from the brook bed and to drive the big off-road trucks on the public right-of-way, including a stream alteration permit from the Vermont Agency of Natural Resources and overweight and overdimension permits from the Department of Motor Vehicles. If those agencies would waive permitting requirements, it would speed up the process.

"It makes perfect sense to me," replied Nichols. "When can you start?"

"Now," said Casella.

"Do it," said Nichols.

This wasn't the first time that Casella had stepped in to help the Rutland region after a natural disaster. Four and a half years earlier, on Monday, April 16, 2007, an intense low-pressure system blew into New England from the south. The region was expecting high winds, not hurricane-force winds. But that was what hit Rutland. The wind poured down from Killington Peak as if the western flank of the Green Mountains were a giant chute. Winds at the Rutland/Southwestern Vermont State Airport south of Rutland hit 57 mph at 9:30 a.m. But in Rutland — which sits at the foot of East Mountain, a steep-sloped foothill of Killington and Pico — several gusts spun CVPS's anemometer at 70 mph. Thousands of trees in Rutland were flattened by the gusts, their root balls sticking far out of the dirt. Softwood pines snapped in half. One giant tree toppled onto the roof of a house near downtown Rutland, while closer to East Ridge, acres of trees were flattened in the hillside neighborhoods. One house on a wooded lot was suddenly sitting out in the open, the forty or so trees that once dotted the property blown over into the street. The flattened trees created a wall that no one could see over.

Everywhere in the city downed trees and power lines choked streets, and downed phone wires lay in the road like discarded string. Across Vermont, more than sixty thousand CVPS customers lost power, with Rutland County receiving the heaviest damage. Some city residents were without power for sixty hours. Local citizens with chain saws and the city's Public Works Department removed debris from the thoroughfares, and piles of refuse lined streets and filled yards. Casella Waste Systems supplied dumpsters, vehicles, and employees for the clean-up. But there was simply too much debris for homeowners to remove on their own.

Chris Louras, Rutland's newly elected mayor, planned a clean-up day that Saturday and asked for volunteers to help remove the heaps of debris.

At the clean-up day's kick-off on Saturday morning, the mayor found himself standing next to a dark-haired man with a Cheshire Cat grin who introduced himself as Doug Casella.

"Why are you smiling?" asked Mayor Louras. He didn't think the city's situation was particularly funny.

"Nothing," replied Casella, shaking his head but still smiling.

"You're smiling at something," said Louras. "Go ahead, let me have it."

Although the volunteer turnout that Saturday was noteworthy, Casella knew that manpower alone was not going to remove all the remaining woody debris from the city.

"I could have this whole fucking city cleaned up in two days," Casella said, still smiling.

"Bull—," replied Louras.

"I do it all the time," replied Casella, the smile still on his face.

"OK, that would be great," said Louras, still thinking Casella had underestimated the job.

Casella and his crews went right to work. He sent his company's payloaders around the city to scoop up the debris and empty it into the Casella Waste dumpsters. On Monday morning, at 6:30 a.m., Mayor Louras drove around the city to see what clean-up work remained. Everywhere he looked, piles were gone. And the sun wasn't even up yet.

"It was like Grant took Richmond," remembered Mayor Louras, still dumbfounded. "He just went through the town and cleaned up everything in a day and a half. Piles of stuff disappeared."

So when Doug Casella said he could have U.S. 4 fixed in weeks, not months, Louras believed him. So did Nichols.

Later that same day, Governor Shumlin arrived at the Rutland City Reservoir. He was there to hug Tommy Garofano and assure him that he was behind every effort to find his younger brother. Shortly after the governor arrived, John Casella pulled him aside and said that Doug had a plan to reopen U.S. 4 within three weeks. Could they talk? The governor was skeptical but agreed to chat. Although Doug had already run his construction plan by Nichols and received the transportation manager's OK, he needed the governor on board.

Standing next to Mendon Brook along with Tommy Garofano, Doug Casella told the governor that Casella Construction had big equipment that he could move into Mendon to rebuild U.S. 4. Garofano chimed in and asked if the state could lift the permitting requirements for bringing oversize construction equipment into the state. With that equipment, Casella could load up the road material that had washed down the Mendon Brook during the storm and deposited in its alluvial fan below the Rutland City Reservoir intake valve. But he would need permission from several state agencies to do the job. If he did not have to jump over all the permitting hurdles, Casella said that his company, along with the other local contractors already on the project, would team with VTrans and the National Guard and get the road open in three weeks.

"I had all my east-west corridors [in the state] shut down," said Governor Shumlin. "I looked at him, and I recognized as a fellow Vermonter who knows something about construction that he meant it and that he wasn't telling me something that he couldn't do. I just saw it in his eyes."

Back in the helicopter, Governor Shumlin called Rob Ide, commissioner of the Department of Motor Vehicles, and Secretary of Transportation Brian Searles and told them to lift their oversize vehicle permits and get Doug Casella what he needed. The governor also called the Agency of Natural Resources and told them Casella's plan.

"Let's partner with these guys and trust them," said the governor. "Get them digging."

10

ONWARD

We are more connected to each other than ever. While we were working at a breakneck pace to re-establish households and share gasoline, electricity, propane, food, medical needs, clean-up duty, outside communications, accounting for every citizen, FEMA paperwork, and the list goes on, we didn't have time to judge each other negatively, and as a result we were all mightily impressed with our neighbors.

    ⑂ Angelique Lee, "Postcard from Pittsfield: The new normal," in VTDigger.com

WHEN OUTSIDE HELP REACHED MONTPELIER after the 1927 flood, Vermont governor John E. Weeks reportedly said, "Vermont can take care of its own" (though according to D. P. and N. R. Clifford, in their book *"The Troubled Roar of the Waters": Vermont in Flood and Recovery*, that phrase did not become part of flood lore until well after 1927). Although outside help did assist the state in its recovery after the 1927 flood, Weeks's supposed declaration is a sentiment that prevailed in that recovery as much as it did after Irene. On September 1, 2011, President Barack Obama approved Governor Shumlin's major disaster declaration, and although more than 700 FEMA employees and 1,300 National Guardsmen (including 724 from Vermont) responded to Vermont after Irene — airlifting 93 pallets of supplies to sixteen towns and trucking in another 334 pallets to forty-five other towns (to give a sense of the scale, a tractor-trailer truck can carry twenty-four of the four-foot by four-foot pallets) — Vermonters were working above and beyond to take care of their own.

In Woodstock, Phil Camp managed to salvage a few of the *Vermont*

Standard's computers from the muck that filled the weekly's former headquarters, and Justin Macourt, a Woodstock local, removed the hard drives and managed to save 90 percent of the information stored on them. Later in the week, a local realtor who had never advertised with the weekly walked into the new office south of town, put a $2,000 check on Camp's picnic table desk, and said, "You guys could use this." Camp and his staff managed to get the *Standard* published by Friday—only two days late.

Just west of Woodstock in Bridgewater Corners, the Ottauquechee had flooded the Long Trail Brewing Company's property, but clean-up was quick. The brewery opened its doors to the community, offering free food—"good, hot comfort food," said one local—and free Internet access in its popular pub. The brewery's owners also chartered a helicopter to ferry supplies to isolated Rochester, and many brewery employees carried food into other isolated towns on their personal ATVs.

At Bethel Mills, Lang Durfee continued to take orders for building supplies even though the lumberyard had lost almost a half-million dollars in inventory, as well as its retail space. He worked shoulder to shoulder with employees, their families, friends, and neighbors to clear the lumberyard of destroyed inventory and mud—shoveling it into piles with snowplows. As he worked, Durfee thought about what his grandfather had told the wife of the lumber company's owner in 1933 after the owner suddenly died, "You can always go bankrupt later. Let's see what we can do right now."

In Rutland, more than two hundred people responded to Restoring Rutland's request for volunteers to help clean up the hardest hit neighborhoods on Saturday, September 3. They swept streets and sidewalks of dried mud and helped homeowners remove flood debris from their lawns (without liability insurance, the organization could not allow volunteers to go inside people's homes).

Around the state, donations of food, supplies, and money kept pouring into relief organizations. Groups like the Chittenden Volunteer Fire Department continued to ferry donations into the now quasi-isolated towns (roads existed into the towns, but traveling those sometimes treacherous paths could take hours), and some groups began working together. Restoring Rutland's Alexis Voutas, a Chittenden resident, asked Jan Sotirakis if the Chittenden Volunteer Fire Department's convoys could help distribute the vast amount of donated food and supplies that Restoring Rutland was receiving. Yes! replied Sotirakis. Volunteers drove carloads of Restoring Rutland's donated supplies ten miles to the Chittenden Fire Station, where they were unloaded by more volunteers and organized by product type in the fire station. From there, more volunteers loaded everything from canned peaches to condoms into the convoy of pickup trucks—with town names listed on specific supplies. One day, a bucket brigade of men filled a truck with cardboard boxes marked "feminine supplies." Other trucks were loaded with horse feed and prescription pet foods. From August 31 through September 15, the Chittenden Volunteer Fire Department drove 120 pickup truckloads of supplies to the mountain towns above Rutland. In addition, Sotirakis collected over $52,000 and donated every cent to families in Pittsfield and Stockbridge.

Even local veterinarians donated their services, treating and in at least one case rescuing pets in the trapped towns. An avid cyclist, Bruce LeGallais, who owns Eastwood Animal Clinic in Rutland, loaded a backpack with veterinary supplies and a laptop and rode his bicycle with a friend from his vet clinic to the Killington Fire Station—a distance of about thirteen miles with more than 2,000 feet of elevation gain. He held a veterinary clinic at the fire station, and people holding their cats and dogs formed a line that ran out the door—in that line was Heather Grev with her old dog Cody, who had not quite been himself since he was rescued from their flooded house in Pittsfield during the storm. When LeGallais had finished treating this line of pets, he rode his bike another couple miles up the mountain to put down a gravely ill elderly cat. The distraught owner wanted her beloved kitty cremated. So LeGallais put the eighteen-pound deceased cat in his backpack and rode fifteen miles back to his vet clinic in Rutland. The ride back to Rutland was not all downhill. It included a mile climb back over 2,155-foot Sherburne Gap.

With the initial disaster winding down in the mountains and the recovery effort taking over, people in the quasi-isolated towns began resuming their normal lives. Schools started up, and many children went to great lengths to attend class. Two brothers in Stockbridge did not want to miss the first few days of school at Rutland High School, so they packed rolling suitcases and began walking to Rutland. The twenty-five-mile trip normally takes about forty minutes by car. Walking, hitchhiking, and hiking around the devastated sections of road, it took them three hours to reach Mendon. After pulling their bags down the Woodchip Parkway in Mendon, they were met by friends on the Rutland side. They attended school during the day and boarded at a friend's house at night.

In Braintree, the Third Branch of the White River took out the western end of the Riford Brook Bridge, leaving a fifty-foot-wide, thirty-five-foot-deep chasm between the road and the bridge. To reach their school bus stop, children who lived up Riford Brook Road were faced with a choice: either climb two ladders from the bottom of the chasm to the top of the bridge, or drive across the river in a John Deere tractor farther downstream. The evening news showed a high-school-age boy wearing a backpack and holding another bag in his hand as he climbed thirty-five feet up the ladders.

Regular commuters on the Woodchip Parkway in Mendon included thirty-three elementary-school students who attend the Barstow Memorial School in Chittenden. Every morning their parents drove them to Journey's End Road. Then they walked or rode golf carts over the Woodchip Parkway. A small yellow school bus picked them up on the Rutland side and drove them two miles down the road to Meadow Lake Drive, where they met another school bus. In the afternoon, they reversed the trip.

Although people in the isolated towns could now get out, it was often a long drive, so errands such as grocery shopping were not done as regularly as normal, with MREs filling in the gaps. But the ready-to-eat meals delivered to the towns by the Army National Guard provided as many laughs as they did calories. With donated food reaching many of the towns within a few days of the storm, and people sharing with their neighbors from their gardens and freezers, food was not as scarce as it can be in other natural disasters. So people jokingly argued about which MRE tasted better, the pesto sauce with chicken and noodles or the Southwestern-style chicken with beans and rice. Some guffawed about the calories in each meal (1,450 for the pesto chicken, only 1,190 for the Southwestern chicken), the fat (71 grams in the pesto chicken, or 109 percent of the U.S. recommended daily allotment), and the 1,000 or so grams of sodium. Others opened the meal packages and ate only the peanut M&Ms or other candy. In Cavendish, where the Black River had taken out both the sewer and water systems (forcing residents to use portable toilets trucked into downtown), residents were required to take one MRE for every bottle of water from the supplies brought in by the National Guard.

But not everyone made fun of them, at least not all the time. After a long, hard day of clean-up, when she and her husband, Peter, were too tired to cook, Verna Borden was thankful for the MREs. They provided a satisfying hot meal. And a week or so after the storm, Pittsfield town clerk Patty Haskins and her husband, Vern, celebrated their wedding anniversary by sharing an MRE in a candlelit dinner on their porch.

Despite good spirits and hard work, not everyone was recovering quickly. The sense of loss was everywhere. Just about every Vermont town south of U.S. 2 had experienced flooding. Lawns were littered with filthy, mud-caked possessions. In streets and yards, the mud soon dried and turned to dust blown into the air by wind and vehicle traffic. Huge roll-off dumpsters were part of the landscape. Businesses wore closed signs. And homes across the state teetered in various states of collapse, some with signs asking passers-by and potential looters to leave them be — that this was all that remained of what they owned. For those people and others tragically touched by the storm, the name Irene will forever cause them to flinch.

ဖ ဖ ဖ

WITH THE Rutland Reservoir draining rapidly, and city residents counting how many days' water they had left, Casella Construction employees worked as rapidly as they could to rebuild the intake pipe to the reservoir. Signs were up around the city encouraging people to save water, and daily newspaper articles gave tips on how to conserve. Still, the reservoir was draining fast. Mayor Louras estimated that daily consumption was 2.0 million gallons per day, just a little under the usual rate of 2.3 million gallons per day. Local car washes were shut down.

On the banks of Mendon Brook downstream from the reservoir intake construction, searchers continued to hunt for the body of Young Mike Garofano. They worked twelve- to fourteen-hour days — from before sunrise to well after sunset — and other local contractors besides Casella, including Belden, Markowski Excavating, and Fabian Earthmoving, contributed heavy equipment to the effort. But no amount of horsepower yielded any clues. New England K-9 Search & Rescue responded with five dogs and their handlers three additional times during the week after the storm. These dogs can normally search about eighty acres in three to four hours. But along the brook, the huge piles of tangled trees and other debris slowed their progress.

FEMA arrived at one point during the week—with what deputy fire chief Fran Robillard described as an armada of people, trucks, and equipment. The armada filled the Rutland Town School parking lot. But after assessing the situation by Mendon Brook, FEMA personnel realized that they could contribute nothing to the effort that wasn't already being done.

"We really turned over every stone, every log, every brush pile, everything had been turned over," said Robillard.

The deputy fire chief prowled the woods around the brook like a man obsessed. The brook's silt had settled into all the low spots that usually dot a forest floor and made the entire floodplain look as if it had been paved over with concrete. With every step, Robillard was haunted by the fact that he could be walking over Young Mike and would never know it. The dogs couldn't get a scent through the cementlike silt.

"How is this ever going to end?" he wondered, close to tears.

The state police were the ones who finally called off the search at the end of the week. Everyone needed a rest. New England K-9 agreed to return at a later date. But Robillard knew it was far from over.

"I kept thinking what if it was my kid," he said. "I didn't want someone to tell me they weren't going to look anymore."

☙   ☙   ☙

BY THE END of the week, businesses in Wilmington that had been flooded began considering their futures. Even the few with flood insurance, like Bartleby's, would need additional funding to restore their businesses (flood insurance covers only the cost of building damage, not inventory, and in some cases, it offers only partial coverage). FEMA does not provide grants to commercial entities. So many of them turned to the Vermont Economic Development Authority.

VEDA was created by the Vermont General Assembly in 1974. Its mission: to partner with Vermont banks and other lenders to provide low-interest loans to Vermont businesses and farms. Since its inception, the organization has loaned more than $1.8 billion to Vermont businesses to grow and also to recover from devastating losses. For example, after Pete's Greens in Craftsbury suffered almost $1 million in damages from a fire in early 2011, VEDA provided financing to help the popular farm rebuild (insurance covered only part of the losses). Other well-known Vermont companies that have benefited from VEDA financing include Green Mountain Coffee Roasters, Cabot Creamery, and the light-fixture manufacturer Hubbarton Forge.

After Irene left much of the state in tatters, VEDA's staff asked Governor Shumlin for emergency funding so the agency could make loans to businesses needing to rebuild (through VEDA's affiliate, the Vermont Small Business Development Corporation). On Wednesday, August 31, Governor Shumlin announced that VEDA had allocated up to $10 million in special low-interest financing for Vermont businesses and farms that suffered physical damage from Irene.

By Thursday, VEDA had the Hurricane Irene Assistance Loan Program—or "HI" program—applications online. The program would provide loans up to $100,000 at 1 percent interest for two years, with no payments due the first year. And VEDA would provide these loans to people who had essentially no business assets left—whose buildings and their contents were either destroyed by the floodwaters or washed downstream. They could use their homes as collateral. With real estate to back up the loans, businesses could then have up to thirty years to repay them, which would keep payments as low as possible. Business owners simply had to file copies of their property deeds along with their applications.

But in Wilmington, those deeds were in assistant town clerk Pat Johnson's barn. Or on the second floor of the destroyed town office. And without a filing system, neither Johnson nor town clerk Susie Haughwout could find anything. Meanwhile, businesses in Wilmington, including Bartleby's Books, were waiting for VEDA financing.

Unaware of the true extent of the disaster in Wilmington, Louise Anair, a senior loan closing officer with VEDA, started emailing Haughwout asking if she could please send copies of the deeds for the Wilmington businesses that were applying for loans. Haughwout looked at Johnson, shrugged her shoulders, and asked, "What are we going to do?"

Anair's phone number was included in the message, so Haughwout sat down on Johnson's porch and dialed the loan officer. The town clerk explained to Anair that the Wilmington Town Office had been flooded and that the town land records sat on the floor in a barn. Haughwout then explained that any computer records were on a hard drive on a computer that was also sitting in the barn. Even if she plugged it in, she couldn't connect to the town's server. She could hunt for the proper books and go through each town record one by one. But given the crisis, Haughwout told Anair she did not think that was the best use of her time.

"I just couldn't do anything for her," was Haughwout's first thought.

But the town clerk wasn't ready to give up. An outgoing, accommodating person who knows almost everyone and cares about the people in her hometown, Haughwout asked Anair if the loan process could begin if the town clerk promised to backfill the needed information as soon as the town office was up and running again. She suggested that Anair could access Wilmington's grand list on the town's website (which is hosted on a server offsite). This list would at least affirm who owns what property.

Anair could have stonewalled and insisted that bureaucracy does not normally work this way. Instead, she agreed to try the approach.

In Haughwout's words, Anair "kicked it up the food chain" and received permission to proceed with the applications without official citations.

On September 19, Haughwout and Johnson opened the temporary town office in a shopping center about a half-mile east of downtown Wilmington. Two days later, another band of volunteers moved all the records and salvaged office equipment from Johnson's barn and from the second floor of the old town hall into the temporary office. The new office space once housed a pharmacy, so it had a locked-off section where prescription drugs had been stored. Haughwout put the sensitive town records into this locked section, which would serve as the temporary vault. As soon as the office was open, she and Johnson began backfilling citations so that VEDA had legitimate references to ownership for the loan applicants.

Of the forty businesses in Wilmington that suffered flood damage, thirty-two applied for VEDA loans. People also came into the town office looking for their deeds so they could apply for loans from the Small Business Administration or from their banks. If Haughwout had not saved the town records, borrowing would have come to a screeching halt.

Many in Wilmington are grateful to Haughwout for all she did to help them start over—and for all she did for the town. She not only saved the town records, she also stopped into their businesses in the days and weeks after the storm to check on them. The Quaigh Design Centre's Lilias Hart cannot imagine Wilmington without her.

Haughwout downplays her role in the town's recovery, though, saying only that her chronic worrying finally paid off.

"It's very hard to remember the first three weeks [after the storm]," said the town clerk. "I just know I went home every night really dirty, smelly, and tired. And I threw away my boots at the end."

§   §   §

FOR TRACY PAYNE, it wasn't just her house that was gone. Her life was gone too. Everything that she owned, collected, and that identified her had washed down the Ball Mountain Brook and into the West River in Jamaica. Her passport was gone, a good deal of cash, photos, her guitars and amplifiers, favorite clothes; she didn't even have her toothbrush. It wasn't so much a flood that hit her house, it was like a tidal wave, said Jennifer Dorta-Duque.

Payne and her partner, Kelly Esposito, spent weeks scouring the riverbed and banks of the Ball Mountain Brook and West River downstream from Jamaica, looking for any trace of her life. Mostly, she wanted to find her safe. Inside it was cash, jewelry, and all of her grandmother's pictures.

Instead, along six miles of riverbank from Jamaica down to the Townshend Dam, Payne and Esposito found an odd assortment of possessions, mostly kitchen items. Her new dishwasher lay on top of a heap of riverside debris. Inside was a teacup, part of a whole set she had brought to Jamaica from her mother's attic just two weeks prior to the flood. The teacup was all that she found of the set. She also rescued a frying pan from the dishwasher and her French press. Far downstream, she found some of her underwear hanging high in a tree. In the cobbles, boulders, and mud along the riverbanks, she found a spindle from her porch railing, a piece of exercise equipment, and the pedestal bathroom sink from her master bathroom now battered and beyond salvage. Someone else found one of her guitars and some photos. Payne was happy to have the guitar back, beat up as it was.

"I loved that river," she said. "Now I hate that river."

Waves of loss began washing over her. She would feel a sharp pain, like a dagger, when she remembered something she no longer had — like a favorite jacket or the new North Face winter coat and hat that she had received for her birthday from Kelly (they still had the tags on them) or a necklace that her grandmother had given her.

"I would wake up in the middle of the night and my brain would hurt, like it was aching," she said.

She also had to deal with the fact that she and Esposito had nowhere to live. The Dorta-Duques were kindly letting them stay in the Three Mountain Inn's cottage. But she knew they couldn't stay there forever. She called the Stratton Foundation, which at the behest of state representative Oliver Olsen had immediately begun accepting the donations that were pouring into the area for flood relief. The foundation also offered to help victims fill out FEMA paperwork. When Payne telephoned, Stratton Foundation coordinator Tammy Mosher gave her a phone number to call to get started with FEMA.

"I don't have a pen," replied Payne.

Struck by the stark sadness of Payne's reply, Mosher asked what she could do to help. Payne said she could use dry sneakers.

But every nice gesture was immediately countered by another hurdle. Payne applied for FEMA's Individuals and Households Program (IHP), which provides money to people whose property has been damaged or destroyed by a natural disaster. The maximum grant in the IHP is $30,200. But Payne's former roommate, whose furniture had gone down the river with the house, also filed a claim with FEMA. And the relief agency provides assistance for only one application per address. Payne called FEMA repeatedly to explain the situation and asked her former roommate to please stop.

"I was just trying to get the money from FEMA so I could take a breath and not be out on the street with a cup," she said. "I was not capable of finding a job. I was homeless."

All she had were summer clothes, and the fall air was developing a chill. But she had very little of her own money to buy anything new. She heard that a few local stores were going to offer new clothes to flood victims, but it proved to be only a rumor. Donations of used clothes, furniture, household supplies, and toiletries were pouring into the Jamaica church. Payne was grateful for the tubes of toothpaste, shampoo, shaving cream, and other simple necessities. But she could not find much that fit her small frame.

"I had Patagonia clothes, I had jeans that fit me," she said. "I'm a size zero. It's not easy to find things for free that feel good on you or to you."

When new items were offered, Payne felt conflicted about accepting them. Karen Ameden put a donation jar in D&K's Jamaica Grocery and money came pouring in; food and supplies poured in as well. Ameden donated it to the people in Jamaica who had lost everything, and she let them take whatever they needed from the store. Payne was very grateful and called Ameden an angel. But after a couple of weeks, she felt awkward about continuing to take without paying.

"I'm not very good at taking things for free," she said. "It doesn't feel very good. You don't want to be a walking charity person. But I didn't have anything. I had to allow myself to accept. It's very, very hard."

With very little money, no place to live, and no idea when she would find either, Payne became angry, "impossibly angry." One night, she left the Three Mountain Inn's cottage at midnight and walked down to the Depot Street Bridge. A big construction light was shining on her barn and illuminated construction on the new road, which crossed the area where her house had once sat. She collapsed on the bridge and wept for hours.

One of Esposito's friends in Massachusetts offered an apartment to rent, so Esposito returned to the Boston area. Payne needed to stay in Jamaica. But she needed to move from the inn, so it could become an inn again, not an emergency shelter. She stayed with a friend for a few nights. Then the Stratton Foundation put her in touch with a couple who own a vacation condominium at Stratton Mountain. They offered the place rent free to Payne until Thanksgiving. They also offered her anything she wanted to eat from the freezer, and they paid for all utilities, even Internet access.

"They were wonderful," said Payne. "They didn't know anything about me. I could have been a crazy person. They just handed me the key and said don't worry about anything."

About a week after Irene ravaged Jamaica, the Dorta-Duques finally put back up the wooden Three Mountain Inn sign. They had taken it down on the Saturday before the storm because they feared it might blow over. Then in the week after the storm, there was no need to put it back up. The inn was serving as a command center and emergency shelter, not a place of hospitality.

By Labor Day weekend, Oliver Olsen encouraged the Dorta-Duques to hang the sign back up. "People might be looking for a place to stay," he told them.

But they did not start answering their phone again as "Three Mountain Inn" instead of "emergency command center" until September 15. They had lost almost three weeks worth of business — including a holiday weekend. The Dorta-Duques will not say how much income they lost, but it was significant. Even if the inn were only half full on weekends with no one staying midweek from August 29 through September 15, they lost at the very least $10,000. FEMA does not offer money to private businesses, even if those private businesses serve vital roles during an emergency.

֍   ֍   ֍

MARY RUSS first met Geo Honigford at the Tunbridge World's Fair. He was running the booth for the White River Partnership, a community-based nonprofit that works to improve the health of the White River in Vermont. The partnership has a water quality monitoring program and over the past fifteen years has worked with eighty-five landowners to restore twenty-five miles of stream channel, riverbank, and streamside vegetation, among other programs. On the partnership's board, Honigford recruited Russ and her husband, Greg, to get involved about ten years ago.

"He's a very active community member and a very active, enthusiastic volunteer," explained Russ, who's now the executive director of the White River Partnership.

And Honigford is comfortable directing people. He once worked with fifty Boy Scouts to plant hundreds of trees as part of a White River Partnership program. He quickly figured out the most efficient way to plant the trees and then explained it in a way that was fun — and that made the Boy Scouts feel part of something larger, says Russ.

"He's a natural," she explained. "He's got a big presence and a big voice. When he talks, people listen. I'm not sure if that's a skill you can develop or a skill you're born with, but he has it."

In addition to working with Honigford in the White River Partnership, Russ has also helped the farmer sell Hurricane Flats' produce at the Norwich Farmers' Market. And she realized that Honigford puts as much thought into farming as he does into organizing river restoration programs. For example, Honigford didn't let Russ work the stand without first listening to a tape on direct marketing and customer service techniques for open market situations. And when it comes to pricing his produce, he sells items like his cucumbers by the piece rather than the pound, because it costs as much to grow a small cucumber as a large one.

So it was no surprise to Russ that Honigford took a leadership role in Hurricane Irene recovery in South Royalton. The farmer, along with Edsell, Sarah Buxton, and other townspeople involved with Operation Revive Royalton, rallied eleven hundred volunteers to help clean up flooded properties in town. The restoration effort started at the Murphys' house and the rest of the small development on South Windsor Road, and then took on a life of its own. Bill Murphy called the recovery effort and outpouring of support "an amazing experience."

By Friday, Operation Revive Royalton volunteers had cleaned out seventeen flooded homes in South Royalton. "We were feeling pretty good," said Honigford, who set out in his truck that afternoon to help clean up a house far from the village. With bridges and roads still in tenuous shape, he had to drive a circuitous route that passed through the neighboring town of Bethel. As he drove by houses there, he was stunned by what he saw. Six days after the flood, homeowners in Bethel were still carrying wet furniture from their flooded properties. They hadn't torn out soaked drywall, insulation, or flooring, and mold was no doubt starting to grow.

"They were nowhere close to us," said Honigford. "There was no organization in Bethel, no one was doing anything. People were telling me the select board was fighting any offers of help, that the board was turning away help."

That evening, back in South Royalton, hundreds of people gathered on the town green for a benefit concert and community dinner. Originally planned by Bill Murphy as a thank-you concert for all the townspeople who had helped him and Nancy clean up after the flood (Murphy plays in a band called "Snakes of Ireland"), Operation Revive Royalton asked Murphy if they could promote a dinner and fundraiser along with the concert. Murphy agreed, and hundreds converged on the town green for the festivities. Seth Stoddard, a local sound engineer and handyman who had lost the majority of his sound equipment in the flood and whose parents lost their entire house, ran the band's sound for free.

As "Snakes of Ireland" rocked the green, everyone let out a week of pent-up emotion. It was, in Honigford's words, an overexuberant blow-out party.

"I've never seen anything like it," said Honigford, with a smile. "There's an open container ordinance, but no one was paying any attention — beer, kegs, bottles of whiskey. People were saying, 'Look how far we've come, we've pulled together, this is amazing.' People were patting each other on the back."

During the party, Honigford told Edsell what he had seen in Bethel and asked if Edsell could spare any volunteers on Saturday. Operation Revive Royalton had recruited two hundred volunteers for clean-up on Saturday, but most of the work was already finished in South Royalton. Sure, said Edsell.

On Saturday morning, Honigford set off for Bethel with seventy-five volunteers. He wasn't sure what kind of reception awaited them. He did not know anyone in Bethel and would have to develop a rapport quickly with homeowners and gain their trust. When he first offered help, some of the homeowners asked Honigford how he was able to obtain permission to help them clean up their properties.

"We didn't ask," he told them. "You don't have to ask permission to help people. You just help them."

An older couple in Bethel had mud in their basement, and Honigford told them it was urgent that it be removed, and that he and his volunteers were willing to help. The couple kept asking Honigford what he wanted in return for the work. They seemed to fear that a bill for the clean-up would arrive at some future date.

"I don't want anything," he assured them. "I just want to help you."

Later that day Honigford returned to South Royalton where Edsell told him that Operation Revive Royalton was shutting down the command center and sending the volunteers to other towns. Bethel, said Edsell, had finally set up a recovery group. The group leader was a guy Honigford knew from an impromptu basketball league.

"Did you tell him what we've learned?" asked Honigford.

"No, not really," replied Edsell. "He didn't want to hear it."

On Saturday evening, Honigford called his basketball-playing friend and offered to tell him what he had learned about cleaning houses and organizing volunteers.

"Oh, we've got it," the friend assured him. "We've identified houses, and we're going to send volunteers there and get them fixed up."

"Who's going to lead the volunteers?" asked Honigford.

"The homeowners," replied his friend.

"It won't work," stated Honigford. "You're going to have five people doing active work, ten milling around doing nothing, and five doing totally useless stuff."

His friend disagreed, and the conversation ended. Still stewing, Honigford called him back later that night. He asked his friend to come to the houses in Bethel where Honigford and the volunteers had worked on Saturday, meet the landowners, and see what else needed to be done. His friend kept assuring him that he could handle it.

"No! No, you don't have it handled," Honigford snapped. "You don't understand, you haven't seen it."

Honigford was at his breaking point. He was exhausted and knew he couldn't keep going. And he needed to gather energy and emotional strength to face the mess on his own farm.

"I was cooked, this far from breaking down," he said, holding up his thumb and forefinger and almost pinching them together. "I had my own shit to deal with. I'd come back here every day and see my mess, and it would just bring me down."

But at the same time, he couldn't step aside while people still needed help. Then he suddenly remembered two women, named Sophie and Jasmine, who had responded to Operation Revive Royalton's many requests for volunteers. He'd never learned their last names. They were from out of state, but one of them had a parent who lived nearby in Thetford and they had come to help the recovery. Edsell had sent them to work with Honigford during the previous week, and they were natural leaders. Honigford phoned them and asked if they would meet him in Bethel the next morning.

On Sunday morning, he drove back to Bethel, met Sophie and Jasmine, and introduced them to the volunteer crew in Bethel. Then Honigford got into his car and drove away. With one of his daughters in the copilot seat, he drove north on I-89 to Stowe and climbed Mt. Mansfield.

"I wanted to get as far away from it as I could," he said.

By now, he knew that the produce saved from the muck in his greenhouses was not saleable. The U.S. Food and Drug Administration considers crops that come into contact with floodwaters to be adulterated. He could not even give the produce away. It was a $45,000 loss in income and would add to the $75,000 in property damage to Hurricane Flats from the storm.

On Thursday the following week, about 125 people gathered at Honigford's farm. They were neighbors, friends, and customers who bought his produce at the farmers' markets each summer — people recruited by fellow South Royalton farmer Jennifer Megyesi, as well as Edsell's wife, Liz, and other friends. The volunteers walked shoulder to shoulder down Honigford's long, flat field and picked up trash and flood debris. On the trip back up the field, they pulled up irrigation tubes and the black plastic that Honigford had placed around heat-loving plants to improve soil temperature. Much of the plastic was buried under inches if not feet of mud. It was a herculean effort to get it all up, said Mary Russ. And they had to get it all, even the little inch-square pieces. They also pulled up the ruined vegetables that hadn't been harvested and all the limp vines. Another group of volunteers dug choking mud from around the roots of the young hardwoods that Honigford had planted a few years earlier to protect the riverbank. They had the farm cleaned up in three hours, then had a big lunch.

"What I learned from working with people who got flooded is that it's very hard to ask for help," said Honigford. "It's agonizing to acknowledge that you need help. One of the things I learned to do was say to the homeowner that it's ok to ask for help. And then I would say I'm here to help you. It took me a while to get that message through my own head."

He calls his friend and colleague Mark Edsell the real hero of storm recovery. The farm manager lost his job when the storm wiped out Hurricane Flats. Yet he did not hesitate to help.

"He saw a community in crisis and figured out what to do," said Honigford. "He was a visionary. He saw the whole thing before the rest of us did."

Edsell continued working with Sarah Buxton and others in Operation Revive Royalton through the fall. By selling $20 "Hillbilly Highway, Exit 2½" T-shirts and other fundraisers, such as a benefit concert in December, Operation Revive Royalton raised more than $80,000 for flood victims.

After the dust settled, Russ thought back on the experience and the role Honigford had played as part of Operation Revive Royalton. He had the leadership and construction skills to help people. And helping them allowed Honigford to deal with his own disaster—to put it in perspective and let him face it when he was ready.

"Some people, you know what they're capable of," she said. "He saw a need and he took it very seriously and dumped 100 percent of his time into it. That's just the kind of guy he is."

Bill Murphy agreed: "He's a great neighbor. His heart is in the right place."

§ § §

THURSDAY, SEPTEMBER 1, was a big day in Pittsfield. For starters, CVPS restored power that afternoon, and the cheering could be heard throughout town. Verna Borden was at her house when the power came back on.

"Oh, the light's on," she thought to herself as she walked down the hall by the bathroom.

Then she stopped in her tracks and happily screamed, "The lights are on!"

The first thing she did was a load of laundry. Her eldest son, Andrew, had other priorities. He flushed the toilet.

That same day, local contractors managed to fill the chasm where Gary and Janice Stumpf's house had been swept into the Guernsey Brook. The town opened the road with a "big huge whoop-dee-do," said Peter Borden, and now Route 100 was passable in both directions. But the route north, beyond where Route 107 intersected Route 100, was still rugged. With two huge sections obliterated from the landscape, Route 107 had become literally the road to nowhere. Still, people living north of town could now reach Pittsfield and Killington without hiking around the chasm.

Joe De Sena and a dozen laborers—including some Death Race participants—worked for three straight weeks around the clock rebuilding the covered bridge to the Riverside Farm (using beams from a flood-damaged home in Pittsfield). They also helped rebuild other bridges in town and cleared debris from along the Tweed and West Branch rivers so it would not clog bridges and culverts in the next bad storm.

With Pittsfield recovering from the emergency remarkably well, some were almost enjoying the adventure. With very little traffic in town, and a strict speed limit set by constables Hunt and Mianulli to keep ATVs from racing around, parents let their kids wander.

"Everyone walks, rides their bikes, smiles, waves, introduces themselves, offers help; it is like we live in the 1800s — but with electricity," wrote Angelique Lee in an article on life in Pittsfield for VTDigger.com.

With the road passable, Casella Waste brought giant dumpsters to town. On Saturday a group picked up debris along the river. Kelly Ziegler pitched in along with her son Jackson. In tangled heaps along the riverbank they found skis, textbooks, trashcans, a jewelry box, and a big pair of bloomers. Looking at the little white house by the river tipped into the mud as if dumped there by a tornado, its owner, Tim Pins, asked Ziegler if she could click her heels together like Dorothy in the *Wizard of Oz* and make it right.

Heather Grev and Jack Livesey, who had rented the little house from Pins, needed to find another place to live. They had spent the past five days at their friends' house in Pittsfield. But Grev knew that if they were going to remain friends, she and Jack needed to figure out their own living arrangement. They had heard they could drive to Killington on Route 100, so they borrowed Jack's mother's car, loaded up the two dogs — Cody and Irie — and drove south. They planned to fuel up the car at a gas station in Killington and buy some supplies. But mostly, they just wanted a change of scene.

They bought what they needed at the Killington market, then went to the Grist Mill Restaurant for a bite to eat. They walked into the restaurant with the two dogs and asked for a table on the deck. Grev apologized for bringing the dogs but explained that, after the week they had just lived through, they were "one unit traveling together." Someone overheard them discussing their housing situation and suggested they call John Hurley, who owns Woodstock's White Cottage snack bar, which was wiped out by Irene. Hurley, they said, had a furnished apartment available in Killington. Grev and Livesey knew Hurley and called him immediately. He explained where the apartment was and said the door was open, go in and look at it.

With the power back on in town and the road situation improving, townspeople began to talk about returning to their normal lives. Many of the kids who attended schools "on the other side," as Pittsfielders referred to the outside world, had already missed the first few days of classes, so parents began to discuss how to get their children to school after Labor Day.

Angelique and Sean Lee's teenage daughters attend Sharon Academy, twenty-five miles west of Pittsfield. With Route 107 gone — and with no hope of its reopening for months — the Lees could reach Sharon only by driving narrow dirt roads that added significantly to the commute. In early September, when more rain threatened to soften the makeshift roads or wash them out again, the Lees decided they did not want their daughters traveling that route daily. So they arranged for them to live with friends. For a few weeks, their girls would attend a boarding school of sorts.

Parents of younger children were less willing to split up the family, particularly in view of the tenuous road situation.

"Peter and I had long discussions about the family," said Verna, who as a teacher knows how important it is for kids to attend the first couple of weeks of school. Barstow Memorial School, where the Borden boys attend school, had opened on Wednesday, August 31, so her boys had already missed the first three days. "Were we going to break our family apart? And if we're broken apart, and we don't have access to our kids, would we be comfortable with that?"

The Bordens decided that the boys would head to Barstow when Verna went back to work on the Tuesday after Labor Day. Then, if they became stuck on the Rutland side, the boys would have their mom with them.

Peter Borden also went back to work after Labor Day. He had taken personal time from his job at the *Times Argus* to serve as Pittsfield's full-time emergency management coordinator for eight days after Irene. During that time he burned through twenty-three hundred minutes of cell time. That's more than thirty-eight hours spent talking on his phone, or about five hours a day. And Pittsfield has good cell service only from the center of the village green.

On the Tuesday after Labor Day, Borden announced to the Pittsfield select board that he had to step down and transition back to his life. The town was still dealing with eight projects — mostly removing debris, replacing culverts, filling holes, and cleaning up the river. He assigned every project to a contractor, handed his list to the select board at 10:00

a.m., and then paced around his house and around town for a few hours. The next day, he drove to work in Barre. Normally a forty-five-minute drive on Route 107 to I-89, he had to pick his way along narrow, muddy roads up and over several mountain ridges. The commute took him two hours each way.

Verna and the boys had an even rougher trip. In their two-hour commute to Rutland, they slowly drove twelve miles south on Route 100, which was eroded down to one lane in at least five places, then west on U.S. 4 to Mendon, where they parked at the boarded-up Tyrol Motel. From there they were shuttled to the end of Journey's End Road, where they were dropped off near the Woodchip Parkway. They walked the quarter-mile or so through the woods to Helvi Hill Road, where the boys boarded a school bus bound for Meadow Lake Drive. There they waited for another school bus that took them to Barstow Elementary. Verna was met at Helvi Hill by a friend who drove her to the shoe store she worked at in Rutland. There Verna waited for another friend to drive her the rest of the way to Rutland's Northeast Elementary School. She likened her commute to a combination of the movie *Planes, Trains, and Automobiles* and the reality TV show "The Amazing Race." On rainy days, she would arrive at work with mud splattered up the back of her pant legs. The school principal would take one look at her and ask, "Verna, tough morning?"

The commute home in the evenings was even worse. The boys played after-school soccer, so Verna had to arrange rides for them back to Helvi Hill Road, where she met them after hitching a ride from a friend. Together, Verna and the boys walked back uphill to Journey's End, where they were shuttled back to their car at the Tyrol. They did not get back home until six or seven at night. After a week of this schedule, the whole family was exhausted.

With no time to grocery shop in Rutland, Verna sent the boys to school with MREs for lunch, and thirteen-year-old Andrew quickly developed a system of preparing his noontime meal. These ready-to-eat meals take about twelve minutes to heat — a process that causes a small amount of smoke to rise from the packages. He would activate the heater before the prelunch recess. Then the meal would be hot and ready to eat by the time he came back inside for lunch. But after a day or two of nervously watching the ready-to-eat meals smoke, the school principal asked the Bordens if they could find an alternative lunch for the boys.

But how to get to the grocery stores in Rutland, then get the bags of food home without having to walk back up the Woodchip Parkway? A couple of weeks after the storm, Kelly Ziegler hatched a plan to grocery shop in Rutland. Her friends, the Jareckis, who own Vermont Fresh Pasta in Proctorsville about thirty-four miles south of Pittsfield near Ludlow, told her how to bypass a section of washed-out road on Route 100 south of Plymouth. If Ziegler could drive Route 100 all the way south to Route 103 in Ludlow, then she could drive 103 west to Rutland and the grocery store.

She made it to Killington, then kept heading south on Route 100. In West Bridgewater, she stopped at the "Road Closed" sign and called Tricia Jarecki to ask what she should do. "Just keep going," urged Jarecki. She followed her friend's advice, driving slowly around all the road construction. Two hours later, Ziegler drove into the Hannaford parking lot in Rutland. She filled a shopping cart to overflowing with everything she needed. As she paid for it, she wondered if she would make it home to Pittsfield.

She drove southeast on Route 103 with no problem. But when she turned north on Route 100 near Ludlow, a police officer stopped her. Ziegler explained to the officer that she had made her first foray into Rutland since the storm to buy groceries, and that if she were not allowed home, her husband and two sons would have no food. He let her pass. She reached home six hours after she'd left. Grocery shopping had become an all-day event.

§   §   §

WITH THE STATE'S PERMISSION to rebuild U.S. 4 with gravel from Mendon Brook's alluvial fan, Doug Casella began mobilizing his company's biggest trucks. They were at construction sites in New York and had to be dismantled, then trucked to Rutland. It would take time. But another local contractor could help. Markowski Excavating in Florence, Vermont, ten miles north of Rutland, owns much of its own equipment, including several large off-road trucks. Markowski employees, including Sam Markowski's daughter Denise, drove the trucks from the company's headquarters in Florence twelve miles to Mendon. Under normal circumstances, these giant trucks are not allowed on public rights-of-way.

"We bent a lot of rules," said VTrans District 3 manager Bruce Nichols—a theme that helped restore the roads in the first few weeks after Irene destroyed them.

Markowski Excavating officially joined Belden and Casella Construction working on U.S. 4 on Saturday. Like the other two contractors, Markowski Excavating is a local company, established in the fall of 1962 when Peter Markowski decided to get out of the dairy business. From his farm in Florence, north of Rutland, he sold a mare and her colt and used the money as a down payment on a bulldozer. Then, on January 13, 1963, he sold the milking herd—and his four sons rejoiced. No longer would their lives be tied to the daily chores of farm life. But they weren't on permanent holiday. The four Markowski boys—David, Greg, Marty, and Sam—now helped their dad on landscaping and construction jobs. In 1974, when the four boys were all in their twenties, their father invited them to join the construction company as equal partners. Since then, the four Markowskis have built their company to the point that they do site work for major corporations and other organizations in the area, including Middlebury College.

Markowski Excavating had been running construction triage around Rutland County since the height of the storm on Sunday, when CVPS asked them to reinforce the embankments at Patch's hydroelectric dam in Rutland. The morning after the storm, Bruce Nichols had asked Markowski Excavating to rebuild a section of State Route 103 in Cuttingsville—about ten miles southeast of Rutland. Route 103 is a heavily traveled road across the state, bringing people from U.S. 7 on the western side of Vermont to I-91 on the eastern side. The Mill River had washed out 103 in several spots, including a high embankment in the village of Cuttingsville, home to Over Easy's, a diner where U.S. senator Jim Jeffords used to enjoy breakfast when he was home in Vermont. Sam Markowski spent the week repairing that section of road.

Then Nichols asked Sam if he would help Beldon and Casella rebuild U.S. 4 in Mendon. Markowski loaded up his excavator in Cuttingsville and drove it over to the washouts in Mendon. Normally competitors, Casella, Belden, and Markowski were now on the same job. Except that no one was talking money. Even more unusual, their kids joined them. Doug's son Joe, Kent's son Justin, and Sam's daughter Denise were on site every day driving heavy equipment. A veterinary technician at Eastwood Animal Clinic in Rutland, Denise took a three-month leave of absence to help rebuild the roads. And joining all three companies were a collection of former and retired employees, family friends, and experienced machine operators looking for work. A guy from North Carolina called Belden soon after the storm and asked if they could use another heavy equipment operator. "Yes," said Belden. The guy hopped a plane to Vermont that afternoon.

At the blowout on U.S. 4, the three competitors divided the job and did not bicker over who was doing what. With Casella spearheading the gravel excavation from the brook, Belden — with experience in pipe work — began rebuilding the road's drainage system and culverts. Someone needed to keep Mendon Brook from undermining the new roadbed, so Markowski volunteered. He put his excavators down in the brook and began reestablishing the brook's channel.

"I basically said, 'Hey, Sam, keep that frigging river away from us,'" said Casella, half joking.

"It wasn't a complicated job, it was just a lot of repetition," Markowski said. "It had to be done."

Markowski worked with Fred Nicholson, who had recently retired from the Vermont Agency of Natural Resources. Nicholson gave Markowski stream parameters so the brook could still meander in the narrow valley without taking out the road as it was being rebuilt.

By Labor Day the three companies "got it down to a flow," said Belden. A steady parade of sixteen huge off-road trucks were running from the brook below Meadow Lake Drive up to U.S. 4, dumping the dirt and gravel wherever it was needed along U.S. 4, then returning for more. At one point in the rebuild, Nichols counted fourteen excavators, six or seven bulldozers, and fifty dump trucks, in addition to the sixteen or so giant off-road dump trucks working on U.S. 4. Every day, crews started working very early in the morning and often worked well past sunset. There were no days off. Casella worked through the night on at least three or four occasions. Other days, he logged twenty-hour days, going home only to change his clothes and grab a couple hours' sleep.

In eighteen days they moved a tremendous amount of dirt — 100,000 yards total. "You can normally move around 30,000 yards a month on a big job," said Belden. "This was three times that, and we did it in half the time."

Asked why they worked so hard, Belden said: "It wasn't a job to get done. We all viewed it as an emergency to get the road open. Everyone just flowed to whatever had to be done."

"There is a very big reason that the job got done in the amount of time that it did," added Casella. "It isn't just because of the contractors and what we did. It's because everybody was trying to make sure that whatever we needed, we got. Everyone asked what could they do? I don't know how many cups of coffee or how many cookies got brought up that hill to us when we were working. Half of them I didn't know. It was pretty neat." (Although Markowski, working down in the Mendon Brook, said he did not get one cookie!)

The road was rebuilt quickly—and the job done correctly—because three Vermont companies that "know our regulations and are responsible" did the work, said Casella.

"They didn't have to tell us don't do that and don't do this because we wouldn't do it that way anyway," he continued. "It's not the way we run our businesses. We aren't trying to save a nickel or shave here and there. We know how the job should be done."

Bruce Nichols applauded the contractors who saw what needed to be done and just started working. By Friday after Irene, VTrans had 150 contractors working on roads in Rutland County alone. To keep tabs on the progress, Nichols was driving eighteen hundred miles each week. VTrans supervisors from other districts, like Carl Senecal, Doug Petterson, and Bill Jewell, also came to Rutland County to help, though contractors rebuilding U.S. 4 all agree that they did not need to be babysat. Nichols particularly commended Craig Mosher, who, along with his "miracle men," single-handedly rebuilt U.S. 4 in Killington without nearly the resources that Casella, Belden, and Markowski had on the Mendon side.

After rechanneling the Mendon Brook, Markowski left a giant rock in the brook's small floodplain. On that rock, he wanted to install a plaque to read something like this: "On August 28, 2011, this river came through here. It took two lives downstream. The road was re-created in 18 days to open up traffic. Long may this rock and plaque stand here, until the next storm takes it away." Then he wanted to list on the plaque the names Michael J. Garofano and Michael G. Garofano, Doug Casella, Kent Belden, and Sam Markowski—"Two men who died in the line of work, and three competitive contractors who collectively worked well together to rebuild this section of highway."

ʕ ʕ ʕ

ON SEPTEMBER 15, 2011, U.S. 4 officially reopened in Mendon and Killington. On the Mendon side, the road was only two lanes wide—not three. But the road was open, and the entire region seemed to breathe a sigh of relief. The next day, Governor Shumlin flew by helicopter to Killington to cut the ribbon, first on the Killington side, then at Sugar & Spice on the Mendon side.

In Killington, a small crowd gathered on the road outside Our Lady of the Mountains Church and stood next to the wide swath of new black asphalt laid across the three lanes that Mosher and his men had rebuilt. No white or yellow lines were painted on the road yet. That work was still to come. But the road was open, and that was cause for celebration. On a cool, sunny September day, Governor Shumlin addressed the crowd, thanking the region's elected officials, Chris Nyberg, president of Killington Mountain Resort, and Mosher. Joking that the state was going to erect a statue of Mosher in town, Governor Shumlin then added in all seriousness, "He's the one who saved this road."

When the governor announced Mosher's name, the crowd applauded and cheered. Dressed in a Mosher Excavating shirt, canvas Carhartt work trousers, and dirty work boots, Mosher smiled almost bashfully.

"We're going to continue to make Hercules look like a wimp," added the governor.

Then he told of a conversation he had had recently with New Jersey governor Chris Christie. The New Jersey governor had called Shumlin to commiserate over the recovery process, saying it was going slowly in his state.

"It's going pretty fast up here," replied Governor Shumlin. "But I've got something you don't have. Every Vermonter has a tractor and a backhoe, not a Mercedes and BMW."

Half an hour later, down in Mendon, the governor joined a large crowd at Sugar & Spice. Casella had driven two of his Euclids, the big green off-road trucks, and parked them at one end of the parking lot. He stood in front of his trucks with his son Joe, wife, Maureen, and a number of Casella Construction employees, along with members of the Army National Guard, Kent Belden, Sam Markowski, and Governor Shumlin—the huge haul trucks dwarfing the group. Casella's smile seemed even wider than usual, as if it were going to take over his whole face. Not comfortable as the center of attention, Casella chided the photographers who kept asking him to pose for photos. "It took less time to rebuild the road!" he joked.

When the road reopening ceremony started, Eric Mallette and Lyz Tomsuden presented Governor Shumlin with an "I Am Vermont Strong" T-shirt. The governor took off his sweater and pulled the T-shirt over his blue button-down shirt and tie. Then he told the crowd that when he first flew over the devastation in Vermont on Monday, August 29, he thought it would be eighteen weeks before U.S. 4 could be rebuilt—at the earliest. And he talked of meeting with Doug Casella at the Rutland Reservoir.

"Doug said, 'Governor, if we could use Vermont common sense and wash the red tape down the river and get into the brook and dig up the gravel that washed down there from the road, then we could get this road done,'" recounted the governor.

The governor said that he called Brian Searles, the state's secretary of transportation, and the secretary agreed.

"If we were in New Jersey, it would have taken eighteen weeks," declared the governor. "In eighteen days, they got it done."

And it cost only $2 million to rebuild, said Casella.

Asked if he'd thought U.S. 4 would open a mere eighteen days after the storm, Bruce Nichols said yes.

"Knowing Vermonters like I do—and I've lived here my whole life—and knowing the capability of the people I've got working for me, my goal was to have every road open again by the end of the month," said Nichols, whose father was a road commissioner in Braintree, Vermont. "And we made it."

After the ceremony, Governor Shumlin talked to the contractors individually, and he thanked Maureen Casella for "sharing" her husband with Irene. When everyone had left, Maureen was marveling at the size of the trucks. The tires alone are taller than most people. Casella had to get the trucks back to Casella Construction's headquarters just down the road. So he said to his son Joe, "Give your mother a ride."

Mother and son climbed the ladder into the sixty-ton Euc and set off down U.S. 4.

PART III

THE RECOVERY

11

VERMONT WAS LUCKY

There's something deeply Yankee about this place in that
hardscrabble resourceful Vermonty way. You live in these hills for
hundreds of years, and you're isolated. You cut your own wood. You
shovel your own driveway. But you also understand that when push
comes to shove, you can't do it alone. It's tough to live in these hills
by yourself, which is why community is so strong here. People expect
you to pull your own weight. But when things get beyond what you
can handle on your own, people rally.

    ≶ Mark Edsell, Hurricane Flats' former farm manager and
        Operation Revive Royalton organizer

IN SOME WAYS, VERMONT WAS LUCKY. Long before Hurricane Irene
swirled into the state, the storm's winds had lost their punch, and she
was downgraded to a tropical storm. Trees came down, but wind did not
cause the damage many had feared it would. Also, the storm could have
hit on a weekday, when people were at work in far-off towns, or driving
to or from work. Instead, Irene arrived in Vermont on a Sunday, when
many were at home. And in most of the state, the worst of the rain fell
during the day, not at night, so those in low-lying areas could see floodwaters rising and knew if their neighbors needed help. Had the storm
reached its peak at night, when people were sleeping, Vermont might
have had more than the four reported fatalities on that Sunday.

The state was also lucky because destruction was not total. While
Irene's floodwaters devastated 1,405 homes and washed out more than
2,300 road segments, many properties, even in the isolated towns, were
left unscathed. Without having to deal with their own messes, people
who suffered no property damage during the storm were available to

help their neighbors. They could offer food and shelter, help muck out homes and businesses, and look for belongings. They could also organize volunteer relief efforts, from small-scale to large — as in Pittsfield, where someone dropped off a new Rubbermaid toy box at the end of Marion and Wilbur Abrams's driveway. Inside were two baseball bats and gloves, two shovels, two life jackets, and two toy bows and arrows for their young sons, whose outdoor toys had swept downriver. The gesture brought Marion to tears.

"It was just sitting there, no note," she said. "But it wasn't about . . . ," she paused, choking up again. "That's what's so great. It wasn't about who gave it or being beholden to someone else."

On a larger scale, volunteer efforts like Lyz Tomsuden's and Eric Mallette's "I Am Vermont Strong" theme raised $60,000 from T-shirt and sweatshirt sales by October 1. They donated the money to the Vermont Foodbank and kept raising more. On February 3, 2012, the Vermont legislature passed a bill allowing for the sale of "I Am Vermont Strong" commemorative license plates. Governor Shumlin bought the first $25 plate and presented it to a family whose mobile home had been destroyed by floodwaters in Berlin, Vermont. The goal of the "I Am Vermont Strong" license plate effort was to sell fifty thousand plates and raise $1 million for the Vermont Disaster Relief Fund and the Vermont Foodbank. Other relief groups also continued their fundraising efforts, such as Restoring Rutland, which held a silent auction and concert in May 2012, with funds going to Irene-affected families.

FEMA representatives who came to Vermont after Irene were impressed by Vermonters' independence, resilience, and generosity. They found that many people did not ask for help — at least not at first. Or else they said, "Just get me on my feet, and I'll take it from there," said James "Nick" Russo, the FEMA federal coordinating officer in Vermont after Irene — or the lead FEMA guy in Vermont.

Irene was disaster number eighty for Russo, who had worked as an emergency responder in Boston for thirty years before joining FEMA a decade prior to Irene. One of those disasters was Hurricane Katrina in New Orleans and Mississippi. Although he does not compare disasters or the response to disasters, Russo was impressed by neighbor helping neighbor in Vermont.

What was especially remarkable was the help given by people who needed it the most. People who had lost part or all of their belongings helped their neighbors clean up their own properties, pitched in at local shelters, directed traffic—whatever needed doing.

"Nine times out of ten, I'd give a hug to someone who'd lost their home, lost their belongings, lost it all, and after consoling them for awhile, they'd say, 'You know, Governor, I've got to go. I've got to help my neighbor across the street who got hit harder than I did,'" said Governor Shumlin.

So why did so many people pitch in after Irene? Social media played a key role. People were able to post photos of the devastation as it was happening on Facebook and Twitter, the two most popular social platforms, with exponential growth in users starting in 2006 (the year Facebook opened to the public and Twitter launched). These photos helped rally support for the state while the rain still poured.

Beyond social media, Vermont's size and the character of its people were instrumental in the state's recovery. Vermont is a small state, and many people knew at least one person who was trapped in the isolated towns or who was severely affected by the flooding. And they knew that even small gestures, like baking cookies for road workers or sending baby formula to an isolated mountain town, would make a difference.

Government is also small and accessible in Vermont, so Vermonters are accustomed to having an impact. Each of the state's 150 representatives brings the voices of about 4,200 people to Montpelier's legislative sessions, and many Vermonters know their state rep personally. He is the local school custodian, or she is an innkeeper who greets her kids at the school bus stop every afternoon. Likewise, state reps tend to know their constituents, and if trouble arises in their districts, the state reps are often the first to roll up their sleeves and help. By comparison, California's lower house has 80 representatives from districts with about 420,000 people; Massachusetts's state legislature has 160 house members each representing roughly 41,000 people.

Local government in Vermont is even more accessible. County government is nonexistent, leaving municipalities and their select boards as the primary governing bodies within Vermont's fourteen counties. And town governments are often microcosms of democracy. At annual town meetings, held the first Tuesday in March, townspeople can stand up and voice their opinions or raise issues of town importance, even if not everyone in the room agrees. Although not perhaps the most efficient form of civic rule, town meetings keep politics personal and bring the community together, albeit only once a year.

"I've seen how our democracy works being a legislator and going to national conferences and realizing we're really different and really special," said Sue Minter, who was Vermont's deputy secretary of transportation during Irene, then appointed Irene recovery officer. Prior to her appointment with VTrans, she had been a state representative. "Our democracy is so accessible. People really know their representative, they have access to the system. In general our process is one of consensus building and working toward a common goal as opposed to conflict."

And the common goal after Irene was clear: get the state and its people back on their feet.

Vermonters also responded to Irene because volunteering is part of the state fabric. Studies have shown that people in rural settings volunteer more than urban dwellers. They also more readily volunteer if they identify with a place and the cause. They will run for town office—and often multiple town offices. George Deblon in Pittsfield is a perfect example. Not only is he the town's road commissioner; he is also a selectman, justice of the peace, cemetery commissioner, a civil defenseman, and the town fence viewer. Elected and appointed town officials might not necessarily want all those jobs, but someone has to do them. Townspeople are also called upon to join the annual Old Home Week committee, the historical society, school organizations, the library board, or whatever organization will help enhance town life. In fact, Vermont has the highest percent of people volunteering for secular groups of any state in the nation: 28.42 percent, almost 2.5 percentage points higher than Montana, the second highest. (Interestingly, only 4.12 percent of Vermonters volunteer for religious groups—the lowest in the nation and far below Utah's high of 23.02 percent.) So when Irene created havoc in Vermont, it was only natural for people to pitch in and help their neighbors.

When it came to digging out and getting along without basic infrastructure such as roads, power, water, and sewer, Vermont character cannot be overlooked. Vermonters are, in general, known as rugged, resourceful, stubborn, independent characters—traits no doubt handed down from early Vermonters who lived in what was then a mountainous, wooded frontier and, until 1791, an independent republic. And these are traits common to those who have moved here since then—and stayed. (Only 51.5 percent of the people who live in Vermont are native born, according to the 2010 U.S. Census.) No matter how far technology has advanced, winters in Vermont are still cold and snowy, and the mountains still steep. Temperatures have dropped as low as –50 degrees Fahrenheit, and snow can fall over a yard deep.

Roads over the mountains can reach 10 to 15 percent grades for stretches longer than a mile—and up to 25 percent on Lincoln Gap (the steepest paved road in the nation). By comparison, roads over the Continental Divide in Colorado are typically 6 to 8 percent. And many of Vermont's roads are not paved: 55 percent of the state's 15,820 miles of public roads are still dirt, reportedly the highest percentage of unpaved roads of any state in the nation. Cell phone coverage, ubiquitous in most states, is still limited in Vermont. Just ask anyone who has tried to call for a tow truck on a narrow mountain road. And some Vermont towns were still without electricity long after satellites began orbiting the earth. Residents in Victory, Granby, and Jamaica used candles and kerosene lamps until 1964, when they were finally hooked into the electric grid— eighty years after electricity first came to the state. To live here happily, many Vermonters have the tools, patience, and often the skills to deal with inconveniences that can cause other places to grind to a halt.

"For generations and generations, we were pretty self-sufficient long after others were plugged in," said Governor Shumlin, when asked why he thought Vermonters responded so quickly to the Irene damage. "And there's a real sense that you don't wait for government to come help you out of a crisis. You get the chainsaw out of the shed, you get the tractor, you get the truck, you get your neighbor's backhoe, and you go to work."

And that, more than any other reason, is why Vermont's infrastructure was rebuilt so quickly after Irene.

§   §   §

MAUREEN CASELLA once joked that her husband started a construction company because he loves driving heavy equipment. Doug Casella does not disagree. But he did actually have a good reason to buy a bucket loader and dump truck back in the mid-1970s. When he started Casella Waste in 1975, Killington Resort was one of his first customers. With heavy snowfall on the mountain, and most of the resort's trash created during the ski season, Casella needed heavy equipment to reach his dumpsters in deep snow and to ferry the dumpsters off the mountain when full. The following summer the heavy equipment sat unused, and "it's not good for this stuff to sit," Casella said. So he began working construction in the summer months to keep the equipment running. Thus was born Casella Construction.

Of all his construction jobs since the summer of 1976, Casella is perhaps most proud of the U.S. 4 rebuild after Irene, as are Kent Belden, Sam Markowski, and Craig Mosher. They are proud that they could reconstruct this major thoroughfare in less than three weeks and open up the mountain towns. And they are proud that they saved the state money.

"It was a real true story of how Vermonters pulled together, helped each other out, and with a can-do attitude, worked 24-7 to put this state back together," said Governor Shumlin. "And they did it for 23 cents on the dollar. In other words, in most states, you'd hear, oh yeah, they did that, then they ripped you off in the process. These guys were working blood, sweat, and tears on the cheap. They never took advantage of anything. In fact, they gave more than they took."

After U.S. 4 officially reopened on September 16, 2011, the contractors who had put the road back together stayed to tidy up loose ends, such as installing a permanent sewer line for the Alpine Pipeline and seeding the new road embankments. Around the same time, a sculpture mysteriously appeared next to the new roadbed. Someone piled boulders into a snowman, spray-painted a smiley face on the top rock, and capped it with a black top hat. Casella credited Markowski with making the sculpture; Markowski said Belden did it.

Casella Construction stayed heavily involved in road rebuilding throughout the fall. Crews rebuilt town roads in Mendon; Doug Casella sent a crew to remove the damaged bridge on Route 100 south of Pittsfield, while Craig Mosher's crews installed a temporary bridge there. Casella Construction also continued to rebuild the intake pipe to the Rutland City Reservoir, as well as reconstruct a diversion dam off Killington Peak that directs water to Rutland's water supply (the earthen dam was washed away by Irene's floodwaters pouring off the peak). They finished laying the new intake pipe by mid-September—about a week before the city would have run out of drinking water.

Then, without really taking a breath, Casella took his two sixty-ton

Eucs, as well as other heavy equipment, and headed into the mountains to rebuild Route 107 between Stockbridge and Bethel. The ten-mile-long road was in even worse shape than the "Cavendish Canyon" (Route 131 outside Cavendish) and Route 100 in Wardsboro. Over two long sections of 107, the White River had simply erased almost every indication that a two-lane highway—with shoulders, guard rails, culverts, and hundreds of thousands of tons of roadbed—had ever existed there, where the steep, tree-filled mountainsides plunge straight into the river. Casella counted sixty-three places along a five-mile stretch of 107 that were damaged.

The National Guard worked on Route 107 in the storm's immediate aftermath, building a narrow temporary road into the mountainside that made drivers feel as if they were navigating the Peruvian Andes rather than Vermont's Green Mountains. People who lived in the area needed a better route to the outside world. So before he began rebuilding 107, Casella did triage on River Road, a dirt road that parallels Route 107 from Gaysville to Bethel on the opposite side of the White River. River Road had been swept away in some places; in other sections there were thirty-foot holes. (Near Bethel a narrow iron bridge still stood, but the roadbed on either side was gone.) Casella started fixing River Road the same way he and the other contractors had fixed U.S. 4. "I just got in the excavator and started working," he said.

Three days after he started, River Road was passable. Then Casella and his crews tackled Route 107. Along the two long sections that had completely disappeared, his crews had to build back the roadbed to a level thirty-five feet above the river. But that amount of material—roughly 300,000 yards, or three times the amount needed to rebuild U.S. 4 in Mendon—was not readily available. The White River was full of the gravel that had once been the 107 roadbed, but Casella needed big rocks to make that much road—big rocks that would not easily wash away in the next flood. He found the material at a large quartzite quarry in Colchester, adjacent to I-89 north of Burlington. The rock at the quarry was hard, pink-tinged Monkton quartzite (the same rock used to build northern sections of I-89), and the pit had a permit to quarry the amount of rock needed. Since the pit opened in 1954, its owners have quarried up to a million tons of rock per year—or about three thousand tons every day.

The rock was loaded into open-topped train cars and pulled seventy-six miles southeast along railroad tracks to Bethel. There the train cars dumped the rock down a steep embankment into a pile. Casella's Eucs carried the stone through the White River (the trucks were too heavy to cross the rickety River Street Bridge over the White River in Bethel), then up onto 107 to the washouts. Load by load, they began re-creating a road from a riverbed.

§ § §

THROUGHOUT THE FALL of 2011, Geo Honigford worked on repairing his farm along the White River in South Royalton. He re-covered the two greenhouses in his field with plastic and planted a cover crop to prevent erosion during the winter: by late November it was starting to grow in the spongy brown silt that still covered his field. No longer visible were the huge gouges that the river had taken from his field. During the clean-up, locals had dumped truckloads of silt scooped up from their fields—and the school ball fields—and filled in the house-size holes. However, with no barrier protecting this four hundred feet of new riverbank, Honigford worried that another rainstorm or spring runoff would raise the White River to the point that it would once again create craters in his field. He did not want to place riprap along the bank. Rocks reflect heat back into the river water and inhibit tree growth along the bank. He wanted to stabilize the riverbank by first burying about a hundred trees that the flood had swept onto the toe of his field, so that the trees lay perpendicular to the river and the roots were facing out toward the water. That would create a natural logjam and slow the river's flow near the bank. On top of the buried trees he would then restore a thirty-five-foot riparian buffer between the river and his field. But he had to pay for immediate needs first—like fixing the greenhouses and irrigation system.

On a damp November day, he spent a couple of hours cleaning fine silt out of an electric panel that powers his irrigation pump. The box sits on a pole in the middle of his field. It is on this pole that Honigford can see how high the water rose at Hurricane Flats: eight feet. He wryly joked that they were now calling the farm "Hurricane Flattened."

§ § §

OF THE TOWNS that were cut off from the outside world by Irene's floodwaters, Pittsfield became a poster-child for how a town can successfully handle a crisis. Part of the town's ability to cope so well with the disaster was simply its geography. Unlike neighboring Stockbridge, which has no real village center and is sparsely populated, with houses scattered along webs of dirt roads, Pittsfield is a compact village with a downtown that serves as a hub for the community. Two general stores, the post office, town office, and church all sit within a stone's throw of each other and draw people downtown. And even though Irene had washed out Route 100 both north and south of the village, most of the town's residents could still reach downtown after the storm.

But the biggest contributing factor to Pittsfield's success was its people. Between the two washouts on Route 100 live people with skills and equipment, and they served the town well in crisis.

"Everybody had some talent," said Peter Borden. "Like Greg Martin; [he and his family] run cv Oil. He can fix a furnace, he can fix anything with his hands. He's also an amazing heavy equipment operator. The fact that we had these amazing people in town with the skills and with the hydraulics, it was the 1800s with hydraulics. We could rebuild anything. We didn't have horses, we had bulldozers. We didn't have carriages, we had dump trucks."

Those in charge were also well served by common sense and the ability to communicate well. Or as Borden said, overcommunicate. Constable Mianulli stayed visible day in and day out in downtown Pittsfield as much to answer questions, coordinate supply chains, and just give townspeople a sense of order in the chaos as to maintain order. And, when needed, to give a hug.

"I didn't leave town until I collapsed," said Mianulli, a lovable town character who usually carries a sidearm, wears a necklace made of partridge feet, bear claws, and yak bone (all animals he has shot), and once patched an accidental gunshot wound in his own abdomen with duct tape. "Doing that job and making those people feel comfortable and safe was big to me. Putting your arm around people, loading their cars, some days I emptied garbage for people."

"If I didn't have those people to work with, we would have had a totally different situation," said Borden of his fellow town officials and others who stepped in to help.

Town leaders were constantly on the phone — once cell phone service returned — gathering information and then sharing it through official notices posted at the town office and two general stores, and at the daily town meetings, which most people attended. Rumors were dispelled before they could gain traction — such as when roads would or would not open, and when the power might come back on. And everyone trusted that everything that could be done, was being done.

"It felt so good to do things you knew how to do and to know they were important," said Angelique Lee, who helped in myriad ways, posting signs around town, offering Internet access at her house, lending a sympathetic ear to anyone who needed to talk, and helping townspeople in any way she could (leading some to refer to her as "the flood whisperer").

"It was like the world's best committee," Lee added. "No one ever questioned what you were doing. You just did it. You had a huge sense of responsibility."

After U.S. 4 opened in Mendon in mid-September, most people in Pittsfield returned to their pre-Irene lives — at least in terms of commuting to work and school. On September 10 the town held the last Irene town meeting. No one remembers specifically what they discussed at that meeting, only that they really needed to have it.

"The whole energy of the town changed because people were starting to go back to work," said Lee. "It deflated."

With life back to "normal" in Pittsfield, some people admitted that they almost missed the days after the storm, when the town as a whole had a collective goal, when life was zeroed in on digging out, acquiring basic needs, and helping neighbors meet those same needs. Such intense focus pushed the usual white noise of life into the background and brought clarity and a true sense of purpose. The experience of being isolated, of having to come together as a community and solve their own problems without outside help, has become a badge of honor. Pittsfield is proud of how the town weathered Irene — and a "Pittsfield Proud" bumper sticker shows it. After the storm, most people in Pittsfield said that there was no place they would rather be. In comparison, the 2010 census showed that New Orleans's population shrank by 29 percent after Hurricane Katrina.

"We couldn't have staged it any better," said Peter Borden. "We were lucky to have the equipment we had in town and the talent pool we had in town. We just lucked out."

"And it was good it didn't happen during hunting season," added Verna Borden, with a laugh.

§ § §

THROUGHOUT THE LATE FALL, not far from Pittsfield, Casella Construction and crews from forty-five other companies rebuilt Route 107. Heavy equipment crawled up and down the White River Valley, and truckload by truckload they put the road back where it had been. By the end of November one of the long destroyed stretches had been paved, while the other still needed ten more vertical feet of roadbed material. Temperatures in the forties were not ideal for paving, but what could they do? Casella said that they would put down a coat of asphalt knowing they would have to repave again in the future.

On December 29, 2011, four months and one day after Irene ripped it apart, Route 107 reopened. Weary from the storm and continued recovery, only a handful of people showed up for the ribbon-cutting at the Stockbridge school. Nonetheless, it was a milestone—literally.

Looking out over the fresh tarmac, Casella said that rebuilding U.S. 4 and 107 gave him a new perspective on the word "permanent." Like the crafty pig who builds his home from bricks in the "Three Little Pigs" fairy tale, Casella knows that structures built of stone, concrete, and asphalt feel permanent. And safe. But it's not a wolf huffing and puffing that will bring the house down. It's a violent serpent of fast-moving water that can demolish anything in its path. Picturesque as they may be, flowing placidly through meadows, babbling around mountain boulders, and tumbling over bands of gneiss and schist, Vermont's rivers and streams are not to be trusted.

"Before, I was a little naive to think that we could build stuff that Mother Nature can't rip out," Casella said. "After seeing what I saw, I will definitely say that there's nothing we can build that Mother Nature can't tear out if she wants to."

12

THE HUMAN TOLL

It is clear that even as recovery continues, new challenges emerge,
and there remains a long road ahead to full recovery.

⸙ Governor Peter Shumlin in a memorandum to "Vermont
Recovering Stronger: Irene Recovery Status Report,"
June 2012

WALLACE STEGNER ONCE SAID THAT HE was attracted to Vermont
because "it heals." A Pulitzer Prize–winning author known as the "dean
of Western writers," Stegner grew up in Montana, Utah, and Saskatch-
ewan, and taught writing at Stanford University in California for twenty-
six years. But he and his wife, Mary, also spent half a century of summers
living in Greensboro, Vermont. In that time he noticed how scars in the
landscape, such as old logging roads and clearcuts, were soon over-
grown, with spring mud helping to fill in the ruts, and grasses and trees
seeding themselves in fields and openings in the forest floor.

"The rest of the country—the West—when you damage it, you get a
wasteland," said Stegner. "Here we spend half our time cutting trees just
to keep a view of the lake open. Then you turn your back, you come back
the next year, and it's woods again."

In the months after the storm, the scars that Irene left behind in
Vermont's landscape—the bare dirt of collapsed embankments, the
scoured riverbeds and cobbled deposits, the silt-filled fields, and the
toppled houses—were constant reminders of the storm's devastation.
But already by late spring of 2012, some areas were beginning to "heal."
Grasses and trees were sprouting in the fresh dirt of the exposed riverbanks, and corn and other crops were rooting in the fields. Several
collapsed houses still remained, but most of those will eventually be

dismantled or rebuilt. In a few years, the damage to the landscape will be hard to see. At least until the next major meteorological event. The only places that may not "heal" as quickly are the sections of stream that were channeled to keep them away from roads and bridges, and where embankments were reinforced to support and protect the state's transportation infrastructure. With the challenges of building and maintaining roads and bridges (and railroads) in a state where topography offers few options, we are forced to make compromises.

But ruts in the human psyche are not as easily healed, and many Vermonters will not recover as quickly as the landscape. Irene was a rude reminder that Nature can do what she wants, when she wants, no matter what stands in her way. Months after Irene blew through Vermont, many survivors were still suffering from post-traumatic stress disorder (PTSD). Symptoms ranged from recurring dreams or nightmares about the flood to feeling numb or withdrawn or disconnected, or having bursts of anger or irritability, and avoiding reminders of the storm and flood. PTSD sufferers can also have trouble concentrating and remembering what they need to do, physical ailments (persistent headaches, digestive problems, muscle tension), and difficulty making decisions.

A good social support system may protect disaster victims against PTSD. And the host of volunteers who assisted those affected by Irene no doubt helped many in the storm's immediate aftermath. But after the initial waves of support had moved on, many were left almost alone to sift through the debris of their lives, in some cases with little remaining. While the many Vermonters who were not grievously affected by Irene resumed their lives shortly after the roads and bridges were put back together, those who had lost homes and businesses were left to relive the disaster every day. For them, the flood did not occur solely on August 28, 2011. They were confronted and reminded daily of their loss—whether it was bills they were uncertain if they would be able to pay, or the sudden memory of a family heirloom they would never see again.

"[The flood] didn't, past tense, happen," said Paul Fraser, Jamaica's emergency management director and a retired psychologist and social worker for the U.S. Air Force. "They are still living the disaster. While most folks are going about their lives and getting a little disaster fatigue, these people are living it, it's still ongoing."

"This isn't just that they lost their front yards or their houses burned down," he added. "[This disaster] erased their entire house, it erased the traces and erased their lives."

To help people affected by Irene, FEMA funded Starting Over Strong (SOS) Vermont. SOS Vermont began providing free support to those affected by Irene on September 1, 2011, and three teams of crisis counselors went door to door in affected communities — even those towns still reachable only by tenuous temporary roads — to find people interested in receiving support ranging from individual counseling, stress reduction strategies, and assistance filling out paperwork, to finding contractors to deal with specific reconstruction issues like mold remediation. SOS Vermont also started support groups, like a stress reduction series with yoga events and spa days, a bowling night, financial planning workshops, and story circles. The sessions aimed to show people that they were not alone in disaster recovery — either physically or emotionally — and to teach them mechanisms for coping, such as an exercise called Six Senses, in which people learn to put stress aside by focusing on what they can hear, feel, see, and smell in their immediate surroundings.

"It pulls somebody into the moment and helps them be present," said Ellia Cohen, an SOS Vermont team leader. "It takes them out of whatever stress they were feeling in the previous moment. It's something people tell us they've continued to use."

Although they do not know how many Vermonters were affected by Irene-related PTSD, SOS Vermont counseled more than twelve hundred individuals in the nine months after the storm. And more than forty-three hundred attended the group sessions.

"[Irene] was a very huge event in a lot of people's lives," said Cohen, adding that a year is not enough time to recover from such a devastating event — and in fact, the anniversary of the storm can plunge people even deeper into despair. "Even a year later, they're not back to normal."

SOS Vermont's FEMA grant ended on October 29, 2012. But the group did not fold up shop completely. On their website, startingoverstrongvermont.org, they included a link to several resources for recovery, including lists of techniques to cope with worrying and tips to help children heal from a natural disaster, as well as lists of counseling and long-term recovery committees throughout Vermont.

Financial concerns have exacerbated the frustration and hopelessness that those who lost everything — or nearly everything — have felt.

While state and federal money will, for the most part, pay for rebuilding the state's infrastructure, citizens with damage to their private property are not as lucky. Those without flood insurance — and there were many (FEMA estimated that only 2.5 percent of destroyed and damaged residences were covered by flood insurance) — were left with nothing but the FEMA individual household grant of $30,200 plus whatever money was directly donated to them by generous friends, neighbors, and relief groups. After registering with FEMA, many spent months chasing down grants (or rumors of grants) and filling out paperwork to tap into the millions of dollars donated to the many flood relief groups in the storm's aftermath. But grants from these groups were small in comparison to what home and business owners needed to restore their properties. As one homeowner whose property was trashed by the flood put it, the $25 gift cards to Home Depot and Hannaford were very much appreciated, but what they really needed was a $250,000 gift card to buy a new home out of the floodplain.

To help with long-term recovery, groups like Upper Valley Strong and ReBuild Waterbury formed in the weeks and months after the storm. These groups worked with individuals and families that struggled to rebuild and guided them through the hoops of finding funding. Caseworkers and project managers assessed needs and asked individuals to provide a list of assistance received to date (FEMA grants, bank loans, and other funding), specific unmet needs such as damaged or lost appliances that had yet to be replaced, and resources at their disposal. The caseworkers then worked with local contractors to begin repairs, such as installing new insulation or wallboard.

But the amount of money required to return families to an adequate living situation was staggering. In the Upper Valley alone — comprising towns along the White River and vicinity — twenty-five homeowners had damage totaling more than $2 million. Half that amount was covered by FEMA grants and other volunteer donations. After subtracting homeowner loans and other sources of local support, almost $500,000 was still needed to return families to "normalcy" in just the Upper Valley. Statewide, roughly seven thousand Vermonters registered with FEMA after Irene, with 1,405 residences suffering significant damage (433 of those residences were mobile homes). The Vermont Long-Term Disaster Recovery Group estimated that unmet needs around the state would total $10 million. And that did not include businesses, which FEMA does not include in disaster relief programs. Although many local business owners received money from local flood relief organizations, most were left to take out loans.

To cover homeowners' "unmet needs," groups like Upper Valley Strong have applied to the Vermont Disaster Relief Fund, the primary fund created after the flood to provide relief to individuals and families who had exhausted all other forms of funding. The fund awarded money *not to the individuals* but to the contractors and other vendors who performed repairs or provided equipment and services — and only after local fundraising was tapped out.

Administered by the Vermont Long-Term Disaster Recovery Group, the fund raised $3.6 million by the one-year anniversary of Irene and had allocated more than $1.7 million toward the estimated $10 million in unmet needs. Funds collected included $1 million from ninety-four-year-old Burlington businessman and philanthropist Tony Pomerleau for displaced mobile home residents, as well as money raised from the "I Am Vermont Strong" license plate sales. But $6.4 million in unmet needs remained, and as of August 2012, the Vermont Long-Term Disaster Recovery Group was still strategizing ways to raise it.

A few homeowners in the state were lucky — if that word can be applied to people whose homes and belongings were swept downstream. Several Vermont towns applied for FEMA's Hazard Mitigation Grant Program (HMGP) in behalf of the homeowners whose property had been destroyed by the floodwaters. Under the buyout program, the town purchases the properties at 75 percent of their preflood assessed value, not including the contents of the homes. The purpose of the program is not to help homeowners but to ensure that they do not rebuild in flood-prone areas and thus apply for FEMA funding in future natural disasters. First the state has to approve the town plans. Then the state has to apply to FEMA for the Hazard Mitigation Grants and wait to hear the government's decision. If the government approves the grants, the state repays the towns, which would reimburse the homeowners. For those who have mortgages, some or all of the money goes straight to the bank. They are left with no money, no home, no land, and no equity. But at least no more mortgage payments on property that no longer exists. For well over a year after Irene, ninety-nine homeowners in Vermont hung in the balance, waiting to hear if FEMA would approve the Hazard Mitigation Grant buyouts.

"The hardest thing is just waiting," Dave Kaneshiro told Vermont Public Radio at the end of May 2012. Kaneshiro owned one of the four houses swept away by the Ball Mountain Brook along Jamaica's Water Street. "Waiting to see what the results are so I can go on with life. I'm still trying to get over it. It's gone. It's gone. It's gone. Now you gotta start a new life. And the finalization of the mitigation program would be the first step after the flood."

Waiting for months to hear from FEMA, those who were most affected by Irene were left in limbo and in debt—a homeless purgatory in which they could not see more than a day or two ahead. Nor could they look back. For nothing remained and the nightmare continued.

§   §   §

EVEN WITH a place to stay during the fall of 2011—the borrowed condo at Stratton—Tracy Payne's life spun helplessly in circles. Her days were filled with paperwork and salvaging what bits of her life she could. Some days she would randomly dial some of the groups that were raising money for flood victims, such as the band Phish, which brought in more than $1.2 million at a benefit concert on September 14, 2011 (proceeds from the concert were put in the band's WaterWheel Foundation, which worked with the Vermont Community Foundation to develop a grant-giving strategy).* Townspeople in Jamaica and the Stratton Foundation had helped Payne immediately after the storm, giving her cash, clothing, food, and temporary housing. But where was the long-term support?

*On November 14, 2011, the WaterWheel Foundation announced that the initial round of support from the Phish benefit concert was composed of grants ranging from $50,000 to $150,000. The grants were given to groups such as the Vermont Farm Disaster Relief Fund and the Vermont Farm Fund Emergency Loan Program to support farmers affected by Irene's floodwaters; the Vermont Irene Flood Relief Fund to support small businesses that suffered flood damage; the Special and Urgent Needs—Irene Recovery Fund to support nonprofit and public sector organizations affected by the flood (such as the Boys & Girls Club of Brattleboro to repair and replace items lost in the flood); and the Vermont Foodbank. The fund also donated money to support immediate relief efforts at mobile home parks. The foundation then made a second round of smaller grants to twenty-eight local relief groups in Vermont towns. These grants were aimed at helping families and individuals, as well as town services and infrastructure, hardest hit by the storm.

Where was all the money that these groups had raised? Why wasn't it immediately dispersed to those who needed it most? Five months after the storm, she had yet to receive a penny from any organization in the state raising money for flood victims.

And then she had to deal with a second disaster in her life. About a month after Hurricane Irene took her house, Payne's mother called from an ambulance in Maryland. Her sixty-nine-year-old father had fallen off a ladder. He couldn't move, and paramedics thought he might be paralyzed.

Payne barely had money to pay for gas (she had yet to receive any IHP funds from FEMA). But she knew she had to be with her mom. She jumped into her car and headed for Maryland. When she arrived at the hospital, she learned that her father had broken his back and had undergone a six-hour operation. Another flood of emotion slammed her hard. When would the disasters end? When would she be able to catch her breath?

She finally caught a small break in October. During one of her many trips to Maryland, Payne's high school friends held a fundraiser that brought in around $1,500, and they gave her the money directly. And finally in mid-October, Payne received the full IHP grant from FEMA. But with clothes, furnishings, gas, and food to buy, plus other expenses, $30,200 did not go far. And she was told to keep receipts for everything she purchased, from a pack of gum to clothing. Part or all of the $30,200 might be deducted from any future FEMA funding.

"I have learned how to stretch a penny," Payne said. "I have squirreled away every bit of cash that I can."

As Thanksgiving 2011 neared, Payne knew that she had to move out of the loaner condo. With the help of the Stratton Foundation, she located a place to rent in Weston. But there was some confusion about Payne's housing situation. Assuming that she had a place to live already (in Massachusetts, with Esposito), the foundation had found someone else to rent the place in Weston.

At that point, Payne made the decision to leave Vermont. It was difficult, she said, and she did not want any of her Vermont friends to know.

"I felt ashamed that I was leaving," she said. "I had people that I loved tell me that I needed to stay plugged into Vermont. But how? I didn't have anywhere to stay. I didn't have a job."

By leaving the state, Payne may have missed out on some of the programs that were created to help those significantly affected by Irene, such as sos Vermont. She also moved away from people who knew what she had been through, and away from those in a similar situation. Though it would have been hard to stay in Vermont, it was just as hard to go.

But slowly she began to build a new life. On December 1, 2011, she and Esposito moved into an apartment in a Boston suburb. Ironically, her address once again read Water Street. By January she was ready to look for work and found a part-time job packing greeting card orders. She also learned that the state of Vermont was going to pay for leasing her property as a right-of-way for the temporary Water Street that crossed her land. That payment amounted to $6,500. Finally, she felt like she could take a breath.

Walking into a diner in downtown Boston on a cold, rainy day in January 2012, Payne, in an oversized raincoat and hefting a daypack that appeared to weigh more than she did, looked even smaller than her tiny size zero frame. But she smiled and said she had hope for the future. Her father's condition had stabilized, and he was now in a nursing home. She talked hopefully about living near her mom one day, maybe in Florida. But she bears deep scars — like a fear that she will lose all her money again. So she carries it around with her everywhere.

"It's probably really stupid, but if you think about it, I don't feel like it's safe to put my cash anywhere now," she said. "I don't want to put it in the bank. I don't know why I don't want to put it in the bank . . ."

And throughout the year following Irene, she and her former neighbors waited to see if first the state, then FEMA, would approve the Hazard Mitigation Grants. If so, they would each receive 75 percent of the preflood tax value of their property. Then, from the $434,600 that the Stratton Foundation had raised for Irene relief—70 percent donated by second homeowners in the area—the foundation pledged to give the homeowners who had lost everything in Jamaica the remaining 25 percent. But when word came that the state would cover the remaining 25 percent from the HUD-funded Community Development Block Grant (CDBG) program, the foundation waited to see how it would play out. In April 2012 the foundation dispersed some of the funds to two families who found permanent housing in the area and needed money for a down payment. A month later, the foundation fronted $20,000 to the four waiting to hear about the FEMA buyout. The organization then waited to learn the fate of the FEMA grants and matching state donations before dispensing further funds. The homeowners were originally told that FEMA would make its decision in June 2012. Then the date was moved to September.

The lag of more than a year between Irene and the pending buyout was grueling. Financial insecurity deepened Payne's sense of loss and undermined any power she might have felt to move her life forward. Even if the grant was approved, the road ahead seemed daunting.

"To rebuild a life at my age is hard," said Payne, who is in her mid-forties. "I've lived a life already."

Then, in late September 2012, Payne and her former neighbors learned of a major setback. The four houses on Water Street did not sit within the mapped Ball Mountain Brook floodplain for a one-hundred-year flood event. The floodplain in Jamaica was determined during a FEMA-commissioned flood study in the 1970s or 1980s and did not take into account fluvial erosion. In fact, no FEMA flood studies take into account rivers eroding their banks, migrating across the landscape, and taking their floodplains with them. Despite the fact that Brett Morrison's, Karin Hardy's, Dave Kaneshiro's, and Tracy Payne's houses were swept away, along with most of the land on which they had been built—and the fact that these same properties along Water Street had been damaged in previous floods, as evidenced by old photos and a book on town history—these houses sat above what is called the base flood elevation, or BFE. Thus they were above the floodplain and not eligible for the FEMA Hazard Mitigation Grant Program. No one realized this until very late in the process. It seemed obvious that these house *had* to have sat within the floodplain boundary. Why else would the brook have surrounded them with floodwater and swept them away?

Paul Fraser—Jamaica's emergency management director and the person who filled out the FEMA HMGP paperwork—was left with few options, the most obvious being to prove that the floodplain map was wrong and that the four houses were in fact below BFE. A local surveyor offered to remap, for free, the land along Water Street. Unfortunately for the four homeowners, he discovered that all of the properties had been above BFE. Other suggestions included showing that the Ball Mountain Brook's streambed had moved, and thus its floodplain had moved with it. So if the property owners rebuilt on what remained of their land, they would now be within the floodplain and vulnerable to future floods. Another suggestion was to improve Water Street to prepare for future emergencies. Then the agency would have to offer the homeowners buyouts, because the road would take over most of their land.

But what FEMA officials said they needed to approve the Hazard Mitigation Grants was proof that the cost of the buyout would be beneficial—that is, it would cost taxpayers less in the long run to buy out the homeowners now than to pay for future flood damage if they rebuilt on what was left of their land. If the homeowners could show that the agency had had to pay for damages after previous storms, the buyout would be easier to approve. But by all accounts, the last time floodwaters in this section of the Ball Mountain Brook caused significant property damage was during Hurricane Belle in 1976. FEMA was not created until 1979.

Sadly, had the four homeowners purchased flood insurance, they would have received checks for damages shortly after Irene. According to Kevin Geiger, a regional planner working on flood management issues with Vermont Emergency Management, the insurance policies would have run only about $200 to $300 per year, because the properties were not in the mapped flood zone. Fraser urged the four homeowners to encourage their former Water Street neighbors to buy flood insurance immediately.

On December 4, 2012, Morrison, Hardy, Payne, and Kaneshiro convened in Jamaica for a meeting with FEMA, state, and town officials. The four homeowners each carried thick folders of accumulated paperwork, photos, and countless notes about their property, town history, possible funding leads, and whatever else they had learned about disaster recovery in the previous fifteen months. As they sat surrounded by officials who had been working on Irene recovery for months, they were told that FEMA would most likely deny the Hazard Mitigation Grants. The agency had to work within the technical regulations that "unfortunately, are not as flexible as our rivers sometimes are," state rep. Oliver Olsen told the gathering. The officials had turned over every rock they could, but it didn't look as though a buyout would be cost beneficial.

But not all hope was lost. They were told that Vermont's congressional delegation, along with Irene recovery officer Sue Minter and other state and town officials, were committed to finding a way to resolve the issue.

"If FEMA funding is denied, we're going to look as a team at alternative sources of funding on a case by case basis," Ray Doherty, state Hazard Mitigation officer for Vermont Emergency Management, told the homeowners. "We're not going to let it stand as denial and not do anything."

Possible sources of funding included CDBG money and the Stratton Foundation, possibly along with the Vermont Disaster Relief Fund and other local sources. The CDBG money had been slated to cover the remaining 25 percent of the assessed property value for those in Vermont approved for FEMA Hazard Mitigation Grants. Jennifer Hollar, the deputy commissioner of the Vermont Department of Economic, Housing and Community Development, which is tasked with administering the HUD-funded CDBG program, assured the four Jamaica homeowners that the state would try to meet their needs — the full cost of the buyout, if possible.

"We don't know how far we're going to be able to stretch that CDBG money to do more, but as we learn more about how these projects shake out, we'll have a sense of that," Hollar told them. "We'll work with you and the regional commission and the town and try to pull in other sources to try to cover the total project costs so that a buyout can go forward. Our commitment is to keep working on it."

Payne expressed frustration that the four had often been told that there was hope — but "don't hope too much."

"I keep hearing that," she said. "It's hard."

Robert Bohlmann, FEMA's HMGP task force leader, tried to give the group some perspective. He had seen Hazard Mitigation Grants in other states denied in the past, and "that was the end."

"This isn't much consolation, but I can tell you that from working a number of events around the country it's unusual to have a community and the CDBG and the regional planning commissions all coming together to work for you," he said. "It's enlightening to see this Vermont way."

Fraser agreed and was impressed that rather than just sending an email explaining the probable HMGP denial, both FEMA and state officials drove to Jamaica to face a bunch of potentially angry people with bad news. "There is a difference in how the state has been addressing this issue compared to other states," he said. "Even though we don't like the results, and we're still going to fight for them, these officials don't have to be here today."

After the meeting, Payne did not appear deflated. Quite the opposite. She really did feel hopeful again — not that bureaucracy would eventually prevail but that the state and community would rally around the four Jamaica homeowners and try to make them whole again.

"I'm humbled by all of the time and energy that everyone's put in to make sure we don't get left behind," she said. "It makes me miss Vermont that much more."

S S S

FOR OTHERS in Jamaica, life gradually returned to normal after Irene — a new normal. A temporary Main Street Bridge was installed in October 2011, making Route 30/100 once more the main road through town. And they worked on Water Street to raise it again several feet above the brook and protect it with a rock embankment. In what remained of the four homeowners' properties along Water Street, the town hoped that a buyout, no matter who funded it, would allow them to turn the area into a brookside park. At D&K's Jamaica Grocery, Karen Ameden sold more than eight hundred "Fix It Now, Apologize Later" T-shirts and donated the money to the Stratton Foundation, earmarked for Jamaica flood victims. Although everyone in town was weary of talking about Irene, Ameden said the community felt closer now. She described the town as functioning like an ant colony in the days and weeks after the storm. All the people in town were on a mission, knew their job, and did it to the best of their ability. The trust that developed from mission complete — or almost complete — has permanently permeated the town fabric.

"It just all came together so easily," she said. "Some people were devastated. But overall, the town as a whole gained from the experience."

S S S

FOR BUSINESS OWNERS whose shops and offices lay in the flood's path, it wasn't their lives that they had to rebuild as much as their livelihoods. Many people had invested everything they owned into their small Vermont businesses. FEMA does not provide funding to businesses that are damaged in natural disasters, and unless the bank required them to purchase flood insurance as part of their mortgages, most small business owners did not buy coverage. So in order to rebuild, they have had to take out huge loans. In a tough economy, with income dwindling and loan payments calling, this put many businesses on a knife's edge. Lang Durfee, owner/manager of Bethel Mills, said he began running the 231-year-old business like a start-up—patching together what equipment he could and working long hours and even longer weeks. He is deeply thankful to, and humbled by, the customers who helped the lumberyard clean up and slowly move forward. But for Durfee and other businesses that were flooded, a second disaster loomed after Irene: the specter of foreclosure.

Of all the Vermont towns hit by Irene, Wilmington experienced the steepest financial losses: $13 million. As foliage season approached, many of the flooded businesses in the historic downtown district were still in the process of rebuilding. Lilias Hart's Quaigh Design Centre, just up West Main Street from Bartleby's, was the first to reopen. With wall insulation still showing and her gallery walls bare, Hart opened her door about a month after the storm—"to show people we are coming back," she said. Within two weeks, another five or so businesses in various states of repair also opened. Over Columbus Day weekend—when busloads of tourists often flock to Vermont—more downtown businesses opened, some under tents and only for the weekend. For many, it was the first time they had served customers since August 27.

At Bartleby's, Lisa Sullivan and Phil Taylor set up tables in the front part of their store and set out books that they had salvaged and other merchandise donated by publishers. The bookstore had no lights and no cash register (they used a cash box), and Taylor had to unscrew the front door from the frame every morning when they opened. But they were open.

"We felt life again," said Sullivan.

Although donated supplies were plentiful in Wilmington—particularly donated clothing—what the business owners desperately needed was money to help fund their clean-up and rebuilding efforts. Several people and organizations in town quickly stepped up. The owners of Apres Vous, a restaurant on South Main Street, and the Wilmington Inn organized Floodstock, a two-day music festival on September

23–24, 2011, featuring eight bands from three states. The festival raised $67,549.96, which was divided among twenty Wilmington businesses in grants ranging from $880.93 to $5,285.59.

Adam Palmiter, a local realtor, set up the Wilmington VT Flood Relief Fund to help small businesses in town. He knew that FEMA did not support businesses and that flood insurance, for the few businesses that had it, would not be enough to help them get on their feet again. Working with the Deerfield Valley Rotary Club and the Mount Snow Chamber of Commerce, the fund raised more than $300,000 by Christmas—thanks to donations from companies like Mount Snow, which raffled off a "golden chair" from their Grand Summit Express chairlift for $10,000 (the Grand Summit Express had been equipped with new chairs in 2011, allowing guests to purchase the old chairs, and the resort to paint chair #50 gold and raffle it off). By the time the fund wrapped up its efforts in March 2012, it had raised nearly $450,000. Grants to local businesses ranged from $2,000 to $25,000.

Other contributors to the Wilmington VT Flood Relief Fund included second-home owners—who own more than 60 percent of the houses in the area—and locals like Sullivan's and Taylor's children, eight-year-old Ally and five-year-old Zach, who set up a lemonade stand outside Bartleby's on Columbus Day weekend. They sold fresh-squeezed lemonade for $1 per cup—with most people giving them far more than a dollar. By the end of the holiday weekend, Ally and Zach had raised $661.

Thanks in part to a grant from the Wilmington VT Flood Relief Fund, as well as flood insurance money and a VEDA loan, Taylor continued to rebuild Bartleby's throughout the fall. The building's downstairs once again looked like a bookstore, and he made a few building alterations so they can better utilize the space in the two-story building. To "flood proof" it he installed closed-cell insulation (which does not have to be removed if it gets wet), raised the furnace boiler over five feet above the floor, and shored up the front of the building to withstand water pressure in case of future flooding. But Sullivan admits that paranoia creeps in every time it rains.

Bartleby's officially reopened on Black Friday—the day after Thanksgiving. Before the store opened, people brought camping chairs and lined up along the street. Many held signs that read "Bartleby's or Bust" and "We Love Bartleby's."

"It seemed like every person who'd ever come in here before was out shopping," said Sullivan, whose smile still has not faded.

But other business owners in historic downtown Wilmington were not so lucky. Most did not have flood insurance, and though grants from the local fundraising organizations were greatly appreciated, they covered only a small fraction of clean-up and rebuilding costs, leaving many with huge debt loads. As winter approached, several shops in the historic downtown were still boarded up. On a map in Wilmington's Long-Term Community Recovery Plan, about 40 percent of the buildings lining the Main streets (North, South, East, and West) were marked as "unoccupied/for sale building," including Dot's Restaurant.

Town clerk Susie Haughwout confirmed that only about half the businesses in downtown Wilmington had reopened by spring 2012. With so many businesses boarded up, Lilias Hart of the Quaigh Design Centre feared that tourists who came to town would look around and think, "Gee, let's give this place a few more years to recover before we come back." Hart walked around downtown and pulled up dandelions and other weeds sprouting in front of closed businesses so that the village would not look like it was literally going to seed.

Then Wilmington finally cheered with some good news. Standing next to Governor Shumlin and Patricia Moulton Powden, the state's deputy secretary of commerce and community development, John and Patty Reagan announced that they would reopen Dot's. For months after the storm, the iconic restaurant had sat next to the Deerfield River, a battered emblem of what Wilmington had suffered, while the Reagans had tried to figure out how they could afford to reopen. They had flood insurance, but not enough to cover the $800,000 that engineers estimated it would cost to rebuild the restaurant. To flood-proof it (to a degree — there is only so much you can do for a building that is cantilevered over the river), they would need to build the new Dot's on a steel foundation — not the original stone foundation built up from the riverbank. Many of the building's systems, such as heat and electric, would be installed on the second floor — above, they hoped, any future floodwaters.

Over the winter, the Reagans worked with business advisors and several nonprofits and came up with a plan to finance the rebuild. Flood insurance would cover about a third of the cost, loans would pay for the second third. The remaining money would be donated by the Wilmington VT Flood Relief Fund ($25,000), the Wilmington VT Fund ($50,000 matching grant), and Friends of the Valley, another local nonprofit that promised to raise $100,000. The Preservation Trust of Vermont, which aims to build stronger village centers and downtowns and support community gathering places like Dot's (and had helped to establish the Wilmington VT Fund in December 2011), also assisted. The Reagans were aiming to open sometime in early 2013.

"It came down to, if we don't do it, it's gone forever," said Patty Reagan. "But no way we could have done it on our own."

With his arms around the Reagans, Governor Shumlin said, "There is no better example of Vermonters' tenacity, our ability to help each other out to get through a crisis and rebuild better than Irene found us than we're seeing from the spirit and the hearts of John and Patty today."

After the official announcement outside the old and battered Dot's, John Reagan told a *Rutland Herald* reporter that he and Patty chose to rebuild because Dot's is the heart of Wilmington.

"We want to preserve past memories, family traditions, and the opportunities for future generations to have the Dot's experience," he said. "It's more of a stewardship than owning a business."

Like most people in Wilmington, Susie Haughwout was glad to hear that Dot's would reopen. "It's iconic," she said. "It's good for everybody." And at the announcement in March, the town clerk read a series of linked limericks about Dot's written by local resident Bob Pelosi. The first limerick began, "There was a young lassie called Patty" and ended with "John and Patty made Wilmington happy."

In the final limerick, she read, "And after this while . . . We await the great food, When our Dot's returns in style."

But the good news of Dot's reopening overshadowed the stark reality that the Reagans' share of the rebuild totals more than $250,000. That amount might not seem large to young business owners just starting out. But John Reagan purchased Dot's over thirty years ago. At this stage, most business owners are considering retirement, not diving back into serious debt. And the Reagans are not the only long-time business owners in Wilmington. Lilias Hart started Quaigh Design Centre in the 1960s and can count at least seven business owners in town who are over sixty years old.

It's a reminder that the disaster has continued to unfold for many whose livelihoods were taken by Irene's floodwaters. They have been laden with huge, unexpected debt burdens (and an almost snowless winter in 2011–12 that attracted fewer skiers and snowboarders to Vermont), along with a disheartening feeling that recovery may never fully happen.

And an unlucky few have discovered more damage since they rebuilt following the storm. In April 2012 part of a retaining wall on the Deerfield River along South Main Street in Wilmington began to—or perhaps more accurately, continued to—collapse. The force of the flood had moved rocks that previously protected the retaining wall from being undercut by the river. The collapsed wall sits under the Wilmington Village Pub, purchased thirty years ago by Mary Jane Finnegan, who was in her mid-sixties when Irene hit. Before the flood, she had put the building and business up for sale. She was ready to retire.

But Irene stole her retirement, and Finnegan had no choice but to reopen. She remortgaged the property, cleaned up, and rebuilt her restaurant. At the time, she was told that the building and wall were sound. By spring it was collapsing, and engineers estimated that repairs would cost $30,000 to $100,000. Unless she could find someone to fund the repairs, she faced foreclosure. But outside funding was drying up. At a select board meeting in May 2012, Wilmington town manager Scott Murphy said that the town had "turned over every rock in the state" looking for funding to assist business owners with repairs.

၄ ၄ ၄

THE ONLY CERTAINTY in Wilmington's future is that the Deerfield will inevitably flood again. Although Haughwout and other town officials had hoped to move the town office and the police and fire departments from the floodplain, they have once again opened in their previous location at the corner of routes 9 and 100 (or where the four branches of Main Street meet). Haughwout hopes they will soon create a plan to evacuate vital town records and equipment before the next flood. Though not entirely happy with the idea of moving back to the old office, Haughwout said it was the right decision for the taxpayers, who are not in a position to pass a bond to build new offices. Instead, "insurance will pay to put the town hall back in the condition it was," she said.

Parked at the town office is Haughwout's new car—another Mitsubishi—with her old license plate (which she rescued from her destroyed

SUV after it was towed). Against iconic Vermont kelly green, Haugh-wout's license plate reads, "TWNCLRK." And painted on Wilmington's town office is a new marker. Between little wavy lines, the marker reads, "2011 Flood Level." It's about eight inches higher than the wavy lines marking the 1938 flood.

§ § §

ALL WINTER, with his field looking like a beach full of sand and silt, Geo Honigford found it hard to forget Irene, especially when so little snow buried the evidence. His face looked uncharacteristically creased, and he seemed uneasy, with energy to spare but unsure where to expend it. For a man like Honigford, who analyzes every business decision on his farm, a natural disaster must have altered his axis of equilibrium. He'd put his sweat and soul into his farm, done everything right, yet he was still wiped out. Who's to say it wouldn't happen again?

The storm damage to his field was like a bruise that wouldn't heal, he told the *Valley News* in May 2012.

"It's not a massive, gaping wound, but it's still there," he told the reporter. "It's depressing when I look down and see brown here. But by mid-June, if it all greens up like I'm hoping, it will heal."

Honigford did not seem to return to his old self until he started planting again for the 2012 growing season, said his friend Greg Russ. And he received good news from the University of Vermont: a soil test came back clean, so Hurricane Flats would not lose its organic certification. (The University of Vermont's Agricultural and Environmental Testing Lab had offered to test soil from flooded farm fields for free.)

After he planted in the spring Honigford noticed that the plants struggled at first, and he speculated that their infant root systems were working to find nutrients. Although he knows that repeated floods are what built the farm's soil, which he says is twenty-five feet thick, it will take a while to mix the new silt into the soil and build up the nutrients in it again. He fertilized the new plants with a fish emulsion, and they thrived. On May 5, 2012, he returned to the Norwich Farmers' Market with early season greens. And the Hurricane Flats blog reported that Honigford is in a solid place financially and spiritually.

"Given where we were in September, we are very grateful to be where we are now," said the blog in May.

In all, his farm took a $120,000 hit from Irene, including crop loss, damage to his greenhouses, repair of the holes in his field along the river, and protecting the riverbank. The free truckloads of silt to fill the holes probably saved him $30,000, he estimates. To help cover the other $90,000, he received two $10,000 grants from the Vermont Community Foundation, $5,000 from the Northeast Organic Farming Association of Vermont (NOFA Vermont), and two $500 grants from Operation Revive Royalton. Crossroads Farm in Thetford, Vermont, and the Blind Tiger, a beer bar in New York City, also held fundraisers, each netting $2,000 for Hurricane Flats. And donations from faithful customers also helped Honigford recover his farm. Working through Clean Water Future (cleanwaterfuture.org), a Kickstarter.com-like organization that provides a way for the community to invest in what they call "the natural services provided by private lands," he raised $7,000 for the riverbank restoration. But he remained about $50,000 shy of total flood costs.

Still, in many ways Honigford was lucky. Although his crops were destroyed, he did not lose his home or family, or any livestock. Nor did he lose feed. Just downstream from Hurricane Flats, David and Peggy Ainsworth lost six to seven hundred tons of silage intended to feed their forty-six milking cows and calves through the winter. And silage costs about $40 per ton. Ainsworth was able to buy eighty acres of corn from a neighbor and hoped it would get him through until spring, when he turns the cows out to pasture. Luckily, it was a mild winter and early spring. But Ainsworth still estimates that he was out $40,000: about $20,000 for the replacement silage and fixing a flood-damaged silo, and another $20,000 to restore the riverbank. He received $4,500 from the Vermont Community Foundation and $1,000 from Operation Revive Royalton. Irene loans were available to farmers. But with milk averaging $18 to $18.20 per hundredweight during the winter of 2012, and the USDA's Economic Research Service estimating production cost at $22.53 per hundredweight (January 2012), Ainsworth and other farmers like him were reluctant to go more deeply into debt.

"A lot of us had to borrow against our equity to get through the last couple of years (when milk averaged $11 to $16 per hundredweight)," he said. "So we're kind of sitting at the lip of a cup and almost ready to go under. We don't really need to be borrowing any more money."

Ainsworth was a little discouraged. "I wasn't hammered as badly as some people were," he added. "Not all is lost to me. But it makes you wonder some days what you do it for."

NO ONE HAS SUFFERED from Irene as much as the people who lost friends and loved ones.

"It really put the roads and all the rest of it back in perspective," said Doug Casella. "Screw the roads, we can fix the roads."

On September 22, 2011, New England K-9 returned to Rutland to continue searching for the body of Young Mike Garofano. They brought six dogs and their handlers: two German shepherds, one Labrador retriever, a border collie, an Australian shepherd, and a Belgian Malinois named Haven.

Less than two hours after the search began, Haven found a scent on a giant debris pile. The pile was two miles below the reservoir intake and was a tangled mass of trees, grass, branches, and other rubble. Haven's handler, Nancy Lyon, the president and operational leader for New England K-9, called the state police. The police called Casella and asked if he could return to the brook with one of his excavators.

Fran Robillard returned to the brook too. The deputy fire chief looked at the giant pile and remembered trying to search it in the days after the storm.

"It was the biggest pile in there," he remembered. "We thought if he was in there, we'd never find him."

Casella arrived with the excavator and again worked the arm to painstakingly pull apart the pile. It took hours to free Young Mike's body from the tangle.

Emotions hit everyone hard, in part because the loss to Mrs. Garofano and her remaining son, Tom, seemed unbearable. "How do you cope with losing your husband of thirty years and two sons in just over one year's time?" asked Casella.

Even the emergency responders had a hard time putting the loss behind them. For professionals trained in accident prevention, this one came down to a case of two men being in the wrong place at the wrong time. They struggled with the fact that the tragic accident seemed avoidable.

"In a fire, there's a reason," said Robillard, on the verge of tears. "You can trace the cause of death back. I don't know if that clears it in your mind or makes it even or what it does with a death. At least when you have a reason afterward, you put your prevention hat on and say maybe we can prevent that from happening again. Maybe that's why you can leave something like that behind."

But in this situation, he did not think it was prudent for the Garofanos to have been walking an embankment over a raging river in a bad storm.

"They could have stayed home," the deputy fire chief continued. "They could have trusted that the phone call had closed the intake valve. And it wouldn't have mattered if it didn't close it, because of the damage to the intake pipe."

"It's not like they were in a car in the wrong place at the wrong time," added Robillard after a long pause. "Or they were in their house and something malfunctioned, and they had a house fire. They just plain didn't have to be there."

After some thought, Casella disagreed.

"A guy who doesn't give a shit about his job might not have needed to be there," said Casella. "Mike Garofano cared. The reservoir was his place. That was not the City of Rutland's. That was his home for thirty years. If there was something that he could do to stop something bad from happening, he was going to do it, and he wasn't going to wait for someone to tell him to go up there. He was protecting seventeen thousand people's water. He took that very seriously. Thank God for all of us."

§ § §

ON A SUNNY, cold day in December 2011, Heather Grev sat in her office in the Killington Town Library. As she talked about the dramatic rescue from the little white house in Pittsfield and what had happened since that day in August, she choked up.

"I feel like everyone is moving on and getting back to normal and I'm not. I don't really know what that is," she said, trying to hold back tears.

"It's like a new normal," she continued after a pause. "Some days I get up and I just can't . . . come to work. I still get those looks from people."

In the weeks after the storm, Grev and her boyfriend, Jack Livesey, retained some sense of routine, returning to their jobs shortly after they had lost almost everything in the flood and after reacquiring life's necessities — new clothes (or at least, new to them), a place to live, and new vehicles. But nothing yet felt quite like theirs. When Grev walked outside, she pointed at a new Toyota Tacoma pickup and said, "This is my new truck," as if it were a rental car and not something that belonged to her.

Grev missed the home that she'd called her own. Even though they rented, it had been their space. And with Christmas approaching, Grev teared up again when she realized that she no longer had her nutcracker collection to decorate with for the Holidays.

And she deeply missed Cody. The fourteen-year-old German shepherd mix had not recovered from the trauma of the storm. In mid-October, Grev took Cody to Bruce LeGallais's veterinary clinic in Rutland, and the vet put him down. The old dog was in too much pain.

All through the winter and following summer and into the fall, the little white house in Pittsfield and the two neighboring properties lay as Irene had left them—a constant reminder of what the storm had done to the town. And to Vermont and to its people. The little white house was tipped off its foundation, the mobile home drooped on its frame, and Traci Templeton's house looked more and more battered with each passing month—physical metaphors for the damage inflicted on their lives: tattered, broken, upended. Those who lost everything faced not only the indignity of being stripped of their possessions and everything they had worked for but also months of living in limbo while the bureaucracy churned. Many also face years of debt they had never planned to accrue, or in some cases may be incapable of repaying.

If disasters like Irene in Vermont, as well as massive snowstorms, ice storms, and torrential thunderstorms, are going to continue—and given climate change, it's a safe bet they will—the population as a whole needs to look at how the state is rebuilt and who gets reimbursed for losses. Is it fair that the Federal Emergency Management Agency reimburses 90 percent of the cost of rebuilding state infrastructure, yet a homeowner who suffers a complete loss and has no flood insurance gets only $30,200 from FEMA? Should buildings be allowed in floodplains? And if so, should flood insurance be mandatory? And what to do about homes that still sit in the floodplains, waiting like time bombs for the next heavy rain? Not to mention examining what areas are deemed to be floodplains. If fluvial erosion caused so much damage in Vermont, shouldn't floodplain regulations be rewritten for mountain states?

These questions and many others will take years to answer — if they are answered at all. The only guarantee is that when the next natural disaster strikes, Vermonters will no doubt respond as they did to Irene. There is some comfort in that thought. And it is one of the reasons that many people like Vermont and are proud to say they live there. Vermonters don't just save for a rainy day. They have the skills, equipment, and compassion to respond when that rainy day goes to hell and beyond.

Governor Shumlin put it best when he said: "I know some people doubt this outside of the state, but there is a sense of community, a sense of caring for your neighbors, and a work ethic and ingenuity that you don't find in other places. You put those together, and you get magical results."

ACKNOWLEDGMENTS

This book was made possible thanks to the scores of Vermonters who were willing to share their lives and Irene experiences, often in heartbreaking detail. Most people mentioned in this book did not want to be singled out for any heroics, and across the board, they all would much rather have continued working than talk about their work. I appreciated every minute that they spent pointing me in the right direction or sharing their stories. They inspired me to keep writing, even when it seemed like a daunting task.

I am particularly indebted to Marion Abrams, who shared Pittsfield's story even as she was working on her film *Flood Bound—The Flood Story of Pittsfield, Vermont* (www.FloodBound.com), and to Kristen Wilson and Ernie Amsden. I would not have known where to start in Jamaica and South Royalton, respectively, without their direction. I am also grateful to Maureen and Kristen Casella, Mark Edsell, and Mary Russ, who all went above and beyond in correcting my blunders and pointing me in the right direction; Andy Nash, meteorologist-in-charge at the National Weather Service in Burlington, who very patiently gave me a Hurricane 101 lesson; and Nathan Foster, also at the NWS, who reworked the rainfall map to fit in this book. And to Meghan Charlebois—that email address was just what I needed. Thank you all. And to Jane Pixley, Jennifer Leak, and Diane McNamara at the Cavendish Town Office: thanks for the MRE!

Governor Peter Shumlin and Sue Minter took time from their busy schedules to explain how they faced the crisis. I am thankful for their time and consideration, but mostly for helping government work right against impossible odds. And a big thanks to Jo Maguire, who was never too busy to take my calls and answer my questions.

I am forever grateful to Phyllis Deutsch at UPNE for her kind encouragement, guidance, keen editing sense, and for giving me a chance; and to my editor, David Corey, for starting me off in the right direction and then giving me almost every waypoint en route. It was just a bunch of stories until he gave it shape. Then Martin Hanft's meticulous copy-editing made it far more polished and readable.

Countless colleagues and friends offered crucial support in many different ways. I owe a huge thanks to: Rob Greenwald and Nicole Kesselring, who explained what I had long since forgotten how to explain; Bruce Genereaux, who walked me through the many twists and turns of the flood relief process; Katie Meisinger and Kim Jackson, for putting me in touch with exactly the right people; Paul and Alison Buhler, who offered a ride in Killington and Pittsfield when I needed it most; Tom Horrocks, who shared the secret of finding the Woodchip Parkway before many knew about it, and Audra Fairbanks, who offered a backup plan; authors and friends Nathaniel Vinton, who affirmed my hunch that this could be a book, and Lisa Densmore and Kirk Kardashian, for their insight into publishing; Melissa Patterson and Cindy Trevino, for their belief that this really was a book when it was only half finished; and Aimee Berg, who provided unflagging encouragement and support. I am especially grateful to Shelley Lutz, an intrepid, loyal, and patient friend who is always up for an adventure and kept me sane. Everyone needs a friend like Shelley.

I also owe a huge thanks to my father, Ferguson McKay, who dusted off his English professor skills and read countless drafts. He served as an editor but mostly a cheerleader. And I give my biggest thanks to my husband, Andy Shinn, who was one of the first to encourage me to write (not masquerade as a scientist), and who continues to support me emotionally, financially, intellectually, and with humor—even when writing seems more like a hobby than a career.

APPENDIX

Tropical Storm Irene Facts and Damage Report for Vermont

Tropical Storm Irene hit Vermont on Sunday, August 28, 2011.

Six storm-related deaths were reported from the Vermont communities
of Rutland, Woodstock, Ludlow, Brattleboro, and Wilmington. Four
were a direct result of drowning during the storm. Two men died
in the aftermath from injuries sustained in falls in storm-damaged
areas. One person remains missing.

Estimated funds required for recovery and future disaster preparation:
$733.38 million.

COMMUNITIES, HOUSES, AND INDIVIDUALS

A total of 225 Vermont municipalities were affected by Tropical Storm
Irene, 45 of which incurred severe damage.

More than 3,500 homes suffered some damage. Of those residences,
approximately 681 had damages exceeding $10,000.

An estimated 1,405 households were temporarily or permanently
displaced.

Sixteen mobile parks and more than 500 mobile homes (located in
parks and on private land) were damaged or destroyed.

A total of 7,252 people registered for FEMA's Individuals and
Households Program (IHP).

The maximum FEMA IHP grant of $30,200 was awarded to 220
households. By June 2012, FEMA had distributed $22.7 million in
grants to families and individuals.

Average FEMA individual assistance grant provided: $5,500.

The American Red Cross responded with thirteen temporary shelters
and food banks to supplement community efforts.

More than 16,000 meals were provided to Vermonters and volunteers.

More than 600 historic buildings were damaged in over thirty downtowns or villages.

AGRICULTURE

Agricultural losses were estimated at over $10 million.

A total of 463 agricultural producers reported damage to the U.S. Department of Agriculture.

Flooding damaged more than 400 acres of land producing fruit and vegetables and 9,348 total acres of agricultural land.

VEDA approved 305 loans totaling $14.9 million. Of the 305 loans, 249 were commercial loans and the remaining 56 were associated with agriculture.

TRANSPORTATION

A total of 146 state road segments were closed (approximately 531 miles). By September 28, 2011 — one month after Irene — all but six road segments, totaling 13 miles, had reopened to traffic.

During and immediately after the storm, 34 state bridges were closed. A month later, 28 had reopened.

A total of 2,260 local road segments were damaged and 175 closed. By December 21, 2011, all but 21 road segments were repaired.

There were 289 local bridges damaged and 90 closed; 963 culverts were damaged.

More than 200 miles of state-owned rail were damaged, and 6 railroad bridges were closed; 66 separate locations on the privately owned New England Central Railroad were heavily damaged, totaling 13 miles of rail and 6 bridges. Within three weeks, all rail lines were repaired and reopened.

More than 200 private contractors and consultants from Vermont supplied equipment, personnel, and expertise to rebuild the roads immediately after the storm.

Approximately 700 VTrans employees worked from three command centers to quickly rebuild the roads.

Maine's Department of Transportation sent 150 people and 145 pieces of equipment to Vermont to aid recovery efforts.

New Hampshire's Department of Transportation sent 75 people and 60 pieces of equipment.

Assisting in Vermont's recovery effort were 763 National Guard members. These soldiers came from Vermont, Maine, Illinois, Ohio, New Hampshire, South Carolina, West Virginia, and Virginia.

Estimated funds required to rebuild the state's roads, bridges, rail, and infrastructure, including the Vermont State Hospital and the Waterbury State Office Complex: $486.20 million.

Adapted from "Tropical Storm Irene: A Snapshot, The Facts and Damage Reports," vtStrong.vermont.gov/Home/StateRecovery.aspx; and "Vermont Recovering Stronger, Irene Recovery Status Report," presented by Governor Peter Shumlin, June 2012.

BIBLIOGRAPHY

NEWSPAPERS
Burlington Free Press (2011 and 2012)
Deerfield Valley News (2011 and 2012)
Herald of Randolph (2011 and 2012)
New York Times (1927, 2011, 2012)
Rutland Herald (1927, 1938, 2011, and 2012)
Valley News (2011 and 2012)
Vermont Standard (2011 and 2012)
Wall Street Journal (2011 and 2012)

WEBSITES
Flood of 1947, Rutland Historical Society, www.rutlandhistory.com/
    Encyclopedia/Floodof1947.asp.
Flow of History, www.flowofhistory.org/index.php.
U.S. Geological Survey, real-time water data, waterdata.usgs.gov.
U.S. Highways, From U.S. 1 to U.S. 830, www.us-highways.com.
USGS Water Watch Toolkit, waterwatch.usgs.gov/new/index.php?id
    =ww_toolkit.
Vermont's official Irene recovery website, vtstrong.vermont.gov.
Vermont Old Roads, www.vtroads.com.
Vermont Public Radio, www.vpr.net.
Vermont Recovery, vtstrong.vermont.gov.
Weather Underground, www.wunderground.com.

BOOKS
Blackmer, Ramona, Barbara Green, and Gloria Taylor, eds. *A Pictorial History
    of Stockbridge Gaysville, 1761–1976*. Bethel, VT: Spaulding Press, 1976,
    1986.
Central Vermont Public Service. "Hurricane Irene: An Historic Response."
    Rutland, VT: CVPS, September 2011.
Clifford, Deborah Pickman, and Nicholas R. Clifford. *"The Troubled Roar of*

the Waters": Vermont in Flood and Recovery, 1927-1931. Lebanon, NH:
University Press of New England, 2007.

Fleming, Madeline C. "An Informal History of the Town of Sherburne,
Vermont, 1761-1965." Available at the Rutland Free Library.

Fradkin, Philip L. *Wallace Stegner and the American West.* New York: Alfred
A. Knopf, 2008.

Goodspeed, Linda. *Pico: The First 50 Years.* Mendon, VT: Pico Ski Resort, 1987.

Hawkins, Guy C. "An Historical Address." Historical Society of Wilmington,
2010.

Johnson, Luther B. *The '27 Flood: An Authentic Account of Vermont's Greatest
Disaster*, Rev. ed. [Originally published as *Vermont in Floodtime*, 1928.]
Randolph Center, VT: Greenhills Books, 1998.

Ludlum, David M. *The Vermont Weather Book.* Montpelier, VT: Vermont
Historical Society, 1996.

Minsinger, W. E., comp. and ed. *The 1938 Hurricane: An Historical and
Pictorial Summary.* Milton, MA: Blue Hill Meteorological Observatory,
1988.

———. *The 1927 Flood in Vermont and New England, November 3-7, 1927: An
Historical and Pictorial Summary.* Milton, MA: Blue Hill Meteorological
Observatory, 2003.

"Multi-Hazard Mitigation Plan, Town of Jamaica, Vermont: New Annex to
Windham Regional Multi-Jurisdictional Pre-Disaster Hazard Mitigation
Plan." Windham Regional Commission, Brattleboro, VT. December 12,
2011.

Musick, Marc A., and John Wilson. *Volunteers: A Social Profile.* Bloomington:
Indiana University Press, 2008.

Smith, H. P., and W. S. Rann, eds. *History of Rutland County, Vermont.*
Syracuse, NY: D. Mason and Company, 1886.

Vermont Atlas and Gazetteer. Freeport, ME: DeLorme, 1996.

Worthen, Mark. *Hometown Jamaica: A Pictorial History of a Vermont Village.*
Jamaica, VT: Jamaica Memorial Library, 1997.

OTHER SOURCES

Dupigny-Giroux, Lesley-Ann. "Climate Variability and Socioeconomic
Consequences of Vermont's Natural Hazards: A Historical Perspective."
Vermont History 70 (Winter/Spring 2002): 19-39. Vermont Historical
Society. Available at vermonthistory.org/journal/70/vt701_204.pdf.

Faulkner, Rob. "Emergency Preparedness: Dealing with Disasters, Early
Actions Expedite a Successful Recovery." *Talk of the Towns and Topics*
(May/June 2012): 16-17. Association of Towns of the State of New York,
Albany, NY.

"Flood at Rutland, Vermont, June 1947: A Story in Headlines, Text, and
    Pictures." Compiled by Aldo Merusi, *Rutland Herald* photographer.
    No date. Rutland City Hall.

"Irene Recovery Report: A Stronger Future." Presented by Governor Peter
    Shumlin, January 2012. Available at www.vtstrong.vermont.gov/
    Portals/0/Documents/Irene_Recovery_Report_Jan_2012.pdf.

"Limits of 1927 Flood as Compared to Preliminary '100 & 500 Year' FEMA
    Special Flood Hazard Areas" for Rutland, Vermont. Poster in Rutland's
    City Hall.

National Center for Biotechnology Information, PubMed Help. "Post-
    traumatic Stress Disorder." February 13, 2012. Available at www.ncbi.nlm
    .nih.gov/pubmedhealth/PMH0001923/.

National Hurricane Center. "Hurricane Basics." National Oceanic and
    Atmospheric Administration, National Hurricane Center, May 1999.
    Available at hurricanes.noaa.gov/pdf/hurricanebook.pdf.

National Oceanic and Atmospheric Administration, National Climatic Data
    Center. "State of the Climate, National Overview, August 2011." Available
    at www.ncdc.noaa.gov/sotc/national/2011/8.

"Quechee Gorge Bridge." Connecticut River Joint Commissions. Available at
    www.crjc.org/heritage/V11-30.htm.

Schoch-Spana, Monica. "Public Responses to Extreme Events—Top 5
    Disaster Myths." Resources for the Future, First Wednesday Seminar,
    October 5, 2005. Available at www.rff.org/rff/Events/upload/20180_1
    .pdf.

Shelvey, Alan J. "A Short History of the Rutland City Water Supply" and
    "A Description of Rutland's Water Supply." Rutland City Water Filtration
    Plant, Rutland City Public Works Department, Rutland City Hall.

Sherman, Michael, Jennie Versteeg, and Paul Gillies. "The Character of
    Vermont: Twentieth Century Reflections." Occasional Paper #19. Center
    for Research on Vermont, University of Vermont, 1996.

Smith, Stanley K. "Demography of Disaster: Population Estimates after
    Hurricane Andrew." *Population Research and Policy Review* 15 (December
    1996): 459-77. Available at www.bebr.ufl.edu/files/PRPR%201996
    %20(Disaster%20Demog).pdf.

University of Vermont Extension. "Managing Flood Damaged Crops and
    Forage from Tropical Storm Irene." Available at www.uvm.edu/extension/
    flooded_crops_factsheet_%20irene2011_uvmextension.pdf.

———. "Post-Flooding Produce Safety for Commercial Produce Growers."
    Available at www.uvm.edu/extension/agriculture/pdfs/post-flood_
    produce_safety_18oct11ver4.pdf.

U.S. Department of Commerce, Economic Development Administration.

"Vermont DR-4022, Economic Impact Assessment, Economic Recovery Support Function." April 2012. Available at www.wilmingtonvermont.us/vertical/sites/%7BE2DA69A7-840E-4CF1-AC59-A0278D51236E%7D/uploads/4-23-12__Economic_Impact_Assessment_for_T.S._Irene.pdf.

Vermont Agency of Transportation. "Outline History of Vermont State Highways, National Highway Week, Sept. 19–25, 1965." Prepared for informational purposes only by the Vermont Department of Highways. Available at www.aot.state.vt.us/planning/Documents/Mapping/Publications/Outline_History_VTStateHwys.pdf.

——. "Traffic Flow Maps." Available at www.aot.state.vt.us/planning/documents/trafresearch/publications/TrafficFlow_2010.pdf.

——. "TS Irene, August 28, 2011, VTrans Response." Available at www.aot.state.vt.us/Documents/Irene/TropicalStormIrenePresentation.pdf.

——. "VTrans 2012 Fact Book." Available at www.aot.state.vt.us/planning/Documents/Planning/2012VTransFactbook.pdf.

Vermont Department of Environmental Conservation, Watershed Management Division. "Wastewater Status Report, September 2, 2011." Available at www.vtwaterquality.org/ww/om/Overflows/20110902-WWTFStatusReport.pdf.

"Vermont Recovering Stronger: Irene Recovery Status Report." Presented by Governor Peter Shumlin, June 2012. Available at www.vtstrong.vermont.gov/Portals/0/Documents/VTRecoveringStronger%20RptJune%202012.pdf.

Waters, Steve. "Flood Physics." Available through the National Weather Service's "Turn Around Don't Drown" (TADD) program. Available at tadd.weather.gov/images/WaterPhysics.pdf.

Weingroff, Richard F. "From Names to Numbers: The Origins of the U.S. Numbered Highway System." *AASHTO Quarterly* (Spring 1997). Available at www.fhwa.dot.gov/infrastructure/numbers.cfm.

"Wilmington, Vermont, Long-Term Recovery Plan, May 2012." Available at www.wilmingtonvermont.us/vertical/sites/%7BE2DA69A7-840E-4CF1-AC59-A0278D51236E%7D/uploads/WilmPlan__FNL.pdf.

A NOTE FROM THE PUBLISHER

Every person affected by the flooding caused by Tropical Storm Irene has a story. Some of these are simple tales of being inconvenienced by road closings or washed-out bridges. Others are tragic and life-changing: houses collapsed against the crush of brown water and debris, the topsoil of family farms replaced by stones and fine silt, near-death experiences or harrowing escapes, even the loss of loved ones. No single book could ever contain all these tales.

Deluge tells a collective story of the flood through the eyes of a few. But it is in no way comprehensive. For this reason, a website has been created where you can share your own story of Irene, at www.vermontflood.com.

At the time of this publication, many state residents were still struggling financially and emotionally due to flood losses. If you wish to help, Peggy Shinn and the University Press of New England strongly encourage donations to the following Vermont relief and recovery organizations.

Vermont Disaster Relief Fund
P.O. Box 843
Montpelier, VT 05601
www.vermontdisasterrecovery.com

The Vermont Community Foundation
Vermont Farm Disaster Relief Fund
P.O. Box 30
Middlebury, VT 05753
www.vtfloodresponse.org

Vermont Irene Fund
Central Vermont Community Action Council
Attention: VT Irene FRF
195 U.S. Route 302–Berlin
Barre, VT 05641
www.vtirenefund.org